ANIMALS AND THE LAW

ANIMALS AND THE LAW

Jaideep Verma
and
Ritikaa Modee

ZORBA BOOKS

ZORBA BOOKS

Published by Zorba Books, August 2021

Website: www.zorbabooks.com
Email: info@zorbabooks.com

Cover design by Sithesh

Title : Animals and the Law

ISBN Print Book - 978-93-90640-80-5
ISBN eBook- 978-93-90640-85-0

Zorba Books Pvt. Ltd. (opc)
Sushant Arcade,
Next to Courtyard Marriot,
Sushant Lok 1, Gurgaon – 122009, India

TABLE OF CONTENTS

Mrs. (Justice) Sujata Manohar (retd.)

M. A. (Oxon), Barrister-at-Law

Former
Judge, Supreme Court of India
Chief Justice, Bombay & Kerala High Courts
Member, National Human Rights Commission

FOREWORD

It is a pleasure to write a foreword for this unusual book "Animals and the Law". It is a user-friendly readable book which starts with "Did you know?". It asks unexpected questions like "Is testing of cosmetics on animals in India legal?" or "Is Elephant a performing animal?". It tells the reader about prevailing legislation in India about animals such as "Prevention and Control of Infections and Contagious Diseases in Animals Act 2009" or "The Prevention of Cruelty to Animals Act" and its various sets of Rules such as those for Pet Shops or for Transport of Animals on Foot.

The author Jaideep Verma, a well-known lawyer and animal lover has asked the basic question, whether we are doing enough for the welfare of animals. As we realize the importance of protecting and preserving the environment, its flora and fauna for our own preservation, this question raises one of the fundamental issues central to preservation of a liveable earth.

It is time we look at the extent of legal protection we give to our rich wealth of diverse life forms still existing in our country. Apart from dealing with legislation in the field, like a true lawyer, the author has also dealt with fairly extensive case law on the subject – itself very interesting.

The book also contains other useful information, for example, about Dog Breeds, protecting street dogs, guidelines for laboratory animal facilities, even slaughter house rules and many other aspects of perils faced by animals everywhere.

As the author has put it, "This manual will help one to understand the rights of animals better, irrespective of whether it is a simple right of a pet dog to be taken for a walk in public parks or a complex right pertaining to conducting experiment on animals and the like". The book fills a gap in less visited area of law and will be useful to environment and animal lovers in addition to lawyers.

Sujata Manohar

Date: 10th June 2021 Mrs. Justice Sujata Manohar (Retd.)

Goenka House, 16, Walkeshwar Road, Mumbai - 400 006.
Tel.: 022-2363 3899 Telefax : 022-2363 4100 E-mail : sujatamanohar@gmail.com

ACKNOWLEDGMENTS

I dedicate this book to:

My father Dr. Bhanushankar Verma and my mother Prof. Amita Verma

> They both taught me the importance of reading, academics and keeping alive the quest for knowledge. They were both acknowledged experts in their fields and forever engaged in learning.

My wife Dr. Sharmila, whose love for dogs is unparalleled;

My daughter Aayati, who at the tender age of 3 decided to become a Veterinary Doctor and has followed her passion by passing her Veterinary Course in 2020-21. She is currently working as an intern at a Government Veterinary Polyclinic;

My daughter Aalokaa, who spends the most time with the head of the household, my geriatric dog – Mishtee. They are totally inseparable.

To my two Sheeba's, Romi, Jhinnie, Minnie, Bhuriyo, Natkhatlal, Leader, Gayatri, Banno, Roro, Ruby and all the free souls who are / have been, a part of my life.

Jaideep Verma
Advocate

ACKNOWLEDGMENTS

I would like to thank my husband Maulik Trivedi, my mother Mrs. Juhee Modee, my father Vikas Modee, my in-laws Mr Mangal and Minal Trivedi and my grandfather Mr. Rajesh Kumar, my mentor in life.

Ritikaa Modee
Advocate

DISCLAIMER

The book is a compilation of various laws, rules, regulations, guidelines and judgments in the knowledge of the authors and currently prevailing and applicable in India. It is a compilation for ready reference only *and authors do not make any representations or warranties of any kind with respect to this book or its contents. The authors even though exercised diligence to ensure the correctness of the contents of this book, they do not assume any responsibility for any inaccuracies, errors, omissions, or any other inconsistencies or for any loss or damage that may be caused due to such inaccuracies, errors, omission or any other inconsistencies. This book is not intended to provide any legal advice or opinion. The book is not intended to substitute legal opinion and advice, and consultation with an advocate or a legal practitioner. Purchase and use of this book shall imply that you have read, understood and accepted this disclaimer. No guarantee or surety, as to any extent and of any sort is given regarding the contents of this book. All the laws, rules, regulations, judgments and facts specified in the book have been taken from different sources and each such source has been accordingly credited in the footnotes. This book is a compilation of already existing laws and precedence.*

Jaideep Verma
Author

ABOUT THE AUTHOR

Passionate about Animal Welfare, nature and heritage. Forever willing to provide pro bono services for a cause.

Certificate Holder of Course on Private International Law - International Court of Justice, Hague, Netherlands (2016) ;

BSL, LLB (1994) from Symbiosis Law College, Pune

Diploma in Consumer Protection Laws from the University of Poona in 1993-94.

Certificate Holder of Course on Patents jointly conducted by Government of Andhra Pradesh and CII.

Ex- Senior Associate with M/s.Crawford Bayley & Company, Solicitors, Mumbai ;

Previously part of Chambers of Mr Arshad M Hidayatullah, Senior Advocate of the Supreme Court of India.

Pan Gujarat Practice in District Courts, Revenue Courts, Consumer Courts, Judicial and quasi-judicial authorities, Documentation.

Member – Academic Advisory Board – School of Business and Law, Navrachana University, Baroda

Independent Director

Ex-Director (Public Interest) on the Vadodara Stock Exchange appointed by SEBI.

DID YOU KNOW?

Before you proceed to read each law on animals in detail here are some fun FAQs.

- Do you think not exercising your dog is an offence?
  Yes, if one fails or neglects to exercise their dog then it amounts to cruelty under the applicable laws in India.

- When is employing an animal for any work of labour cruelty?
  Employing or allowing any animal to be employed in any work of labour or for any other purpose when such animal is unfit to be so used or employed is cruelty.

- To whom can you sell a dog if you are a breeder?
  Breeder cannot sell a dog to a pet shop operating without a licence or for any other activity which is in contravention of any other law.

- What are the basic liabilities of a pet dog owner?
  The owner of pet dogs is responsible for the controlled breeding, immunization, sterilization and licensing in accordance with the rules and the law for the time being in force within a specified local area.

- Is testing of cosmetics on animals in India legal?
  Testing of cosmetics on animals is prohibited under law and in fact any cosmetic that has been tested on animals after the commencement of the Drugs and Cosmetics (Fifth Amendment) Rules, 2014 cannot be imported into the country.

- Thinking of adopting/buying a dog?
  It is important to understand that a dog does not always remain in its puppy stage. It grows old and at that stage requires investments, veterinary visits, beneficiary diet,

and dedication. Hence, it is only advisable to preferably adopt a dog rather than buying and to buy/adopt a dog only when one has sufficient financial ability to take of the dog for its lifetime.

- Has any animal been sent to space?
  Various animals have been sent to space for purpose of experiment including but not limited to monkeys, dogs, cats, chimpanzees etc.

- Where can one slaughter any animal?
  Any person can slaughter an animal only in a recognised or a licensed slaughter house and in no other place in the municipal area.

- Can any person train and exhibit animal as to be performing animal?
  No person can exhibit or train any animal unless registered. Further no animal can be trained and exhibited as performing animal which the Central Government by notification in Official Gazette specify as animal which cannot be exhibited or trained as performing animals.

- Is Elephant a performing animal?
  Vide its circular dated 6th September, 2016 AWBI issued an advisory to the Ministry of Environment, Forest and Climate Change to ban the training, exhibition and use of elephants for performances in India. So the answer is yes and cruelty on this giant animal continues.

- Can the animals be transported freely or are there any rules regulating the same?
  The Transport of Animal Rules, 1978 regulate various conditions subject to which different animals can be transported by rail, road, inland waterway, sea or air and provide as specified below. The Prevention of Cruelty to Animals (Transport of Animals on Foot) Rules, 2001 regulate the transport of animals by foot when distance from the boundary of village or town or city of the origin of such transport to the last destination is 5 km or more than 5 km.

- Is there any law to own and run pet shop?
  Prevention of Cruelty to Animals (Pet Shops) Rules, 2018 set out the rules and regulations which must be complied with for running a pet shop in India. Any person can carry on or continue the business of sale or trade in pet animals after obtaining a certificate of registration which must be prominently displayed in the pet shop. It prescribed criteria of registration for individuals, corporations and association of persons.

- Have you heard of pet insurance?
  Yes pet/animal insurance is a thing and several insurance companies have now started to offer insurance for pets/ animals ranging from pet dogs, to goat, pigs, camel, poultry, duck, rabbit, elephant, horse etc.

- In times of bird flu are you concerned if there is any law to contain and curb spread of contagious diseases by animals?
  Prevention and Control of Infectious and Contagious Diseases in Animals Act, 2009 provide for the prevention, control and eradication of infectious and contagious diseases affecting animals, for prevention of outbreak or spreading of such diseases from one state to another, and to meet the international obligations of India for facilitating import and export of animals and animal products and for matters connected therewith or incidental thereto.

- If female dogs are left unneutered can it be a reason to worry?
  It probably is as just one unaltered female dog and her offspring can produce 67,000 puppies in only six years[1].

- Who owns a wild animal killed or wounded in defence?
  Any wild animal killed or wounded in defence of any person is government property.

1 https://www.peta.org/issues/animal-companion-issues/overpopulation/spay-neuter/

ARE WE DOING ENOUGH FOR THE WELFARE OF ANIMALS?

Mahatma Gandhi has said, "The greatness of a nation and its moral progress can be judged by the way its animals are treated"

This manual is a compilation of various laws, rules, regulations, guidelines, trivia, judgments passed for administering better treatment to animals and for their protection, welfare and safety. It gives an insight of the animal rights and laws which currently prevail in India. It is a compilation for ready reference only and is not to be taken as advice. India is a country with a unique culture embodying different beliefs and practices. It is one country which has exclusive temples to worship animals. But the question is that are we doing enough to actually safeguard and protect the interest of the animals or have we created a make belief world with large number of laws which actually are not so effective in protecting the rights and interest of animals. The question is worth exploring.

With new laws being enacted and old being amended, the rights of the animals have been in conundrum now forever. It cannot be said with certainty whether the existing laws are doing enough. The treatment that has been meted out to the animals in India and the treatment which must be given to them has always been logger heads. Despite the plethora of laws, rules, regulations and circulars animal wellbeing remains a concern.

Be it be a question of right to take a dog in public parks, right to keep a pet, guidelines to breed animals, to experiment on animals, to run a pet shop, to transport animals, restrictions on engaging in animal fights, conditions on sacrifice of animals, slaughtering of animals, keeping and maintaining cattle premises, keeping of draught and pack animals, dealing in ivory, fur and animal skin, prohibition on keeping trophies etc. all have been discussed at length herein with supporting case laws. It is a never-ending trial and is likely to continue for several years.

However, it would be interesting to understand the laws which are currently in place and what can be done by people in order to achieve the desired objective of these laws and regulations. This manual will help one to understand the rights of the animals better, irrespective of whether it is a simple right of a pet dog to be taken for a walk, in public parks or a complex right pertaining to conducting experiment on animals and the like. In this manual some interesting facts pertaining to animals have also been compiled from various sources. All the credits have been given in the footnote the manual is the compilation of laws and precedence which are in the knowledge of the authors and currently prevailing and applicable in India.

ANIMALS AND TEMPLES OF INDIA[2]

Animals have been integral part of the culture and religion in India. As an interesting fact, below is the list of temples in India where animals are worshiped, are believed to be the children of god, are considered sacred, visit the temple every day for Prasad, or have simply made the temple premises their home:

a. Dog Temple – Channapatna, Karnataka
b. Eagle Temple – Thirukazhukundram, Tamil Nadu
c. Monkey Temple – Jaipur, Rajasthan
d. Bear Temple- Mahasamund, Chattisgarh
e. Rat Temple- Bikaner, Rajasthan
f. Crocodile Temple - Ananthapura temple
g. Sringeri - Holy Fish
h. Kali Singh Temple (to pray for wellbeing of pets) – Sisauli
i. Bull Temple- Bengaluru Karnataka
j. Kapaleeswarar Temple - Peacock Temple – Mylapore, Tamil Nadu

2 https://www.nativeplanet.com/travel-guide/temples-dedicated-to-animals-in-india-002071.html; andhttps://www.nativeplanet.com/travel-guide/animal-temples-in-india-002084.html; last visited on 14.07.2020

THE PREVENTION OF CRUELTY TO ANIMALS ACT, 1960 (PCA)

PCA has been enacted to prevent cruelty to animals. The Act prohibits infliction of unnecessary pain or suffering on animals. The term 'animal' has been defined under the Act to mean any living creature other than a human being[3]. The term has been given a very wide connotation to include within its ambit every living creature except human beings making the compliance only stricter. This section out the acts which may amount to cruelty making a person liable for punishment under the provisions of PCA, the acts which are exempted from the ambit or cruelty, the duty to care, punishment for inflicting cruelty and the circumstances in which an animal may be killed in order to release it from unnecessary pain and suffering.

1. **Acts which amount to cruelty to animals**[4]
   a. Beating, kicking, over loading, over-riding, over-driving, torturing or otherwise torturing an animal in such a manner which causes unnecessary pain or suffering to such animal or being the owner allowing such treatment of animal.
   b. Employing or allowing any animal to be employed in any work of labour or for any other purpose when such animal is unfit to be so used or employed.
   c. Willfully and unreasonably administering or causing or attempting to cause any injurious drug or substance to be taken by any animal.
   d. Conveying or carrying any animal is such position or manner whether in a vehicle or otherwise which causes unnecessary pain or suffering to such animal.

---

3 Section 2(a) of PCA

4 Section 11 of PCA

e. Keeping or confining any animal in any cage or otherwise which is not of adequate height, length, breadth to give the animal reasonable space for movement.
f. Where a person being the owner neglects or fails to exercise a dog that is habitually chained or kept in close confinement.
g. Keeping an animal chained or tethered for an unreasonable time by an unreasonably short or heavy chain or cord.
h. Failing to provide sufficient food, drink or shelter to the animal of which a person is the owner.
i. Abandoning an animal without any reasonable cause which is likely to cause pain to such animal because of starvation or thirst.
j. Being the owner, allowing any animal infected with contagious or infectious disease to go at large in any street or permitting any diseased or disable animal to die on street.
k. Possessing or offering for sale any animal which is suffering from pain due to mutilation, starvation, thirst, overcrowding or other ill-treatment.
l. Killing or mutilating any animal by using the method of strychnine injections in the heart or in any other manner which is unnecessarily cruel.
m. Solely for entertainment purposes:
   - Confining or causing confinement of any animal to make it object of prey for any other animal;
   - Inciting any animal to fight or bait any other animal.
n. Organizing, keeping, using or acting in the management of any place which is used for animal fights or baiting of any animal, permitting/allowing any place to be so used, receiving money for admission of any person into such place.
o. Participating in or promoting shooting match/completion where animals are released from captivity for such purpose.

2. **Punishment for inflicting cruelty on animals**[5]
   a. If the offence is committed for the first time then person is punishable with a minimum fine of Rs.10 and maximum of Rs.50. If the second or subsequent offence is committed

5 *ibid*

within three years of previous offence then the person becomes punishable with a fine of not less than Rs. 25 which may extend up to Rs.100 or with imprisonment for a term which may extend up to three months or both.

b. The owner is deemed to have committed the offence of cruelty if he fails to exercise reasonable care and supervision with a view to prevent such offence. In a case where offence of cruelty is committed only because the owners fails to exercise care and supervision then in such case he is not liable to imprisonment without the option of fine.

3. **Acts which will not amount to cruelty are as listed below**[6]
   a. Dehorning of cattle, or castration of branding or nose roping of any animal in the prescribed manner;
   b. Destruction of dogs in lethal chambers or by other prescribed manner;
   c. The extermination or destruction of any animal under the authority of law for the time being in force;
   d. Experiment on animals as per the prescribed rules and regulations;
   e. Commission or omission of any act in the course of the destruction or the preparation for destruction of any animal as food for mankind unless such destruction or preparation is accompanied by infliction of unnecessary pain or suffering.

4. **Destruction of suffering animals**[7]
   a. Where the owner of an animal is convicted for the offence of cruelty then in such case if the court is satisfied that it would be cruel to keep the animal alive it may direct that the animal be destroyed and assign the animal to any suitable person for such purpose.
   b. Any such person who is assigned the animal has to destroy or get the animal destroyed in his presence as soon as possible without causing unnecessary pain or suffering to such animal.

6 *ibid*

7 Section 13 of PCA

c. Any expense incurred in destroying the animal is recoverable from the owner as if it were a fine.
d. Where any magistrate, commissioner of police, or district superintendent of police has a reason to believe than the offence of cruelty has been committed he may direct immediate destruction of the animal if it would be cruel to keep the animal alive.
e. Any police officer above the rank of a constable or any person authorized by the State Government in this behalf who finds an animal which is so diseased, or so severely injured, or is in such physical condition that it cannot be removed without cruelty may, if the owner is absent or refuses to give his assent summon veterinary doctor in charge of the particular area and if the veterinary doctor certifies that the animal is mortally or so severally injured, or is in such physical condition that it would be cruel to keep the animal alive, after obtaining orders from the magistrate destroy or cause to be destroyed such animal in the prescribed manner.

5. **Duties of a person who has care or charge of any animal**
Any person who has the care or is in charge of any animal is duty bound to take all the measures as may be reasonable to ensure the wellbeing of such animal and to prevent unnecessary pain or suffering to such animal[8].

State Amendments

a. **Karnataka**: Subject to the fulfillment of the conditions specified in the paragraph 5 above and such other conditions as may be specified by the state government by notification from time to time a person who has the care or charge of any animal may be allowed to conduct Kambala[9] or Bulls race or Bullock cart race[10].

---

8 Section 3 of PCA

9 Kambala means the traditional sports event involving buffalo's (male) race normally held as a part of tradition and culture in the state on such days and places, as may be notified by the State Government.

10 Bulls race or Bullock cart race means any form of bulls race including race of bullock cart as a traditional sports involving bulls whether tied to cart with the help of wooden yoke or not (in whatever name called) normally held as a part of tradition and culture in the state on such days and places, as may be notified by the State Government.

When any person conducts Kambala or Bulls race or bullock cart race with a view to follow and promote tradition and culture and ensure preservation of native breed of buffalos/cattle as also their safety, security and wellbeing then such act will not amount to cruelty.

b. **Maharashtra**: Subject to the fulfillment of the conditions specified in paragraph 5 hereinabove and such other conditions as may be specified by the state government bullock cart race[11] may be conducted with prior permission of the Collector.

   Any person in charge of the animals if conducts bullock cart race in contravention of the aforesaid requirements resulting in pain or suffering to the animals then such person becomes liable to be punished with fine a which may extent up to rupees five lakhs or imprisonment which may extent up to three years.

   When any person conducts bulls race or bullock cart race with a view to follow and promote tradition and culture and ensure preservation of native breed of bulls as also their purity, safety, security and wellbeing then such act will not amount to cruelty.

6. **Concept and legality of practicing *phooka* or *dhoom dev***

   "*Phooka*" or "*Dhoom dev*" includes any process of introducing air or any substance into the female organ of a milch animal with the object of drawing off from the animal any secretion of milk[12].

   Any person who on a cow or other milch animal performs or allows to be performed the operation "*phooka*" or "*dhoom dev*" or any other operation to improve lactation which is injurious to the health of such cow/other animal is punishable with fine

11 Bullock cart race means an event involving bulls or bullocks to conduct a race, whether tied to a cart with the help of a wooden yoke or not (by whatever name called) with or without a cart with a view to follow tradition and culture on such days and in any district where it is being traditionally held at such places. As may be previously approved by the district collector, and also known as "*Bailgada Sharyat*", "*Chhakadi*" and "*shankarpat*" in the State of Maharashtra

12 Section 2(g) of PCA

which may extend up to Rs. 1000/- or with imprisonment for a term which may extent up to two years or with both. Such animal on which the operation is performed is liable to be forfeited by the Government[13].

7. **Saving**
   Nothing contained in the Act renders it an offence to kill any animal in a manner required by the religion of any community[14].

8. **Establishment of Animal Welfare Board of India (AWBI/ BOARD)**
   For the promotion of animal welfare and for the protection of animals, from unnecessary pain or suffering board called the Animal Welfare Board of India has been established by the Central Government.

13 Section 12 of PCA

14 Section 28 of PCA Act, 1960

ANIMAL WELFARE BOARD OF INDIA V. A. NAGARAJA AND OTHERS; (2014) 7 SCC 547

Issue: In the present case the court was concerned with examining the rights of the animals under the constitution, laws, culture, tradition, religion and ethology in connection with the conduct of Jallikattu, bullock cart races etc. in the states of Tamil Nadu and Maharashtra with particular reference to the provisions of the PCA, Tamil Nadu Regulation of Jallikatu Act, 2009 ("**TNRJ Act**") and Notification dated 11.07.2011 issued by the Central Government prohibiting all bullock cart races, games, training, exhibition etc.

The Court observed that:

> "36. Section 3…casts a duty on the person in charge or care of animal to prevent the infliction upon an animal, unnecessary pain or suffering… Considerations which are relevant to determine whether the suffering is unnecessary include whether the suffering could have reasonably been avoided or reduced, whether the conduct which caused the suffering was in compliance with any relevant enactment. Another aspect to be examined is whether the conduct causing the suffering was for a legitimate purpose, such as, the purpose of benefiting the animals or the purpose of protecting a person, property or another animal, etc…
>
> 42. … Parliament, by incorporating Article 51A(g), has …. reiterated and re-emphasized the fundamental duties on human beings towards every living creature, which evidently takes in bulls as well.
>
> PERFORMING ANIMALS
>
> 43. All animals are not anatomically designed to be performing animals. Bulls are basically Draught and Pack animals. they

are live-stock used for farming and agriculture purposes, like ploughing, transportation etc…

47.... It may be noted that when Bull is specifically prohibited to be exhibited or trained for performance, the question whether such performance, exhibition or entertainment is conducted with sale of tickets or not, is irrelevant

49. … Performing Animals (Registration) Rules, 2001... Rule 8 deals with the general condition of registration... Rule 8(vii) specifically cautions that the owner shall train the animal as a performing animal to perform an act in accordance with the animals' natural instinct. Bull is trained not in accordance with its natural instinct for the Jallikattu or Bullock-cart race. Bulls, in those events, are observed to carry out a "flight response" running away from the crowd as well as from the Bull tamers, since they are in fear and distress, this natural instinct is being exploited…

53. …**Welfare and the well-being of the bull is Tamil culture and tradition, they do not approve of infliction of any pain or suffering on the bulls, on the other hand, Tamil tradition and culture are to worship the bull and the bull is always considered as the vehicle of Lord Shiva. Yeru Thazhuvu, in Tamil tradition, is to embrace bulls and not over-powering the bull, to show human bravery**...

54. …This Court, in N. Adithayan v. Thravancore Dewaswom Board and Others (2002) 8 SCC 106, while examining the scope of Articles 25(1), 2(a), 26(b), 17, 14 and 21, held as follows:

"18……… Any custom or usage irrespective of even any proof of their existence in pre-constitutional days cannot be countenanced as a source of law to claim any rights when it is found to violate human rights, dignity, social equality and the specific mandate of the Constitution and law made by Parliament. No usage which is found to be pernicious and considered to be in derogation of the law of the land or opposed to public policy or social decency can be accepted or upheld by courts in the country."

55. As early as 1500-600 BC in Isha-Upanishads, it is professed as follows:

"The universe along with its creatures belongs to the land. No creature is superior to any other. Human beings should not be above nature. Let no one species encroach over the rights and privileges of other species."

Non-essential activities

Right to life

72. ... So far as animals are concerned, in our view, "life" means something more than mere survival or existence or instrumental value for human-beings, but to lead a life with some intrinsic worth, honour and dignity. Animals' well-being and welfare have been statutorily recognized under Sections 3 and 11 of the Act and the rights framed under the Act. Right to live in a healthy and clean atmosphere and right to get protection from human beings against inflicting unnecessary pain or suffering is a right guaranteed to the animals under Sections 3 and 11 of the PCA Act read with Article 51A(g) of the Constitution. Right to get food, shelter is also a guaranteed right under Sections 3 and 11 of the PCA Act and the Rules framed thereunder, especially when they are domesticated. Right to dignity and fair treatment is, therefore, not confined to human beings alone, but to animals as well. Right, not to be beaten, kicked, over-ridden, over-loading is also a right recognized by Section 11 read with Section 3 of the PCA Act. Animals have also a right against the human beings not to be tortured and against infliction of unnecessary pain or suffering. Penalty for violation of those rights are insignificant, since laws are made by humans. Punishment prescribed in Section 11(1) is not commensurate with the gravity of the offence, hence being violated with impunity defeating the very object and purpose of the Act, hence the necessity of taking disciplinary action against those officers who fail to discharge

their duties to safeguard the statutory rights of animals under the PCA Act.

...

89... PCA Act, therefore, cast not only duties on human beings, but also confer corresponding rights on animals, which is being taken away by the State Act (TNRJ Act) by conferring rights on the organizers and bull tamers, to conduct Jallikattu, which is inconsistent and in direct collision with Section 3, Section 11(1)(a), 11(1)(m)(ii) and Section 22 of the PCA Act read with Articles 51A(g) & (h) of the Constitution and hence repugnant to the PCA Act, which is a welfare legislation and hence declared unconstitutional and void, being violative of Article 254(1) of the Constitution of India.

90. **We, therefore, hold that AWBI is right in its stand that Jallikattu, bullock-cart race and such events per se violate Sections 3, 11(1)(a) and 11(1)(m)(ii) of PCA Act and hence we uphold the notification dated 11.7.2011 issued by the Central Government, consequently, bulls cannot be used as performing animals, either for the Jallikattu events or bullock- cart races in the State of Tamil Nadu, Maharashtra or elsewhere in the country**..."

ARE YOU LEGALLY ENTITLED TO TAKE YOUR PET DOGS IN THE PUBLIC PARKS?[15]

AWBI has set out guidelines for taking the pet dogs to public parks. While setting out the guidelines for allowing pet dogs in public parks the AWBI observed that the number of people keeping dogs as companions has been increasing every year. Most of the owners live in apartments where there is no space to exercise the dog. Walking them on the pavement is difficult because of the pedestrian traffic, because the pavements are narrow and often the pedestrians feel scared to come in close proximity with dogs. Thus, it is only prudent that the dogs are allowed to be taken to parks for exercise as it is illegal to deny them the exercise they require and also it can turn them aggressive if they do not exercise properly.

Guidelines for taking/allowing pet dogs in public parks:

1. **For Owners**:
   a. Dogs must be duly leashed and walked by adults.
   b. Leash should not be longer than 6 feet.
   c. Dog must be leashed in all common areas, but authorities in charge of park cannot insist on use of muzzles.
   d. The owners may however assess the nature of their dog and voluntarily muzzle their dog if they feel the same is required for additional safeguard.
2. **For DDA/local authorities that own and manage parks**:
   a. As per the guidelines the sign boards which prohibit the entry of dogs/pets in the parks ought to be removed.
   b. Timings must be specified for the morning and evening hours when dog can be taken to the park for a walk and may be changed as per the season. The timings have to

15 Guidelines for Allowing Pet Dogs in the Public Park dated 15th November, 2016 issued by Animal Welfare Board of India

be reasonably long to allow the dog owners to walk their dog.

c. Parks may put up a board requiring the dog owners to carry scoops and pick up dog excreta and deposit it in the garbage provided for the said purpose.
d. The DDA and all the other local authorities that own and manage parks must withdraw bans/prohibition ordered vis-à-vis pet dogs being exercised in parks. All the signboards and notings on website or elsewhere to that effect ought to be removed.

AWBI in its notification observed that all over the world public spaces are common grounds for both people and their companion animals. We must co-exist and deal compassionately with our animal friends.

GUIDELINES-WITH RESPECT TO PET AND STREET DOGS, AND THEIR CARE-GIVERS, AND FOR RESIDENTS' WELFARE ASSOCIATIONS AND APARTMENT OWNERS ASSOCIATION

AWBI vide circular dated 26th February, 2015 laid down the guidelines with respect to pet and street dogs and their care-givers and for residents' welfare associations and apartment owners association. While doing so the Board observed that number of people keeping dogs as household companions is increasing, and as animal lovers/activists are increasingly showing compassion for street dogs by feeding them, and providing veterinary and other support, conflicts sometimes occur between the pet owners and care-givers of street dogs on one hand and Resident Welfare Association and Apartment Owner Association on the other hand. The duty to show compassion to all living creatures is a fundamental duty under Article 51A (g) of the Constitution conferred upon all the citizens of India and law of the land protect rights of non-humans.

1. **Guidelines for Pet Owners**
    a. Must ensure that the pets are not a source of nuisance to others.
    b. They should not abandon the pet animal under any amount of pressure as the same is not lawful.
    c. Barking is a natural form of expression for a dog and must and has to be tolerated in society. However, incessant barking can disturb neighbours. Pet owners must therefore make every effort to keep their dogs quiet, particularly during night hours.
    d. Must ensure that the pet is healthy and clean. Adequate health care and regular vaccinations must be given to the pet. Sterilisation is advisable.

e. Must clean up when the pet defecates in public premises and participate in other solutions for maintenance of cleanliness.
f. Discuss with their RWAs the ways and means to dispose of pet excreta. E.g. Have designated corners in which pets can be trained/encouraged to relieve themselves and designated corner/area where pet poop can be collected, deposited and composted, using saw dust etc.
g. Leash the pets in public places.
h. Pet owners cannot be debarred by RWAs or Apartment Owners' Association from using the lifts or elevators for the dogs. However, Pet owners must not object to use of 'alternate' lifts if there is more than one working lift or elevator in a building, which is conveniently accessible.

2. **Guidelines for care-givers to street dogs**
   a. Participate in sterilisation and yearly vaccination of street dogs.
   b. Provide, or assist animal welfare organisations in providing health care to street-dogs
   c. Do not feed the street dogs near the residences of other people
   d. Do not feed the street dogs immediately adjacent to the areas in which children play, or people take walks, or that are otherwise crowded.
   e. Do not feed in a manner that contributes to littering or dirtying any feeding site.
   f. Clean up feeding sites after feeding is over.
   g. Keep the status of sterilisation and vaccination of the dogs, one is feeding and taking care of, updated and accessible. Share the same with RWA or other residents to generate positivity and greater acceptability of the dogs.
   h. Participate in solutions for maintaining cleanliness even though one cannot control the defecation habit of the stray dogs.

3. **Guidelines for RWAs and AOAs etc.**
   a. Even upon obtaining consensus of majority of residents and occupiers RWAs and AOAs cannot legally introduce

any sort of ban on keeping the pet dogs or on the number of pets. No restriction can be imposed on the basis of the size of the dogs. If done so it will amount to interference with the fundamental freedom guaranteed to the citizens of India. i.e. freedom to choose the life they wish to live, which includes facets such as living with or without companion animals.

b. Dog barking cannot be cited by them as a valid and compelling reason for any proposed ban or restriction
c. If no municipal or other laws are violated by pet owners then it is not permissible for RWAs and AOAs to object on having pets. Their general body cannot frame bye-laws or amend them in a manner that is at variance with laws of the country.
d. Cannot disallow pets from the use of lifts and no charges can be imposed for the same.
e. Seeking a ban on pets from garden and parks is short-sighted as the RWAs and AOAs may or may not have any right over the garden or park in question. It is better to arrive at timings acceptable to all residents, when pets can be walked without inconvenience to other residents and the said timings may be intimated to the general body.
f. Cannot insist on the use of muzzles.
g. In absence of central or state laws requiring cleaning of pet excreta by pet owners, RWAs and AOAs cannot impose any rule, regulation or by-laws with respect to the same or impose special charges or fines on pet owners. However pet owners are advised to accept reasonable and lawful requests to participate in solutions aimed at peaceful community living.
h. Should not intimidate a pet owner into 'giving -up' or 'abandoning' a pet.
i. Cannot beat and drive away street dogs. Though they may be sterilised, immunised, vaccinated and released into same locality/territory.
j. No prohibition can be lawfully imposed prohibiting feeding of street dogs whether inside or outside the community premises and gated complexes.

k. Animal cruelty is an offence under section 11 of PCA and Section 428 and 429 of the India Penal Code-punishable with imprisonment and fine.
l. Attempts to interfere with or harass persons who choose to look after and feed community dogs can tantamount to very grave offence of criminal intimidation (Under Section 503 read with 506 of Indian Penal Code).
m. Any aggression or hostility that dogs may be subjected to may render them aggressive and hostile to human and they may then resort to snapping and biting in self-defence. If the same happens, human aggressors shall be liable for the blame.

SH. AJAY MADHUSUDAN MARATHE V. NEW SARVODAYA CO HOUSING SOCIETY LTD; CONSUMER COMPLAINT NO: 166/2008

Complaint: The Complainant had a pet dog named "Shimu". This dog was staying with the family of the complainant since 1997. The dog was registered with Navi Mumbai Municipal Corporation and the registration and license number showed that dog was pet dog of complainant.

Respondent was registered Co-operative housing society. The society had sent a notice to complainant on 11/5/2008 informing him that he cannot use society's lift for the movement of the dog. When complainant protested, the society communicated to complainant that use of society's lift by the dog may result in spread of diseases. The society informed the complainant on 28/5/2008 that he should get a certificate about the health of the dog from a veterinary doctor. The Bombay Veterinary College at Parel Mumbai issued a certificate that the dog has no infectious or contagious diseases. Even after submission of this certificate, the society continued with its stand of not allowing the dog to use the lift.

Society went even further and passed a resolution in the General Body Meeting (GBM) held on 3/8/2009 in this matter. The contention of the Complainant was that the society did not give an opportunity to the complainant to explain his side. The dog was old and was suffering with osteoarthritis, hence it was very difficult for him to use the stair case and use of lift was a must for the dog.

Consumer Forum held that:

> "Item no 1:-- Is the respondent responsible for deficiency in service to the complainant?
>
> Answer: Yes

Item no 2:-- Is the complainant eligible for getting compensation and legal expenses from the society for mental agony / harassment?

Answer: Yes

Explanation for Item no 1: ... The forum is of the view that society is registered co-operative housing society, and that complainant is member of the society. He pays the maintenance charges to society ...as a member of the co-operative society, the complainant is definitely eligible to lodge a complaint with this forum regarding deficiency in service and he is consumer of the society as per section 2 (1) (d) of the consumer protection act.

In this matter, whether the dog is a consumer of the society is not a pertinent point, and only the point to be checked is whether the complainant is consumer of the society. Hence the arguments put forward by the society are being rejected since the forum does not find any substance in it."

On merits, the forum observed that; "the complainant is a resident of the building for a long time. The society is registered in 1982. Complainant has valid license for the dog issued by the Navi Mumbai Municipal Corporation. The dog is staying in this building with the complainant for the last 11 years. The dog is now old and is suffering with osteoarthritis. Complainant stays on top floor of the society and hence it is very difficult for the dog to use the stair case. Complainant has attached a certificate from the Bombay veterinary college dated 16/6 /2008 along with his complaint. He has already been vaccinated against Antirabies, DHLPPI Corona ... With this certificate it is very clear that the dog owned by complainant is not suffering with any contagious disease and thus there is no possibility of anybody else being affected. Hence should be allowed to use the lift of the society.

Society has not brought to the notice of the forum any proof about the dog injuring any resident or visitor to the society. As per the complainant the dog needs to use the lift only 2-3 times a day. The forum feels the stand taken by the society about the dog not being allowed to use the lift is incorrect. The complainant has obtained valid license for the dog and also registered the dog. Society cannot prevent members staying on higher floors from having pet dogs. Taking into consideration the age and health of the dog, the complainant must be allowed to use the lift for the dog. But the society without any justifiable reasons prevented the complainant from using the lift for his dog. Even after getting the certificate about dog's health from the authorities the society refused to allow the lift to be used for the movement of the dog. The forum feels this is deficiency in service by the society as per section 2(1) (g) of the consumer protection act.

Society must allow the lift to be used for the movement of dog henceforth. Complainant should use the lift of the society for the movement his dog when no other person other than his family member is present in the lift. In case the dog urinates and/or dirties the premises of the society in any manner the responsibility of cleaning up will be that of the complainant."

DOGS AREN'T YOUR BEST FRIENDS? YOU MIGHT WANT THEM TO BE AFTER KNOWING SOME INTERESTING FACTS ABOUT THEM!

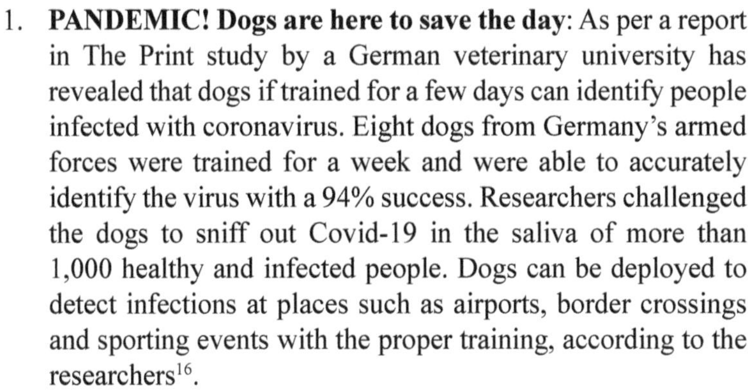

1. **PANDEMIC! Dogs are here to save the day**: As per a report in The Print study by a German veterinary university has revealed that dogs if trained for a few days can identify people infected with coronavirus. Eight dogs from Germany's armed forces were trained for a week and were able to accurately identify the virus with a 94% success. Researchers challenged the dogs to sniff out Covid-19 in the saliva of more than 1,000 healthy and infected people. Dogs can be deployed to detect infections at places such as airports, border crossings and sporting events with the proper training, according to the researchers[16].
2. A study has revealed that owning, walking and playing with a dog may help toddlers in their social and emotional development. Research has suggested that children from dog owning households have better social and emotional wellbeing than children from households with no dogs. As per the research children from dog owning households were 30% less likely to engage in anti-social behavior, 40% less likely to have problems interacting with other children and were 34% more likely to engage in considerate behaviors, such as sharing[17].
3. On the basis of the experiments it has been concluded that dogs are able to tell the difference between happy and angry human facial expressions[18].

16 https://theprint.in/world/dogs-can-sniff-out-coronavirus-infections-with-few-days-of-training-german-study-reveals/467711/; last visited on 27.07.2020

17 Newspaper Report, Times of India, 15.07.2020

18 https://www.nationalgeographic.com/news/2015/2/150212-dogs-human-emotion-happy-angry-animals-science/; last visited on 15.07.2020

4. As per the experts dogs can read facial expressions, communicate jealousy, display empathy, and even watch TV, studies have shown. They've picked up these people-like traits during their evolution from wolves to domesticated pets, which occurred between 11,000 and 16,000 years ago[19].
5. Dog's noses are incredibly sensitive and quite complicated, which makes them excellent at smelling bombs, drugs, and even animal poop, which can help with conservation[20].
6. If trained dogs can detect cancer and diabetes. Dogs can detect bacteria in urine samples with nearly 100 % accuracy[21].
7. A new study has revealed that even stray dogs that have never lived with people can also understand human gestures[22].

---

19 https://www.nationalgeographic.com/news/2015/07/150720-dogs-animals-science-pets-evolution-intelligence/; 15.07.2020

20 https://www.nationalgeographic.com/news/2016/03/160319-dogs-diabetes-health-cancer-animals-science/; last visited on 15.07.2020

21 *Ibid*

22 https://www.nationalgeographic.com/animals/2020/01/stray-dogs-communication-rabies-health/; last visited on 15.07.2020

RIOTS OVER DOGS[23]

So you think animal protection activism is a recent thing. Think again.

In the year of 1832 there were "Dog Riots" which were initiated and led by the otherwise genteel Parsis, against the British authorities. The Magistrates of Police (Bombay) in May 1832, in order to control the increasing menace of stray and rabid dogs in the then Bombay, extended the regulation which mandated the killing of Indian pariah dogs between April to May and September to October within public and government properties.

The dog killers were given 8 annas to kill each stray dog. Many of these dog killers due to the monetary incentive started eyeing dogs which were neither loose nor dangerous. However despite several warnings the police officers in Fort area (Bombay) did not stop from the unscrupulous act of killing which resulted in an outrage amongst the Parsis by whom the dogs are believed to be the gatekeepers of heaven and who believe that gaze of the dogs' wards of the evil. Parsis hold great respect for dogs and their religious text Avesta also has detailed commentary on the virtues of dogs and how they must be taken care of.

The situation became intense and on 6th July, 1832, a holy day for Parsis when a crowd of 200 Parsis came on the streets to mark the protest. By the next day preparations were done for full scale strike and palanquins of Britishers were stopped and pelted with stones. Soon the Parsis gathered the support of the other communities like Hindus, Jains and Muslims and the number of protesters reached close to 500.

The regulation was subsequently withdrawn. Further the demand to only capture the dogs and not to kill them placed before the British by the deputation led by Sir Jamsetjee Jeejeeebhoy, the Baronet, was also accepted resulting in settlement of the dispute.

---

23 https://www.livehistoryindia.com/snapshort-histories/2018/05/09/bombays-riot-over-dogs; last visited on 16.07.2020

INDIAN DOG BREEDS

Our knowledge regarding the different Indian Dog Breed is so limited that we simply refer to all of them as "Indie" without giving a heed to their distinct features, unique histories and behavioral traits. Here are few Indian Dog Breeds that every person should consider adopting dogs and should learn about[24]:

1. **Indian Pariah Dog**
   Found throughout the Indian sub-continent Pariah Dogs are extremely sharp and alert of its surroundings. They make good guard dogs due to their territorial nature. They are also social, highly intelligent and habitable to the Indian climate, which makes them a good fit for families.

2. **Kanni or Chippiparai**
   Ethnic to Tamil Nadu, these dogs for years now have been bred by royal families of Virudhnagar for hunting wild boars and deer. They are robust, resilient against most diseases and do best in warm climate such as of India. These dogs are easy to train and can serve as great security dogs.

3. **Pandikona**
   Initially a breed native to Kurnool District of Andhra Pradesh is now found around India. Pandikona are used for guarding, hunting and are very faithful and good with children. These dogs are adaptable to humans however not so much to other dogs as they are territorial.

4. **Indian Mastiff or Bully Kutta**
   Commonly found in Punjab, Haryana and Delhi. Indian Mastiff is commonly used for hunting and guarding. They are difficult to train but make excellent guard dogs. They are

24 *See* https://www.wagr.in/blog/breeds/native-indigenous-indian-dog-breeds/; *Last visited on 12/12/20*

adaptable to the Indian climate which makes them ideal guard and police dogs.

5. **Rampur Greyhound**
   They too are hunting dog and are bred for hunting. These dogs are extremely adaptable to the climate and possess great endurance. Their wide spaced eyes help them to expand their field of vision and be alert at all times.

6. **Bhakarwal Dogs**
   Ancient breeds found in the Himalayan Range, the Bhakarwal dogs are herding and farming dogs. Since they are extremely alert and strong, they make good watchdogs for sheep and other herd animals. They are suited to mildly cold weather. Unfortunately, these dogs are at the verge of extinction.

7. **Combai or Kombai**
   The Kombai Dogs are extremely faithful and have been bred as watchdogs and hunting dogs since the 9th Century. They need regular exercise and are best raised in large, non-enclosed settings. They need expert training and are highly intelligent and extremely loyal.

8. **Mudhol Hound**
   The Mudhol hound gets its name from a small town in Bagalkot district from the state of Karnataka. It is one of the most healthy dogs to have around. Their lineage and breeding makes sure that they can combat the Indian weather conditions. They do not have any particular health issues attached to them. Their loyalty towards the family makes them good guards and watch dogs. Though their fragile temperament may not make them a good therapy dog.

9. **Rajapalayam**
   The Rajapalayam, draws its name from the small town of Rajapalayam in Tamil Nadu, which is located in the Virudunagar district of the state. The best thing about the breed is that it was bred in India so it is adaptable to all weather conditions. They are very active dogs and require regular and long exercise, whether on leash or without leash. They make excellent guard dogs for the family.

India has been known for diverse bionetwork. When we think of fostering an animal, the first animal that comes to our mind is a dog. They are loyal, provide security and undoubtedly render unconditional love. We have so many Indian Dog Breeds out there however we hardly know anything about them. Instead, we prefer adopting pedigreed breeds from breeders who provide us with custom made dog, matching our societal status at the cost of charging exorbitant prices for our 4-legged friends. In our country people feed the strays but would rather adopt a foreign breed. There is a tendency to forget that for a foreign breed it is extremely difficult to adjust to the climatic conditions in India and can cause tons of health issues. The few people adopting the rescued from the streets also do not realize that adopting a stray involves a lot of patience, attention and emotional support. Many adoptive parents are happy as long as their dogs are little and in the puppy phase. However, the dogs soon grow old and the dog parents realize that they too require investments, veterinary visits, beneficiary diet, and dedication. These dog parents thereafter end up abandoning them due to their inability to give the required attention and emotional support. However, it is not all negative. There are stories of good Samaritans[25] that inspire us every day like the Pudducherry based dog lover who does not just feed the dogs but also gets them vaccinated, de-wormed and sterilized. These are essential, to avoid spreading infections and over-crowding of strays. Many like him may not adopt dogs but foster the injured and then release them once they are up on their feet. It is true that it is not financially possible for every person to take care of a pet however companionate behaviour towards every animal is the least that can be expected living in a civilized society.

25 *See* https://lifestyle.livemint.com/news/big-story/how-pets-helped-indians-get-through-the-pandemic-111606460691693.html; *last visited on 12/12/20*

PROGRESS? STATES OF MIZORAM AND NAGALAND HAVE IMPOSED A BAN ON DOG MEAT[26]!

As reported on the official website of Human Society International (**HSI**) India the state of Mizoram has amended to law to remove dogs from the list of animals which are declared to be suitable for slaughter under the law thereby bringing an end to the practice of consuming dog meat. The state has passed the Animal Slaughter Bill 2020 to end the cruel and illegal trade of dog meat. Though this may not result in complete ban on consumption of dog meat as it is only the slaughter and not sale and consumption of dog meat itself which has been banned. On the other hand, the state of Nagaland has also ended the brutal dog meat trade. The decision was announced on July 3, 2020 by the cabinet to end the import, trade and sale of live dogs and dog meat.

Even though the food safety regulations in India, Food Safety and Standard (Food Products Standard and Additives) Regulation, 2011, already impose a prohibition on the consumption of dog meat the practice of consuming the same has continued in some parts of the country like in the states of Nagaland, Mizoram, Tripura and Arunachal Pradesh, where thousands of dogs are every year illegally captured from the streets or stolen from homes, and cruelly transported from neighbouring states in gunny bags to be brutally slaughtered for consumption by being beaten to death in blatant violation of Prevention of Cruelty to Animals Act, 1960, the Indian Penal Code, and Food Safety and Standard Authority (FSSAI) regulations. Since the law is not imposed strictly the illegal trade of dogs for meat has been rampant. There have even

26 https://www.hsi.org/news-media/mizoram-closer-to-dog-meat-trade-ban/; https://www.hsi.org/news-media/india-nagaland-ends-dog-meat-trade/; last visited on 25.07.2020

been reports of dogs transported from neighbouring countries such as Myanmar and Bangladesh.

Around 30 million dogs and 10 million cats a year are killed across Asia for human consumption, with the trade most widespread in China, South Korea, Indonesia, Cambodia, Laos, Vietnam and parts of northern India. However, Hong Kong, the Philippines, Taiwan, Thailand and Singapore have dog meat bans in place.

DOG BREEDING AND MARKETING RULES

The Ministry of Environment, Forest and Climate Change notified the Prevention of Cruelty to Animals (Dog Breeding and Marketing) Rules, 2016 ("**DBM Rules**") made by the Central Government to regulate breeding, and marketing of dogs and provide as specified below.

1. **Registration for breeding of dogs**[27]
   a. Any breeder[28] can carry on or continue any breeding activity or own or house dogs for breeding and sale of dogs and pups, only after obtaining a certificate of registration in respect of the establishment being used or intended to be used by him for breeding or housing the dogs for breeding, from the State Board[29] in accordance with the DBM rules.
   b. Breeder has to prominently display the certificate of registration in the establishment.
   c. Such establishment has to be kept open for inspection by a person authorised in writing by the State Board.

27 Rule 2(g)of DBM Rules; "dog" includes a pup.

28 Rule 2(c) of DBM Rules, 2017; "breeder" means an individual or group of persons who own dogs of specific breeds for breeding and sale of dogs and pups, and includes boarding kennel operator, intermediate handler and trader. Rule 2(d) "boarding kennel operator" includes an individual or group of persons that keep pet dogs and pups for temporary housing in kennel or any other establishment. Rule 2 (h) "intermediate handler" means any person who receives interim custody of animals during the course of their sale or purchase. Rule 2 (k) "trader" includes an individual or group of persons who sells dogs and pups acquired from any breeder or pet shop, or from his or their own breeding facility, or imported for sale, or acquired in any other manner;

29 Rule 2(j) of DBM Rules, 2017 "State Board" means the State Animal Welfare Board constituted, in a State, by the State Government.

2. **Eligibility for Registration of breeder and establishment**[30]
   a. in the case of an individual:
      - he has attained the age of majority;
      - is of sound mind;
      - is not disqualified from contracting under any law for the time being in force.
   b. in any other case, the person is a corporation, company or other association of persons is duly registered in accordance with any law for the time being in force.

3. **Application for Registration**[31]
   a. An application for registration of breeder in respect of an establishment used or intended to be used by him for breeding or housing the dogs for breeding, has to be made to the State Board in the prescribed format (**Annexure I**) accompanied with a non-refundable fee of five thousand rupees.
   b. A separate application has to be made with regard to every establishment being used or intended to be used for breeding or housing dogs for breeding.
   c. The State Board, if on the inspection of the establishment by a team comprising of an authorised representative of the State Board and a veterinary practitioner and after considering the report signed by all the members of the team is satisfied that the breeder and the establishment complies with the requirements specified under the DBM rules, register the breeder in respect of that establishment and issue certificate of registration and depending upon the available space, facilities and manpower in the establishment, fix the maximum holding capacity for each dog breeding establishment to avoid overcrowding.

4. **The registration will not be granted by the State Board when**[32]**:**
   a. The information submitted by the breeder is found to be false; or

30 Rule 4 of DBM Rules
31 *ibid*
32 *ibid*

b. Material and deliberate misstatements have been made in the application; or
c. Falsified or fabricated records have been submitted to the State Board; or
d. the breeder has, been before submission of application been convicted of any offence under the PCA, or the Wildlife (Protection) Act, 1972 (53 of 1972) or for any offence relating to animals under any other law for the time being in force; or
e. the breeder refused to allow the inspection team free and unimpeded access to the establishment; or
f. the breeder does not meet the requirements as provided in the DBM rules.

5. **Validity, Transferability and Renewability of the Certificate**[33]
   a. A certificate of registration is valid for a period of two years.
   b. A certificate of registration issued under the DBM rules is non-transferable.
   c. It is renewable upon application being made to the State Board together with a fee of five thousand rupees.
   d. An application for renewal of registration has to be made, at least thirty days prior to the expiry of the registration, to the State Board in the format attached hereto.
   e. The establishments registered and covered under the purview of the Breeding of and Experiments on Animals (Control and Supervision) Rules, 1998 for the purpose of experiments, breeding and trading of animals, are exempted from registration under these rules.

6. **Requirements to be met by breeders and establishments used for breeding or housing of dogs for breeding**
   Every breeder must comply with the standards and requirements set out in **Annexure II** hereto.

7. **Conditions for sale**[34]
   a. pups less than eight weeks in age must not be sold.

33 Rule 4 and 5 of DBM Rules

34 Rule 8 of DBM Rules

b. dogs over six months in age must not be sold without first being sterilised (unless sold to another licensed breeder).
c. dogs and pups must not be sold for use in experiments, unless the purchaser is a breeder registered with the Committee for the Purpose of Control and Supervision of Experiments on Animals constituted under section 1 of the PCA.
d. only dogs in good health provided with the medical inoculations must be sold.
e. each pup sold must be micro-chipped and complete record of treatment and vaccination must be maintained.
f. pups must not be displayed in public places for the purpose of immediate sale.
g. Breeder cannot sell a dog to a pet shop[35] operating without a licence or for any other activity which is in contravention of any other law.
h. receipt for sale must be provided to each purchaser and copy thereof must be retained with the micro-chip number of the pup sold, and name, address and phone number of the purchaser.
i. The breeder must furnish to the purchaser in writing, details of feeding, dates of inoculations and de-worming of the pup and the name and address of the veterinary practitioner who was attending to it before sale.
j. Every breeder must screen prospective purchasers to ascertain their potential to take proper care of the breed, especially if it is a large one, to attend to its grooming, socialising, spatial and veterinary needs, and to bear the expense for its upkeep and maintenance.
k. Breeder must keep track of all pups produced and sold and it is the responsibility of the breeder to obtain information regarding the progress and state of health of all dogs sold by him, at least once each year.

35 Rule 2(l) of DBM Rules "pet shop" means a shop, place or premises, including any shop, place or premises in a weekly or other market, where pet animals are sold or housed, kept or exhibited for sale, or where any retail or whole-sale business involving the selling or trading of pet animals are carried out.

l. Every breeder has to rehabilitate a pup not sold within a period of six months, through an Animal Welfare Organisation[36].

8. Record Keeping[37]

a. Every breeder must maintain records of all animals housed in the establishment, including dogs for breeding and dogs for sale and be kept at the establishment for inspection in prescribed format (**Annexure III**).

b. Every breeder must maintain records of individual dogs, both male and female, including the following information, namely:—
   - breed;
   - name and number (or litter number);
   - micro-chip number;
   - sex, colour and markings;
   - date of birth;
   - names and microchip numbers of sire and dam;
   - name of breeder from whom acquired (where applicable);
   - name and address of person from whom directly acquired (where applicable);
   - date of acquisition;
   - date and duration of lease, if any;
   - date and place of mating;
   - names of persons handling the mating;
   - name and number of dog, including micro-chip number, with which mated;
   - name and address of owner (where applicable);
   - date of whelping;
   - number of pups whelped, by sex colour and markings;
   - litter registration number if any;

---

36 Rule 2 (b) of DBM Rules, 2017 "Animal Welfare Organisation" means a welfare organisation for animals recognised by the Board, and includes a Society for Prevention of Cruelty to Animals established in any district under the Prevention of Cruelty to Animals (Establishment and Regulation of Societies for Prevention of Cruelty to Animals) Rules, 2001 made under the Act;

37 Rule 9 of DBM Rules

- date of sale, death or rehabilitation of each pup so described;
- name and address of purchaser;
- cause of death as determined by a veterinary doctor and post mortem report of each dog that dies in the establishment; and
- any other information that is deemed relevant by the Board or the State Board.

c. Every breeder must use clear and concise contracts to document sales, lease arrangements, spaying or neutering contracts, and any other contract pertaining to the dogs at their establishments in prescribed format (**Annexure IV**).

d. Every breeder must maintain health and medical records along with separate vaccination record, of each dog, whether male or female, and of every pup in every litter in the prescribed format (**Annexure V**) and a copy of such record must be provided to the purchaser of the dog or pup.

e. All records maintained by the breeder have to be kept at least for a period of eight years.

9. Reports to be submitted by breeders[38]

a. At the end of each year, a report to the State Board, consisting of the information as to the total number of animals sold, traded, bartered, brokered, given away, boarded or exhibited during the previous year;

b. Provide such other information as may be required by the State Board, from time to time.

10. Effect of death of breeder registered[39]

In the case a registered breeder registered dies before the expiry of the period of registration, the registration shall be deemed to have been granted to his legal heirs in and shall remain effective for a of a period of three months from the date of death of the breeder. Thereafter a fresh application for registration of the breeder in respect of that establishment will have to be made in accordance for continuing the establishment.

38 Rule 11 of DBM Rules

39 Rule 12 of DBM Rules

11. No licence without registration[40]

Unless the breeder does not obtain a certificate of registration from the State Board, for the establishment being used or intended to be used for breeding or housing dogs for breeding, no licence shall be granted by any local authority.

40 Rule 13 of DBM Rules

ANIMAL BIRTH CONTROL (DOGS) RULES

The Animal Birth Control (Dogs) Rules, 2001 (**ABC (Dogs) Rules, 2001**) were made by the Central Government and were notified by the Ministry of Culture vide notification in the Official Gazette to regulate the sterilisation, vaccination, immunisation and release of dogs and provide as specified below.

1. **Classification of dogs and their sterilization**[41]
   a. All dogs are to be classified in one of the following two categories (i) pet dogs, (ii) street dogs.
   b. The owner of pet dogs is responsible for the controlled breeding, immunization, sterilization and licensing in accordance with the rules and the law for the time being in force within a specified local area.
   c. The street dogs have to be sterilized and immunized by participation of animal welfare organizations, private individuals and the local authority.

2. **Formation and Functions of Committee**[42]
   The rules require the local authority[43] to constitute a monitoring Committee for a period of three years for performing the following functions:
   a. Committee may issue instructions for catching, transporting, sheltering, sterilising, vaccinating, providing treatment and releasing of sterilised, vaccinated or treated dogs.
   b. It may authorise veterinary doctor to decide on case to case basis the need to put to sleep critically ill or fatally

41 Rule 3 of ABC (Dogs) Rules, 2001

42 Rule 4 and 5 of ABC (Dogs) Rules, 2001

43 Rule 2 (e) "local authority" means a municipal committee, district board or other authority for the time being invested by law with the control and administration of any matters within a specified local area.

injured or rabid dogs in painless method by using sodium pentathol (and in other manner).

c. It may create public awareness, solicit cooperation and funding.
d. It may provide guidelines to pet dog owners and commercial breeders from time to time.
e. It may get surveys done by an independent agency on the number of street dogs.
f. It may take such steps for monitoring the dog bite cases, to ascertain the reasons of dog bite, the area where it took place and whether it was a stray or a pet dog.
g. It may keep a watch on the national and international development in the field of research pertaining to street dogs control and management, development of vaccines and cost effective methods of sterilisation, vaccination etc.

3. Obligation of the local authority as prescribed under the ABC (Dogs) Rules, 2001:[44]

a. Provide for establishment of sufficient number of dogs pounds including animal kennels/shelters managed by animal welfare organisation.
b. Provide for requisite number of dog vans with ramps for the capture and transportation of street dogs.
c. Provide one driver and two trained dog catchers' for each dog van.
d. Install incinerators for disposal of carcasses.
e. If the Municipal Corporation or the local authority thinks it expedient to control street dog population, it is incumbent upon them to sterilize and immunize street dogs with the participation of animal welfare organisations, private individuals and the local authority.
f. Animal welfare organisation has to be reimbursed the expenses of sterilisation/immunisation at rate fixed by the Committee on fortnightly basis based on the number of sterilisation/immunisations done.

44 Rule 6 of ABC (Dogs) Rules, 2001

4. **Criteria and related duties for capturing/sterilisation/ immunisation/release of dogs**[45]
    a. Specific Complaints (for which the local authority in consultation with the monitoring Committee shall set up as dog control cell to receive complaint about dog nuisance, dog bites and information about rabid dogs)
    b. On receipt of specific complaint about nuisance or dog bite the same has to be attended on priority basis, irrespective of the area from which the complaint comes.
    c. On receipt of such complaint the details such as name of the complainant, his complete address, date and time of complaint, nature of complaint etc. has to be recorded in a register maintained for permanent record.
    d. Capturing for general purpose had to be on such dates and time as specified by the Committee.
    e. The dog capturing squad must consist of:
        - Driver of dog van
        - Two or more trained employee of the local authority who are trained in capturing dogs
        - One representative of any of the animal welfare organisation

        Each member of the dog squad has to carry a valid identity card issued by the local authority.
    f. On receipt of specific complaint or for capturing dogs in normal course the dog squad has to visit the concerned area, capture the dogs identified by the complaint in case of complaint oriented capturing and other dogs in case of general capturing.
    g. All the dogs caught have to be tagged for identification purposes and to ensure that the dogs are released in the same area after sterilization and vaccination.
    h. Only stipulated number of dogs, according to the Animal Birth Control Program target, must be caught by the van.
    i. A record of dogs captured has to be maintained in a register, mentioning therein the name of the area/locality, date and time of capture, names of persons in the dog squads on

45 Rule 7 of ABC (Dogs) Rules, 2001

that particular day and details about dogs captured such as number of male dogs, number of female dogs, number of puppies etc.

j. The dogs have to be captured by using humane methods such as lassoing or soft-loop animal catchers such as those prescribed under the provisions of Prevention of Cruelty (Capture of Animals) Rules, 1979.

k. While the dogs are being captured in any locality the representative of the local authority or of the animal welfare organization accompanying the dog squad has to make announcements on a public address system that dogs are being captured from the area for the purpose of sterilization and immunization and will be released in the same area after sterilization and immunization.

l. In the announcement residents of the area may also be briefly educated about the dog control programme and solicit the support of all the residents reassuring them that the local authority is taking adequate steps for their safety.

m. The captured dogs have to be brought to the dog kennels/ dog pounds managed by the Animal Welfare Organisations (AWOs).

n. On reaching the dog pounds all the dogs have to be examined by the veterinarians and healthy and sick dogs must be segregated.

o. Sick dogs should be given proper treatment in the hospitals run by Society for Prevention of Cruelty to Animals (SPCA)/other recognised institutions and only after they are treated they should be sterilized and vaccinated.

p. The dogs must be sterilized/ vaccinated under the supervision of the veterinarians of the hospital run by the Society for Prevention of Cruelty to Animals (SPCA), Animal Welfare Organization or other dog shelters.

q. After necessary period of follow up, the dogs must be released at the same place or locality from where they were captured and the date, time and place of their release must be recorded. The representative of Animal Welfare Organisations (AWOs) must accompany the dog squad at the time of release also.

r. At a time only one lot of dogs must be brought for sterilization, immunization at one dog kennel or dog pound and these dogs must be from one locality. Two lots from different areas or localities must not be mixed at the same dog pound or dog kennel.
s. The dog kennel must have sufficient space for proper housing and free movement of dogs. The place should have proper ventilation and natural lighting and must be kept clean.
t. Adults and puppies must be housed separately and amongst the adults the males and females also should be housed separately. Adequate arrangement for drinking water and food must be made for dogs while in captivity.
u. Female dogs found to be pregnant must not undergo abortion (irrespective of stage of pregnancy) and sterilization and should be released till they have litter.

5. Identification and Recording[46]

a. Sterilized dogs have to be vaccinated before release and the ears of these dogs are to be either be clipped and/or tattooed for being identified as sterilized or immunised dogs.
b. In addition, the dogs may be given token or nylon collars for identification and detailed records of such dogs must be maintained. Branding of dogs is not permitted.

6. Euthanasia of Street Dogs [47]

a. Incurably ill and mortally wounded dogs as diagnosed by a qualified veterinarian appointed by the committee must be euthanized during specified hours in a humane manner by administering sodium pentathol for adult dogs and Thiopental Introperitoneal for puppies by a qualified veterinarian; or
b. Euthanized in any other humane manner approved by Animal Welfare Board of India.
c. No dog must be euthanized in the presence of another dog.

46 Rule 8 of ABC (Dogs) Rules, 2001
47 Rule 9 of ABC (Dogs) Rules, 2001

d. The person responsible for euthanizing has to make sure that the animal is dead, before disposal.

7. **Furious or dumb rabid dogs**[48]
   a. On the receipt of complaints from the public to the Dog Control Cell of the local authority or on its own, the dog squad of the local authority can catch dogs, suspected to be rabid.
   b. The caught dog must then be taken to the pound where it must be isolated in an isolation ward.
   c. The suspected rabid dog is then to be subjected to inspection by a panel of two persons i.e. (i) a veterinary surgeon appointed by the local authority and (ii) a representative from an Animal Welfare Organisation
   d. If the dog is found to have a high probability of having rabies it must be isolated till it dies a natural death.
   e. Death normally occurs within 10 days of contracting rabies. Premature killings of suspected rabid dogs therefore prevent the true incidence of rabies from being known and appropriate action being taken.
   f. If the dog is found not to have rabies but some other disease it must then be handed over to the AWOs who will take the necessary action to cure and rehabilitate the dog.

8. **Disposal of Carcass**[49]
   The carcasses of such euthanized dogs must be disposed of in an incinerator to be provided by the local authority.

9. **Guidelines for breeders**[50]
   a. A breeder must be registered with Animal Welfare Board of India.
   b. Breeder must maintain full record of the number of pups born/died from individual bitches.
   c. Breeder must maintain record of the person buying the pups.
   d. He should ensure that the buyer has the required knowledge for the upkeep of the pups.

48 Rule 10 of ABC (Dogs) Rules, 2001
49 Rule 11 of ABC (Dogs) Rules, 2001
50 Rule 12 of ABC (Dogs) Rules, 2001

ANIMAL WELFARE BOARD OF INDIA V. PEOPLE FOR ELIMINATION OF STRAY TROUBLES AND OTHERS; (2016) 2 SCC 598

In the present case the contention of the AWBI was that "dogs have various uses for human society and have served the society for centuries and also have constitutional protection under Article 51-A of the Constitution of India and laws made have to be taken care of." Whereas, the Respondents resisted the said contention on the grounds that; "a bite by a stray dog creates a menace in the society and in name of compassion for the dogs, the lives of human beings cannot be sacrificed".

While passing an order in the present case the court observed that "there can be no trace of doubt that there has to be compassion for dogs and that they should not be killed in an indiscriminate manner but indubitably the lives of human beings are to be saved and one should not suffer due to dog bite because of administrative lapse.

The Court analyzed various provisions of PCA, and ABC Rules and observed that; "The local authorities have sacrosanct duty to provide sufficient number of dog pounds including animal kennels/shelters which may be managed by the animal welfare organizations, that apart, it is also incumbent upon the local authorities to provide requisite number of dog vans with ramps for capture and transportation of street dogs; one driver and two trained dog catchers for each dog van; an ambulance-cum-clinical van as mobile centre for sterilization and immunization; incinerators for disposal of carcasses and periodic repair of shelter or pound.

Rule 7 has its own significance. The procedure has to be followed before any steps are taken. Rules 9 and 10 take care of the dogs which are desirable to be euthanized.

...for the present it is suffice to say that all the State Municipal Corporations, Municipal Committees, District Board and local bodies shall be guided by the Act and the Rules and it is the duty and obligation of the Animal Welfare Board to see that they are followed with all the seriousness. It is also the duty of all the municipal corporations to provide infrastructure as mandated in the statute and the rules. Once that is done, we hope for the present that a balance between compassion to dogs and lives of human beings, which is appositely called a glorious gift of nature, may harmoniously co-exist...

Needless to emphasize, no innovative method or subterfuge should be adopted not to carry out the responsibility under the 1960, Act or 2001 rules. Any kind of laxity while carrying out statutory obligations is not countenanced in law."

ARE ABC RULES THE BEST WAY TO PROTECT STREET DOGS?[51]

The increasing population of the dogs in various regions has time and gain posed serious threat to the wildlife and as per the experts can be a probable cause for extinction or endangering of species. The uncontrolled increase of the dog population is also a menace in a lot of communities and societies. As most of the times when not sterilised on time they breed resulting in their increased number. Instead of a scientific and rational policy being implemented in the country, the issue has, most alarmingly, been hijacked by the self-styled "animal welfare" community in India that has promoted the maintenance of un-owned dogs in public places and even areas with wildlife. AWBI has promoted the ABC Rules and funded the sterilisation of free roaming dogs as the panacea to all related problems.

The law prohibits the relocation of dogs and the dogs ought to be released back in the same area from where they are picked after sterilisation and immunisation thereby making it impossible to curb the hazard which may be caused due to large number of dogs in particularly locality particularly near the wildlife regions. The AWBI, however, does not take the trouble to explain why public places and wildlife sanctuaries should be considered 'original areas' for un-owned, domestic dogs and how sterilisation prevents dogs from getting hungry and hunting wildlife. So, while dogs need to be removed from wildlife areas, the ABC rules require that they be released back from wherever they were picked up. In doing so, the ABC policy puts Scheduled species at risk and additionally enables the survival of source population of dogs. In view of the difficulties that are being faced due to the increased

51 https://www.downtoearth.org.in/blog/wildlife-and-biodiversity/india-s-wildlife-is-under-threat-from-free-roaming-dogs-70648 last visited on 06.07.2020

number of dogs, the law needs to be revised to the extent that it serves the dual purpose of wild life protection and ensure health and safety of the free roaming un-owned dogs.

Also, it sometimes so happens that for development purposes there is rehabilitation of humans and in such circumstances they often leave behind the stray dogs for whom they care. Due to the current laws these dogs cannot be relocated and often suffer due to hunger and lack of care. Thus, in interest of dogs, wildlife and people certain exceptions may be introduced in such rules to make them more effective for serving the desired purpose of animal protection, safety and health.

ADMINISTRATIVE DIRECTIONS FOR PROTECTION OF STRAY DOGS

Time and again steps have been taken by the administration to ensure that the public servants and officers act as the protectors of the stray and other animals and do not meet out any cruelty to such animals. Some steps that have been taken and guidelines that have been issued are as follows:

1. **Guidelines issued by Ministry of Personnel, Public Grievances and Pensions for prevent of cruelty to animals dated 26.05.2006**
   a. It provides that in terms of the provisions of the PCA, any government servant who indulges in act of cruelty to animals will make himself liable for action under the PCA. Besides, punishment under the Act, he would also make himself liable for action under CCS (Conduct) Rules for conduct unbecoming of a government servant.
   b. The circular requires that all the problems of stray animals have to be handled within the institutional framework available and no association, recognised or unrecognised, in any government/local-self-government organisation etc. can take recourse to act on their own either themselves or through any person employed by them like security guards etc.
   c. While residents and associations are free to address institutional agencies for redressal of grievances in this matter, no resident/association can interfere with freedom of other residents in tending animals etc. Intimidation, in any form is a criminal offence, apart from action under the appropriate criminal law, such person shall render themselves liable for action under the CCS Conduct Rules.

2. **Delhi Police Act, 1968 (Section 73-79, 99):** The Sections confer special powers on the police officers to take action when offence is committed against an animal. Relevant extract is attached as **Annexure VI** hereto.
3. The SP CID Crime Branch, Gandhinagar issued message to all the police commissioners and District Magistrates dated 12.11.2020 vide message no. Wildlife/CID/22/2020 to issue directions to all the police stations in Gujarat to be sensitive if any complaint for cruelty on animals or offences against the animals is received and register an FIR and issue suitable guidelines for the same.

CAN ANIMALS BE SACRIFICED IN A TEMPLE?

1. **Subhas Bhattacharjee v. State of Tripura, to be represented by the Chief Secretary, Government of Tripura and Others; 2019 SCC OnLine Tri 441**

   Issue: Whether act of offering an animal in a temple can be said to be a secular activity? Whether prohibiting the same would infringe the Fundamental right, as envisaged under Article 25(1) of the Constitution of India? and Whether a religious practice based on a custom, or tradition, not being an essential part of religion, can be allowed to continue?

   The Court observed that:

   COURTS INTERPRETATION OF ARTICLE 25 & 26 - RIGHT TO FREEDOM OF RELIGION:

   …44. On the issue in hand, we stand immensely benefited by the most recent decision rendered by the Constitution Bench (5 Judges-4:1) in Indian Young Lawyers Association v. State of Kerala, (2018) 13 SCALE 75 (5 Judge) (hereinafter referred to as 'Sabarimala")…opined that:

   "Nobody can say that essential part or practice of one's religion has changed from a particular date or by an event. **Such alterable parts or practices are definitely not the 'core' of religion where the belief is based and religion is founded upon. It could only be treated as mere embellishments to the non-essential part or practices**…There has to be unhindered continuity in a practice for it to attain the status of essential practice."

   …46. After discussion, Hon'ble R.F. Nariman, J in Para 21 of his opinion, inter alia, culled out, the following propositions:

   "21.6. ... Superstitious beliefs which are extraneous, unnecessary accretions to religion cannot be considered as essential parts of religion... **One test that has been evolved**

would be to remove the particular belief stated to be an essential belief from the religion-would the religion remain the same or would it be altered?... The Court should take a common-sense view and be actuated by considerations of practical necessity…"

86. …any custom or usage irrespective of any proof of their existence in the pre-constitutional days cannot be construed to be a source of law to claim any right when it is found to be violative of human rights which, in our considered view, would also include the right of animal to live with dignity...

93. The word "life" in Article 21 of the Indian Constitution is wide enough to include every living organism be it humans, animals, insects or bird…

108. In the instant case, sacrifice of animal in temples is not done out of necessity but merely on the unsighted conviction and credence that such activity would please the deity, who in return would bestow them with blessings and wellbeing.

109. … Evidently this particular practice by tradition is merely optional and cannot be figured as an essential and integral part of religion…

110. The ban on sacrifice of animal in Temples… does not infringe the fundamental right as enshrined in Part III under Art 25(1) of the constitution for the reason that such practice is contrary to constitutional morality and health and this activity carried in the name of religion is not intended to be protected.

111. It is only those practices which are fundamental and removing of which, will change the very foundation of the religion which is protected under the umbrella of Art 25 (1) of the Constitution. This practice of sacrifice of animal fails to succeed the doctrine of "essential test…"

…

124. Religious freedom is subject to health. One cannot deny the fact that sacrifice of animal in temple does affect mental and physical health of an individual. It is the duty of a State

to provide legal safeguards to protect individuals' life and to maintain good health of the community. The blood of the animals is allowed to flow in the open drains as a result causing foul smells. Also, it gets contaminated in the open drain, resulting into increase of diseases thus adversely affecting the health of the public at large, more so the residents of the area. Places of worship are considered as most sacred, holiest and cleanliest where people can peacefully connect to its creator. With blood of animals sprinkled around on the ground and the severed heads of the animals stocked infront of the deity, the view remains frighteningly dirty, leaving an impression of deficiency of holiness and peacefulness.

125. In State of Karnataka v. Dr. Praveen Bhai Togadia, (2004) 4 SCC 684 Court observed that the core of religion is based upon spiritual values, which the Vedas, Upanishad and Puranas were said to reveal the mankind seem to be -"Love others, serve others, help ever, hurt never" and "Sarvae Jana Sukhino Bhavantoo". Rig Veda also states "Behave with others as you would with yourself. Look upon all the living beings as your friends, for in all of them there resides one soul. All are but a part of that universal soul. …".

126. ... Religious practice based on a tradition cannot have an overriding effect of the Prevention Act so enacted...The prevention of cruelty Act is a welfare legislation which overshadows or overrides the so-called traditions…

138. In our view, Constitutional values are to be embraced and not to be superseded by personal beliefs. Religious practice, not being an integral and essential part of religion cannot override the provisions, specifically Section 3 of Prevention of Cruelty to Animal Act and other provisions of Part III, Part IV and Part IVA of the Constitution. Section 28 of the Prevention Act merely makes killing for a religious purpose not a punishable crime and more so in the light of the Article 25 does not make it permissible to commit such acts in the temple. Section 28 of the Prevention Act has to be interpreted in the light of Article 21, 48, 48A, 51A(g), 51A(h) and 51(A)(i) of the Constitution…"

MURALEEDHARAN T. AND ANOTHER V. STATE OF KERALA, REPRESENTED BY CHIEF SECRETARY AND OTHERS; 2020 SCC ONLINE KER 2313

Fact: A public interest writ petition was filed challenging the constitutionality of the Kerala Animals and Bird Sacrifices Prohibition Act, 1968 which prohibited the sacrifice of animals and birds in temples and temple precincts.

Issue: Is the Kerala Animals and Birds Sacrifices Prohibition Act, 1968 repugnant to PCA? What is the constitutional validity of Kerala Animals and Birds Sacrifices Prohibition Act, 1968? Does the impugned Act violate Article 25 and 26 the Constitution of India?

The Court after hearing both the parties and upon perusal of all the material on record observed that:

> "31. On a conspectus of the facts and the proposition of law laid down by the Hon'ble Supreme Court...we are of the view that freedom of conscience and free profession, practice, propagation, and management of religious affairs, the fundamental rights guaranteed to a citizen under Articles 25 and 26 of Part III of the Constitution of India are subject to, public order, morality and health, and more importantly, to other provisions of Part III of the Constitution, and therefore, it thus means all persons are equally entitled to freedom of conscience and the right freely to profess, practice and propagate religion. That apart, freedom to manage religious affairs protected under Article 26 of the Constitution of India, as per the law laid down...makes it explicit that such a concept deals with freedom of establishment of the religion itself and not the rituals that are developed by the worshipers, after the formation of religion to satisfy their personal needs. Likewise,

sacrificing animals for propitiating the deity is exactly what the Hon'ble Apex Court has considered in the judgments...and held that unless they are essentials of the religion, such acts are not protected under Article 25 of the Constitution of India. Therefore, merely by stating that freedom of conscience and free profession, practice and propagation as well as freedom to manage religious affairs are protected under Articles 25 and 26 of the Constitution of India, the petitioners are entitled to get the reliefs as sought for, to continue with sacrifices for propitiating any deity, cannot be sustained. So much so, no materials are forthcoming to establish that sacrificing animals and birds are essentials of the religion to drive home the case that Act, 1968 is interfering with Articles 25 and 26 of the Constitution.

32. Article 48 of the Constitution of India states that the State shall endeavour to organise agriculture and animal husbandry on modern and scientific lines and shall, in particular, take steps for preserving and improving the breeds and prohibiting the slaughter of cows and calves and other milch and draught cattle. Reading of the fundamental rights guaranteed under Part III, and the Directive Principles of the State Policy of the Constitution of India, make it clear that there is enough and more compassion extended under the provisions of the Constitution to protect the wellbeing and interest of animals. Moreover, Part IVA of the Constitution deals with fundamental duties, and it imbibes in every citizen of India the duty to protect and improve the natural environment, including forests, lakes, rivers and wild life, and to have compassion for living creatures.

...38. With due regard to the argument advanced to Section 28 of the Prevention of Cruelty to Animals Act, 1960, that nothing contained in this Act shall render it an offence to kill any animal, in a manner required by the religion of any community, there are no materials on record to substantiate which community of the religion is required under the Hindu or any other religion, to kill an animal, for propitiating, if not personal consumption, in the manner required in the religion.

We are also of the view that the expression used in Section 28 is "killing" and not sacrifice and, therefore, the said provision is intended to protect the manner of killing by any particular community, but not for any religious purpose.

40... The constitutional validity of the Kerala Animals and Birds Sacrifices Prohibition Act, 1968 is upheld."

ALIM V. STATE OF UTTARAKHAND AND OTHERS 2018 SCC ONLINE UTT 757

This case gives an insight as to how the rights of animals are protected in India by way of statutes, rules, and regulations, and constitutional and penal provisions.

Facts: The petitioner had sought direction to the respondent nos. 2, 3 & 4 to stop the illegal slaughtering of animals openly in the streets of village. The petitioner had highlighted the plight of cows in the State of Uttarakhand. The petitioner had prayed for construction of modern Goshala or Gosadans and also to provide medical assistance to the cows and stray cattle.

Held: After taking note of the various Acts and rules the Court further observed that; "…56. Uttar Pradesh Municipalities Act, 1916 and the rules framed thereunder.

> 67. There is a complete ban on slaughtering of cows as per Section 3 of the Act. The transportation of cow progeny is also regulated under Section 5 of the Act. It is the duty cast upon the State Government to establish institutions for taking care of uneconomic cow progeny.
>
> 68. The importance of cow as per Arthasastra, reads as under:
>
> "This food is stored the hymn continues in the highest of the upper worlds. All the gods and the deceased ancestors are the guardians of this food. Whatever is eaten, or split or scattered as an offering. Is altogether but a hundredth part of my whole body. The two great vessels. Heaven and Earth, have both been filled. By the spotted cow with the milk of but one milking, pious people, drinking of it, cannot diminish it. It becomes neither more nor less."

69. Section 47 of the Penal Code, 1860 defines word “animal” to include any living creature other than a human being. Section 289, 428 and 429 of I.P.C. reads as under:

“**289**. Negligent conduct with respect to animal.-Whoever knowingly or negligently omits to take such order with any animal in his possession as is sufficient to guard against any probable danger of grievous hurt from such animal, shall be punished with imprisonment of either description for a term which may extend to six months, or with fine which may extend to one thousand rupees, or with both.

428. Mischief by killing or maiming animal of the value of ten rupees.- Whoever commits mischief by killing, poisoning, maiming, or rendering useless any animal or animals of the value of ten rupees or upwards, shall be punished with imprisonment of either description for a term which may extend to two years, or with fine, or with both.

429. Mischief by killing or maiming cattle, etc., of any value or any animal of the value of fifty rupees.- whoever commits mischief by killing, poisoning, maiming or rendering useless, any elephant, camel, horse, mule, buffalo, bull, cow or ox, whatever may be the value thereof, or any other animal of the value of fifty rupees or upwards, shall be punished with imprisonment of either description for a term which may be extended to five years, or with fine, or with both.”

66. ... A milch cattle goes through a life cycle during which it is sometimes milch and sometimes it becomes dry. This does not mean that as soon as a milch cattle ceases to produce milk, for a short period as a part of its life cycle, it goes out of the purview of Article 48, and can be slaughtered…”

The Court by invoking the ‘parens patriae’ doctrine issued following directions to the for the welfare of cattle including cow:

A. No person to slaughter/offer/cause to be slaughtered/ cause offer to be slaughtered any cattle;
B. No person to export cattle for the purpose of slaughter directly or indirectly;

C. No person to sell beef or beef products in any form;
D. Prosecution against the owners of any cattle which are found on the streets, roads and public places;
E. Chief Engineers of all National Highways of the State were directed to ensure that no stray cattle, comes onto the roads;
F. Executive Officers of the Municipal Corporations and Bodies, Nagar Panchayats and Pradhans of the Gram Panchayats were directed to ensure that all the roads passing through their jurisdiction are kept free from the stray cattle to ensure free and smooth flow of the traffic.
G. The functionaries of the State were directed to act with the utmost compassion while removing cattle from road without inflicting unnecessary pain and suffering.
H. The Government Veterinary Officers/Doctors throughout the State were directed to treat all the stray cattle, and provide necessary medical treatment.
I. All the Municipal Corporation/Bodies, Zila Parishads and District Magistrates were directed to construct "gaushalas"/"gausadans" or shelters/homes, within 1 year, for cows and stray cattle, on scientific lines taking into consideration the comfort of animals to be housed there.
J. The State Government was directed to appoint infirmaries within a period of three weeks in order to treat and take care of the animals.
K. The State Government was directed to evict all the unauthorized occupants/encroachers from the gaushalas/gausadans within a period of three months.
L. The Circle Officer of all the Districts were directed to patrol the rural areas once in 24 hours to ensure that no cow is slaughtered.
M. All the Head Gurus of all the religions including Deras were requested to assist the State in construction of gaushalas/gausadans to house cows.
N. The State Government was directed to ensure that the draught animals do not carry more load while driving vehicles than prescribed,

O. The State Government was directed to ensure that all the cattle i.e. cow, bulls, buffalos and calf are kept and transported as per the applicable law

P. The State Government was directed to constitute societies for prevention of cruelty to animals in each district.

Q. The cost of transporting the animal to an infirmary or pinjrapole, to be paid by the owner of the animal.

ESTABLISHMENT OF SOCIETIES FOR PREVENTION OF CRUELTY TO ANIMALS (SPCA)

Prevention of Cruelty to Animals (Establishment of Societies for Prevention of Cruelty to Animals), 2001 (**"SPCA Rules, 2001"**) were made by the Central Government and were notified in the Official Gazette dated 26th March, 2001 for establishment of societies in each district of every state for prevention of cruelty to animals. The rules provide as follows.

1. **Establishment of SPCA**
   a. Each state has to establish a society for every district to be SPCA within 6 months of the commencement of the rules.
   b. The managing committee of the SPCA is to be appointed by the state government or local authority of the district[52]. It is to consist of Chairperson appointed by the state government or local authority[53] of the district in concurrence with AWBI and is to consist of such number of other members as considered necessary by the state government or local authority of the district subject to the condition that:
      - At least two members must be representatives of Animal Welfare Organizations which are actively involved in the work of prevention of cruelty to animals and welfare of animals preferably from within the district; and
      - At least two members must be the persons elected by the general body of members of the society.

52 Rule 3 of SPCA Rules, 2001

53 Rule 2(d) of SPCA Rules, 2001; "local authority" means a municipal board of municipal committee, a State Animal Welfare Board, district board or any local animal welfare organization authorized by any law for the control and administration of any matter relating to animals within specified local areas.

c. Duty of SPCA is to aid the Government, AWBI and local authority in enforcing the provisions under laws and to make such by-laws and regulations as it may deem necessary for efficient discharge of its duties.
d. SPCA or any person authorized by SPAC, if it has reasonable grounds to believe that an offence has been committed by a person under the PCA, may require such person to forthwith produce any animal in his possession, control, custody or ownership, or any license, permit or any other document granted or required to be kept by such person. It may stop any vehicle or enter any premises to conduct search or inquiry and seize the animal in respect of which it has a reason to believe that offence under the Act is being committed and deal with it in accordance with law.

2. **Setting up of infirmaries and animal shelters**[54]
   a. As per the rules adequate land and other facilities have to be provided by the State Governments to the SPCAs for the purpose of constructing infirmaries and animal shelters.
   b. Every infirmary/shelter must have a full time veterinary doctor and other staff for the effective running and maintenance of infirmary/animal shelter and must have an administrator appointed by SPCA.
   c. SPCA has to supervise the overall functioning of the infirmaries and animal shelters under its control and jurisdiction
   d. All cattle pounds and pinjrapoles owned and run by local authority have to be managed by such authority jointly with SPCA or Animal Welfare Organization[55].

54 Rule 4 of SPCA Rules, 2001

55 Rule 2(b) SPCA Rules 2001; "Animal Welfare Organisations" means a Welfare Organisation for animals which is registered under the Societies Registration Act of 1860 (21 od 1860) or any other corresponding law for the time being in force and recognised by the Board or the Central Government.

CPCSEA GUIDELINES FOR LABORATORY ANIMAL FACILITY- 2015

The Committee for Purpose of Control and Supervision of Experiments on Animals (CPCSEA) is a statutory body set up under the Prevention of Cruelty to Animals Act 1960. The goal of the following guidelines is to promote the humane care and conditions of animals used biomedical and behavioural research. The basic objective is to provide specifications providing animal well-being and for advancement of biological knowledge of both humans and animals.

1. VETERINARY CARE

a. Veterinary Care must be provided in such facilities and the responsibility of the same is that of the Veterinarian or the person with training and experience.
b. Daily observation of the animal by someone must be made and reported with frequent communication to the Veterinarian so that the problems in the animal's health and behaviour can be treated with immediate effect.
c. The Veterinarian can help in designing policies, procedures and methods, to prevent and control animal diseases (through Vaccination, etc), for operative or post-operative care of the animals, diagnosis and treatment of diseases as well as injuries. reviewing protocols and proposals, animal husbandry and animal welfare; monitoring occupational health hazards containment, and zoonosis control programs; and supervising animal nutrition and sanitation.

NOTE: The facility/institution needs to determine if a full time or part time Veterinarian is needed in the facility premises or not.

2. ANIMAL PROCUREMENT

a. All animals (like cattle, buffalo, sheep, goat, pigs, etc.) must be acquired lawfully as per CPCSEA guidelines.

b. Small animals like Dogs can be procured from registered breeders.
c. Large Animals can be procured from Farm, farmers or as per guidance of Wild life Department.
d. Cats can be bred separately for their use.
e. Rodents can be imported from foreign countries upon obtaining necessary licence from Director General of Foreign Trade.
f. For every incoming animal a health surveillance programme for the health screening of such animals must be conducted before purchasing the animal to assess its quality.
g. Each consignment of animals procured, must be checked to determine that it complies with procurement specifications. The animals must be quarantined, and stabilized as per the procedure appropriate for the animal and circumstances.

3. QUARANTINE, STABILIZATION AND SEPARATION

a. According to the guideline the newly brought animals must be kept separately from the already existing facility where the other animals are kept to avoid transfer of disease and introduction of new pathogens into an already established colony. The duration of quarantine maybe increased depending on type of infection.
b. For small lab animals (Rodents, etc) - quarantine of one week to one month
c. For large lab animals (Cat, dogs, monkeys, etc) - quarantine allowed upto 6 weeks
d. To limit the exposure of any zootonic infections (Like TB), effective quarantine procedures must be used. The non-Human Primates must be tested and if found positive for consecutive tests, then animal must be euthanized to stop the spread of infection to humans as well as other animals.
e. The newly obtained animals must be given time for physiologic, psychologic and nutritional stabilization before their use. This stabilization period shall be determined on the on the basis of species, type and duration of transport and intended use of animal.

f. It is recommended that animals of different species must be physically separated by housing different species in separate rooms to avoid interspecies diseases, behavioural change, etc. Cubicles, laminar-flow units, cages that have filtered air or separate ventilation and isolators can also be used for such physical separation.
g. Different species may be housed in the same room provided the two species have similar pathogenic status and are behaviourally compatible.
h. Separate care must be taken for sick animals and they also must be housed separately and be provided with constant health supervision for their recovery. Separate set of personnel must be identified for said purpose and such personnel should be restricted from entering any other facility or handling any other animal.

4. SURVEILLANCE, DIAGNOSIS, TREATMENT AND CONTROL OF DISEASE

a. All the animals must be daily observed for the signs of diseases, injury, illness or abnormal behaviour by animal house staff. More frequent observations may be done during postoperative recovery or when animals are ill or have physical deficit.
b. Appropriate methods for disease surveillance and diagnosis must be in place.
c. Post-mortem examination and signs of illness, distress, or other deviations from normal health condition in animals must be reported promptly to ensure appropriate and timely delivery of veterinary medical care.
d. Animals that show signs of a contagious disease should be isolated from healthy animals in the colony. If an entire room of animals is known or believed to be exposed to an infectious agent, the group must be kept intact and isolated during the process of diagnosis, treatment, and control.
e. Animals suffering from contagious diseases like Tuberculosis etc. must be euthanized as is practiced internationally to prevent its spread to other animals and often animal handlers.

f. Proper quarantine and isolation procedures must be employed.
g. Preventive medicine programs (like Vaccination, etc) must be initiated as per the currently acceptable present veterinary practices appropriate to the particular species and source.
h. Only animals in defined health status must be used in research and testing unless specific, naturally occurring or induced disease state is being studied.
i. Systems must be established to protect animals within the institution from exposure to diseases.
j. Transgenic and mutant animals may require special health protection due to them being susceptible to diseases. The transgenic animals are those animals whose germ line is foreign. Thus their proper biological screening must be done and need to be checked specifically for diseases. They may also cause new kind of infections amongst other animals.
k. Disease surveillance must include routine monitoring of colony animals for the presence of parasitic and microbiological agents that may cause overt or unapparent disease.
l. Cells, tissues, fluids, and transplantable tumors that are to be used in animals should be monitored for infectious or parasitic agents that may cause disease in animals.
m. The type and intensity of monitoring necessary must be determined depending upon professional veterinary judgment and the species, source, use and number of animals housed and used in the facility.
n. Diagnostic laboratory services must be available and used as appropriate. Laboratory services should include necropsy, histopathology, microbiology, clinical pathology, serology, and parasitology as well as other routine or specialized laboratory procedures, as needed. It is not necessary that all of these services be available within the animal facility (Facilities from other laboratories with appropriate capabilities may be used).

o. Animals with infectious / contagious disease must be isolated from others by placing them in isolation units or separate rooms appropriate for the containment of the agents of concern.

p. In certain circumstances, when an entire group of animals is known or suspected to be exposed or infected, it may be appropriate to keep the group intact during the time necessary for diagnosis and treatment, for taking other control measures, or for completion of a project.

q. The Veterinarian must have the authority to use the appropriate treatment and control measures, including euthanasia with at least one more veterinarian if required. If possible, veterinarian must discuss the situation with principal investigator to determine the course of action consistent with goals of experiment. If the Principal investigator is not available or of agreement cannot be reached then the Veterinarian must have the authority to do such acts as may be necessary to protect the health and wellbeing of the institutional animal colony and workers.

5. ANIMAL CARE

Institutions should employee people trained in laboratory animal science or provide bot formal and on-the-job training to ensure effective implementation of the program/

6. PERSONAL HYGIENE

a. High standard of personal cleanliness must be maintained by the animal care staff.

b. Facilities and supplies must provide with Personnel Protective equipment (PPE) e.g. Shower, Change of Uniforms, Footwear, etc. to meet the aforesaid obligations.

c. Clothing or Protective Suit gears should be supplied and laundered by the Facility. The same can be cleaned from commercial laundering service but one needs to make sure that clothing is decontaminated of all the hazardous microbial agents and toxic substances. The outer garments wore in the animal facility should not be worn outside. Also gloves, head covers, coats, coverall and shoe covers must be disposed of time to time.

d. Washing and showering appropriate for the program facility must be available.
e. Persons shall not be allowed to eat, drink, apply cosmetic, smoke, etc in the animal area.
f. A separate place for them to finish work with the animals and sit outside the place where animals are kept must be prepared.

7. ANIMAL EXPERIMENTATION INVOLVING HAZARDOUS AGENTS

a. Institutions must have policies in place that govern experimentation with such hazardous agents.
b. Institutional bio- safety committee members are knowledgeable about hazardous agents and must examine the proposal on animal experiments involving hazardous agents.
c. Use of animals in studies where any hazardous agents are to be used require special consideration and hence the procedures and facilities to be used must be reviewed by both the Institutional Bio-Safety Committee and Institutional Animal Ethic Committee (**IAEC**).
d. Disposal of tissues and fluids from used animal must be appropriately governed as per laid in practices of the institution/ bio-safety regulation.

8. MULTIPLE SURGICAL PROCEDURES ON SINGLE ANIMAL

a. Multiple surgical procedures must not to be practiced on a single animal for any experiment or testing unless specified in a protocol approved by IAEC.
b. Individual animals must not be used in more than one experiment, either in the same or different projects, without the express approval of the IAEC.
c. Animals that are used in more than one experiment should be permitted to recover fully from the first experiment before the subsequent experiment is performed.
d. Certification of attending veterinarian is required before the animal is subjected to the second experiment.

9. DURATION OF EXPERIMENT

No animal must be used for more than 3 years for experiment without adequate justification.

10. PHYSICAL RESTRAINT

a. Brief physical restraint of animals for examination, collection of samples and for variety of other clinical and experimental manipulations is allowed either manually or with devices of suitable size and design for holding the animal and operating the animal properly to minimise stress and to avoid injury to the animal.
b. Prolonged restraint of animals in a certain position (eg, chairing of animal) must be avoided unless it's essential to the experiment.
c. Animals must be handled by competent individuals, trained in methods that such that causes minimum distress and injury to the animal.
d. Restraint devices should be used to the minimum extent and only for minimum period required to accomplish the purpose of experiment or if required for the welfare and safe handling of the animal.
e. Animals to be placed in restraint devices must be given training to adapt to the equipment, prior to initiation of the experimentation.
f. Tranquilizers and anaesthetics may be used to initially restraint the animal which can prolong the recovery from the procedure. Thus, when such agents are used recovery of animal must be closely monitored.
g. Provision must be made for observation of the animal at appropriate intervals.
h. Veterinary care must be provided if symptoms or illness associated with restraint are observed.
i. The presence of illness, or severe behavioural change must be dealt with by temporary or permanent removal of the animal from restraint related protocol.

11. LOCATION OF ANIMAL FACILITIES TO LABS

a. Since laboratory animals are very sensitive to their living condition they must be housed in an isolated building far away from human habitations and not exposed to dust, smoke, noise, wild rodents, insects and birds.

b. This separation can be achieved by having animal quarters in separate building, wing, floor or room.

c. Animal rooms should occupy 50-60% the total constructed area and the remaining area must be utilized for various services such as stores, washing, office and staff, machine rooms, quarantine and corridors.

d. Sharp fluctuations in temperature, humidity, light, sound and ventilation should be avoided.

12. FUNCTIONAL AREAS

a. There must be sufficient animal area for:
   - Ensuring separation of species or isolation of individual projects when necessary;
   - Receiving, quarantining and isolating animals; and
   - Providing animal housing.

b. Professional judgement must be exercised to develop a practical system for animal care. If the facility is small or maintain few animals or maintain animal conditions the functional areas listed below may be unnecessary or included in a multipurpose area.
   - Specialized laboratories;
   - Area for activities such as surgery, intensive care, necropsy, preparation of special diets, experimental manipulation, treatment and diagnostic laboratory procedures, containment facilities;
   - Equipment area, if hazardous biological, physical or chemical agents are to be used;
   - Receiving and storage areas for food and bedding;
   - Area for keeping pharmaceuticals and biologics and supplies;
   - Space for administration, supervision and direction of the facility;
   - Area with shower, sinks, lockers and toilets for personnel;
   - Area for washing and sterilization of equipment and supplies;

- Autoclave for equipment;
- Area for food and bedding and separate areas;
- Area for holding soiled and clean equipment;
- Area for repairing cages and equipment
- Area to store wastes prior to incineration or removal.

13. PHYSICAL FACILITIES

a. Housing facility should be:
   - Compatible with the needs of the species housed
   - Designed and operated to facilitate control of environmental factors to exclude vermin and limit contamination associated with the housing of animals, delivery of food, water, bedding and entry of people and other animals;
   - maintained in good condition. Walls and floors should be made of durable materials the surfaces of which can be cleaned and disinfected readily.
   - Kept clean and tidy and operated with maximum hygiene possible.
   - It should have adequate and appropriate areas for food, bedding and equipment.
   - There should be pest control programme to monitor and control vermin.
   - Deodorants designed to mask animal odours should not be used in Housing Facilities and must not be used as a substitute for good cage and equipment cleaning practices and good ventilation.
   - Cleaning practices should be monitored on a regular basis to ensure effective hygiene and sanitation. This may include visual inspection, monitoring water temperatures and microbiological testing of surfaces after cleaning.
   - There should be proper water supply and drainage.
   - There should be adequate contingency plans to cover such emergencies as flooding and fire, or the breakdown of lighting, heating, cooling or ventilation.
   - Access to the housing facilities by unauthorised persons should be restricted.

- Durable, moisture proof, fire resistant, vermin and pest resistant materials must be used on interior surfaces of housing facility.
- The corridors should be wide for movement of equipment and personnel and must be kept clean.
- Utilities such as water lines, drain pipes, electrical connection must be preferably made outside the animal rooms.
- The doors must not be rust and must be dust and vermin proof. The doors should fit properly in their frames and must have an observation window.
- Windows are not recommended for small facilities. However, places where power cuts are frequent and backup power is not available window may be necessary to provide alternate source of light and ventilation.
- Flooring should be moisture proof, non-absorbent, skid proof, resistant to wear, acid, solvents and adverse effects of detergents/disinfectants. They should be capable of supporting racks, equipment, and stored items without becoming gouged, cracked, or pitted with minimum number of joints.
- Floor drains are not essential for rooms housing rodents and can be maintained by wet vacuuming or mopping with appropriate disinfectants/cleaning compounds.
- For using floor drains floor should be sloped and drain taps must be kept filled with water or corrosion free mesh.
- Drainage must be adequate to allow rapid removal of water and drying of surface.
- Inlet and outlet of drains must be fitted with wire mesh guard to prevent entry of wild rodents.
- Walls and ceilings should be free of cracks, unsealed utility penetrations, or imperfect junctions with doors, ceilings, floors and corners.
- Surface materials of wall and ceilings should be capable of withstanding scrubbing with detergents,

disinfectants and the impact of water under high pressure.

- Materials used for construction of roof should cater needs of local climatic condition to provide comfort to the animals.
- Separate storage areas should be designed for food, bedding, cages and materials not in use.
- Refrigerated storage, separated from other cold storage, is essential for storage of dead animals and animal tissue waste.
- An area for sanitizing cages and ancillary equipment is essential with adequate water supply
- All experimental procedures in small animals must be carried out in a separate area away from the place where animals are housed.
- Aseptic surgery for large animals must include separate functional areas for surgical support, like a preparation area, the operating theatre room or rooms, and an area for post-operative care and for treatment of animals.

14. ENVIRONMENT

a. Temperature and Humidity Control- Air conditioning is an effective means of regulating temperature. The same should be controlled depending on the number of animals in one facility.
    - Temperature range should be approximately 18 degree to 29 degree Celsius (at all times)
    - Humidity Range should be within the range of 30% to 70% throughout the year.
    - During extreme summer methods like sprinklers should be adopted

b. Ventilation- consideration must be given to ventilation of the animal's primary enclosure.
    - Heating, air conditioning and ventilation systems must be designed for 12 to 15 air cycles per hour.
    - Animal facility and human occupancy area should be separately ventilated.

c. Power and Lighting- Electrical system must be safe and provide for sufficient lighting.
    - It must provide illumination for people to work in the animals rooms and a lowered intensity of light should be there for animals.
    - Fluorescent lights are efficient and less than 400 lux is preferable for rodent facilities.

d. Noise Control- the facility should be provided with Noise free environment. Preferable less than 85dB is desirable for rodents and non-human primates. Concrete walls are further more effective than metal or plaster walls as their density reduces sound transmission.

15. ANIMAL HUSBANDARY

a. Caging or housing system should be designed carefully to facilitate animal well-being, meet research requirements and minimize experimental variables.

b. The housing system should:
    - Provide space that is adequate, permit freedom of movement and normal postural adjustments for the animal and have a place for resting which is appropriate for species;
    - Provide comfortable environment;
    - Provide an escape proof enclosure that confines animal safety;
    - Provide easy access to food and water;
    - Provide adequate ventilation;
    - Meet the biological needs of the animal (e.g., maintenance of body temperature, urination, defecation and reproduction);
    - Keep animals dry and clean, consistent with the requirement of species;
    - Facilitate research while maintaining good health of the animal;
    - must be constructed of sturdy and durable materials and designed to minimize cross-infection between adjoining units Animals must be caged as per the details specified in **Annexure VII** hereto;

- In order to simply the servicing and sanitation, cages should have smooth impervious surfaces which neither attract nor retain dirt and should have a minimum number of ledges, angles and corners in which dirt or water can accumulate. Feeding and watering devices should be easily accessible for filling, changing, cleaning and servicing.
- Cages, runs and pens must be kept in good condition to prevent injuries to animals, promote physical comfort, and facilitate sanitation and servicing.
- Particular attention must be given to eliminate sharp edges and broken wires, keeping cage floors in good condition. International guidelines can be referred from time to time to improve caging facilities.
- When animals are maintained in outdoor runs, pens, or other large enclosures, they must be protected from extremes in temperature or other harsh weather conditions. An adequate protective and escape mechanism must be provided. Shelter should have sufficient ventilation, and should be designed to prevent accumulation of waste materials and excessive moisture.
- Houses, dens, boxes, shelves, perches, and other furnishings should be constructed in a manner and made of materials that allow cleaning or replacement as per the generally accepted husbandry practices when the furnishings are soiled or worn out.
- To ensure proper sanitation the ground-level surfaces of outdoor housing facilities can be cemented or covered with absorbent bedding, sand, gravel, grass, or similar material that can be removed or replaced when needed.
- Accumulation of animal waste and stagnant water should be avoided.
- It is advisable to cover open pens with additional layers of materials (double fencing) to separate outside animals physically from the animals belonging to the colony to reduce spread of infectious diseases like TB etc.

16. SOCIAL ENVIRONMENT

a. Social environment has been defined to include all interactions among individuals of a group or among those able to communicate.
b. In determining suitable social environment, one has to see whether the animals are naturally territorial or communal, and accordingly the accommodation shall be provided.
c. When appropriate group housing should be considered for communal animals.
d. While grouping animals various factors such as the population density, ability to disperse, initial familiarity among animals, and age sex and social rank must be considered before housing them together.

NOTE: The above factors need to be considered because it has an immense effect on reproduction, metabolism, immune responses, behaviour and psychology.

17. ACTIVITY

a. Provisions should be made for animals with specialized locomotion pattern to express their natural habitat especially when the animals are held for long periods. E.g., artificial trees, ropes, bars and perches are appropriate for non-human primates
b. Pens, runs, other out-of-cage space provide more opportunity for exercise and is recommended for holding dogs for long periods.

18. FOOD

a. The animal must be fed with palatable, nutritional and non-contaminated food daily unless the experimental protocol requires otherwise.
b. The food must be served in adequate portions to ensure the normal growth in immature animals and to maintain, weight, reproduction and lactation in adults and should contain adequate nutrition with proper formulation and preparations.
c. The food must also be free from chemical and microbial contamination and should contain moisture, crude fiber, crude protein, essential vitamins, mineral, crude fat and carbohydrates for providing appropriate nutrition.

d. Feeders should have an easy access to the animal rooms.
e. Laboratory animal diets should not be manufactured or stored in facilities used earlier for farm feeds or any products containing additives such as rodenticides, insecticides, hormones, antibiotics, fumigants, or other potential toxicants.
f. Areas in which diets are processed or stored should be kept clean and enclosed to prevent entry of insects or other animals.
g. Precautions should be taken if perishable items such as meats, fruits, and vegetables are fed, because these are potential sources of microbiological and chemical contamination and can also lead to variation in the amount of nutrients consumed.
h. Diet should be free of heavy metals (like lead, arsenic, Nickel, Cadmium, etc).
i. Meat, fruits, vegetables and all the perishable items must be refrigerated if required. Unused open food must be stored in vermin proof conditions in order to minimize contamination and to avoid potential spread of disease-causing agents.
j. Food hoppers must not be transferred from room to room unless cleaned and properly sanitized.
k. When animals are fed in groups, there should be sufficient trough space or feeding points to cater to the number and size of animals that eat together at one time to avoid undesirable competition for food, especially if feed is restricted.
l. Uneaten perishable food must be removed promptly unless contrary to the eating habits or needs of the species.
m. Any alteration to dietary regimes should be gradual.

19. BEDDING

a. Should be absorbent, free from toxic chemicals and should be made of substances that do not cause irritation or infection to the animal and of type which is not readily eaten by animals.

b. Should be removed and replaced periodically with fresh materials as often as necessary to keep the animals clean and dry. In general, it is ideal to change the bedding twice a week or whenever requires.
c. The desirable criteria for rodent contact bedding is ammonia binding, sterilizable, easily stored, non - withering to the animal, uncontaminated, unlikely to be chewed or mouthed, non - toxic, non - smelly, nestable, disposable by burning, readily available, remains stable during use, manifests batch uniformity, optimizes normal animal behaviour, non - toxic to cage - washers, non - injurious and non - hazardous to personnel, non - nutritious and non - palatable.
d. Nesting materials for newly delivered pups must be provided wherever needed (e.g. Paper cuttings, tissue paper, cotton etc.)

20. WATER

a. The animals must have continuous access to fresh, potable, uncontaminated drinking as per the requirements.
b. Periodical monitoring of microbial contamination in water must be done.
c. Routine examination of watering devices (drinking nozzles and automatic waters) must be done to ensure their proper operation.
d. If required animals must be trained to drink water from automatic watering devices.

21. SANITATION AND WASTE DISPOSAL

a. Animal rooms, corridors, storage spaces, and other areas must be cleaned properly with detergents and disinfectants as and when necessary to keep them free of dirt, debris, and harmful agents of contamination.
b. Cleaning utensils, such as mops, pails, and brooms, must not be transported between animal rooms.
c. Where animal waste is removed by hosing or flushing, this must be done at least twice a day. Animals should be kept dry during such procedures.

d. For larger animals, such as dogs, cats, and non - human primates, soiled litter material must be removed twice daily.
e. Cages must be sanitized before animals are placed in them.
f. Animal cages, racks, and accessory equipment, such as feeders and watering devices, must be washed and sanitized frequently to keep them clean and contamination free.
g. Wire - bottom cages other than rodent cages must be washed at least once in every 2 weeks.
h. Equipment must be rinsed free of chemicals prior to use.
i. Minerals and organic compounds in the urine from animals such as rabbits and some rodents, such as guinea pigs, mice and hamsters often adhere to cage surfaces and necessitate treatment with acid solutions before washing.
j. Water bottles, sipper nozzles stoppers, and other watering equipment must be washed and then sanitized by rinsing with water of at least 82.2□ (180□) or appropriated chemicals agents (e.g. Sodium Hyperchlorite) to destroy pathogenic organisms.
k. Provision must be made for dipping or soaking the water bottles in detergents and disinfectant solutions.
l. Routine sterilization of cages, feed and bedding is essential and care must be taken to use clean materials from reliable sources.
m. Where hazardous biological, chemical, or physical agents are used, a system of equipment monitoring is recommended.
n. Deodorants or chemical agents other than germicidal agents must not be used to mask animal odours.
o. Sanitation practices must be monitored to ensure effectiveness of process and materials being cleaned. Intensity of animals odours such as that of ammonia must not be used as sole means to determine the effectiveness.

22. WASTE DISPOSAL

a. Waster must be removed regularly and frequently and disposed off in a safe and sanitary manner.

b. Waste containers containing animals tissues, carcasses, and hazardous wastes should be lines with leak-proof, disposable liners.
c. Waste storage must be separated from other facilities and must be kept free of vermins.
d. Hazardous waste if any must be rendered safe by disinfection, decontamination or other appropriate means before they are disposed off from an animal facility.

23. PEST CONTROL

Adaptation of programs which are designed to prevent, control, or eliminate the presence of or infestations by pests are essential in an animal home environment. Best results can be achieved by giving contracts to people/firm specialized in pest control.

24. INSTITUTIONAL POLICIES AND DISASTER PLAN FOR EMERGENCY

An institutional policy for care of and to safe guard the wellbeing of animals every day including weekends and holidays must be in place. It must include emergency veterinary care. Emergency procedures, names and telephone numbers must be prominently posted in animal facilities or must be placed in security department or near telephone for better reach. A disaster plan as a part of safety plan for animal facility must be prepared for safety of both the personnel and animals.

25. RECORD KEEPING

Records to be maintained by animal facility are:

a. Animal house plans
b. Animal facility /house staff records - both technical and non-technical
c. Health record of staff and animals
d. All SOPs relevant to experiments, care, breeding and management of animals
e. Breeding, stock, purchase and sales records
f. Minutes of institutional Animals Ethics Committee Meetings

g. Records of experiments conducted with the number of animals used
h. Mortality, Post-mortem Record, wherever required
i. Clinical record of sick animals
j. Training record of staff involved in animal activities
k. Water, feed and bedding materials analysis report
l. Health monitoring Records
m. Rehabilitation Records, wherever required.

26. STANDARD OPERATING PROCEDURES (SOPs) / Guidelines

a. The Institute must maintain SOPs describing procedures / methods adapted with regard to animal husbandry, maintenance, breeding, animal house activities microbial testing and experimentation.
b. A SOP should contain the following items:
    - Name of the Author
    - Title of the SOP
    - Date of approval
    - Reference of previous SOP on the same subject and date (Issue number and Date)
    - Location and distribution of SOP's with sign of each recipient.
    - Objectives
    - Detailed information of the instruments used in relation with animals with methodology (Model no., Serial no., Date of commissioning, etc)
    - The name of the manufacturer of the reagents and the methodology of the analysis pertaining to animals
    - Normal value of all parameters
    - Hazard identification and risk assessment

27. PERSONNEL/STAFF OF HOUSING FACILITY

a. The staff must be provided with all required protective clothing (face masks, head covers, aprons, gloves, gumboots, other footwear etc.) while working in animal rooms.
b. Facilities must be provided for change over with lockers, wash basin, toilets and bathrooms to maintain personal hygiene.

c. A regular medical check-up must be arranged for the workers to ensure that they have not picked up any zoonotic infection and also that they are not acting as a source of transmission of infection to the animals.

d. The persons working in animal house must not eat, drink, smoke in animal room and have all required vaccination, particularly against Tetanus and other zoonotic diseases.

e. Initial in-house training must be provided to all the staff. Few weeks must be spent on the training of the newly recruited staff, teaching them the animal handling techniques, cleaning of cages and importance of hygiene, disinfection and sterilization.

f. They must also be made familiar with the activities of normal healthy and sick animals so that they are able to spot the sick animal during their daily routine check-up of cage.

28. TRANSPORT OF LABORATORY ANIMALS

a. The mode of transport of animals must be determined depending upon the distance, seasonal and climatic conditions and the species of animals.

b. Animals can be transported by road, rail or air taking into consideration the above factors.

c. The transport stress should be avoided and the containers should be of an appropriate size so as to enable these animals to have a comfortable movement and protection from possible injuries.

d. Food and water should be provided in suitable containers or in suitable form so as to ensure that they get adequate food and more particularly fluid during transit.

e. The transport containers (cages or crates) should be of appropriate size and only a permissible number of animals should be accommodated in each container to avoid overcrowding and infighting (as specified in **Annexure VIII**)

29. ANAESTHESIA AND EUTHANASIA

a. Painful procedure must be conducted under appropriate anaesthesia.

b. Anaesthesia must be given for full duration of experiment.
c. Animal must be humanly sacrificed as per the approved method of euthanasia if at any stage of the experiment the experiment has to be abandoned or irreparable injury is inflicted on the animal. The choice of a method will depend on the nature of study, the species of animal to be killed. The method should in all cases meet the following requirements:
    - Death, without causing anxiety, pain or distress with minimum time lag phase.
    - Minimum physiological and psychological disturbances.
    - Compatibility with the purpose of study and minimum emotional effect on the operator.
    - Location should be separate from animal rooms and free from environmental contaminants.
    - Tranquilizers have to be administered to larger species such as monkeys, dogs and cats before a procedure of euthanasia.
d. Animal must be clinically dead before it is sent for disposal.
e. Unless it will affect the results of study sedatives, analgesics and anaesthetics must be used to control pain or distress during experiments.
f. Animals must be prepared for anaesthetics by overnight fasting and pre-anaesthetics.
g. Local anaesthetics for minor and rapid procedures must be used only under expert supervision.
h. Species characteristics and variation must be kept in mind while using an anaesthetic.
i. Side effects such as excess salivation, convulsions, excitement and disorientation must be suitably prevented and controlled.
j. The animal must remain under veterinary care till it completely recovers from anaesthesia and postoperative stress.

30. TRANSGENIC AND KNOCKOUT ANIMALS[56]

a. Housing, feeding, ventilation, lighting, sanitation and routine management practices for such animals are similar to those for the other animals.

b. Special care must be taken with transgenic/gene knockout animals where the animals can become susceptible to diseases where special conditions of maintenance are required due to the altered metabolic activities.

c. The transgenic and knockout animals carry additional genes or lack genes compared to the wild population. To avoid the spread of the genes in wild population, care must be taken to ensure that these are not inadvertently released in the wild to prevent cross breeding with other animals.

d. The transgenic and knockout animals must be maintained in clean room environment or in animal isolators.

e. The transgenic and knockout animals must be first euthanized and then disposed off.

f. For initiating a colony, the breeding stock must be procured from established breeders or suppliers ensuring that genetic makeup and health status of animal is known.

g. In case of an inbred strain, the characters of the strain with their gene distribution and the number of inbred generation must be known for further propagation.

h. The health status must indicate their origin, e.g. conventional, specific pathogen free or transgenic, gnotobiotic or knockout stock.

---

56 Guideline 33; "Transgenic animals are those animals, into whose germ line foreign gene(s) have been engineered, whereas knockout animals are those whose specific gene(s) have been disrupted leading to loss of function. These animals can be bred to establish transgenic animal strains. Transgenic animals are used to study the biological functions of specific genes, to develop animal models for diseases of humans or animals, to produce therapeutic products, vaccines and for biological screening, etc. These can be either developed in the laboratory or procured for R&D purpose from registered scientific/academic institutions or commercial firms, generally from abroad with approval from appropriate authorities."

COMPLIANCES FOR CONDUCTING EXPERIMENTS ON ANIMALS

Central Government on the advice of Animal Welfare Board of India has set up the Committee for the Purpose of Control and Supervision of Experiments of Animals (CPCSEA/Committee). The Committee has formed The Breeding of and Experiments on Animals (Control and Supervision) Rules, 1998 (BEA Rules, 1998) to regulate, control and supervise the experiments being carried out on animals and to ensure that the animals are not subjected to unnecessary pain or suffering before, during or after the performance of the experiment on them.

Any experiment which is performed on an animal is not unlawful if it is done for advancement by new discovery:

a. of physiological knowledge or;
b. of knowledge which will be useful for saving or for prolonging life or alleviating suffering or for combating any disease of human beings, animals or plants[57].

1. **Power to prohibit experiment**

   If CPCSEA on the report made to it, as result of inspection of institution or place where experiment on animals is carried on, is satisfied that the rules and regulations made by it are not being complied with, it may after giving an opportunity of hearing to such person or institution in the matter, by order, prohibit the person or institution from carrying on such experiments for a specified period or indefinitely, or may allow the person or institution to carry such experiments subject to such special conditions as it may deem fit.

2. **Penalties**

   If any person contravenes any order of the Committee or commits breach of condition imposed by the Committee then

57 Section 14 of PCA

he shall be punishable with fine which may extend to Rs. 200/-. If contravention or breach takes place in any institution, the person in charge of the institution is deemed to have committed the offence and is punishable accordingly.

3. **Who can carry on the business of breeding or perform experiment on animals?**[58]

   Only a registered establishment[59] can carry on the business of breeding[60] of animals or trade of animals for the purpose of experiments[61]. No establishment can perform experiments on the animals unless registered[62].

   Maintenance of Register: Every registered establishment has to maintain a register in prescribed format with complete particulars about the animals used from: day to day for conducting experiments, with the number of animals, the species, the age, gender and other relevant particulars [63].

   Permission before acquiring animals/conducting experiment[64]:

   Every registered establishment has to before acquiring an animal or conducting any experiment on animal/animals apply for permission of the Committee or the Institutional Animals

---

58 Rule 3 of BEA Rules, 1998

59 Rule 2(d) of BEA Rules, 1998; "establishment means any individual, company, firm, corporation, institution other than schools up to higher secondary level, which performs experiments on animals.

60 Rule 2(b) of BEA Rules, 1998; "breeder" means a person including an institution, which breeds animals for the purpose of transfer to other authorised institution for performing experiments.

61 Rule 2 (e) of BEA (Amendment) Rules, 2006 '(e) "Experiment" means any programme or project involving use of animal(s) for the acquisition of knowledge of a biological, physiological, ethological, physical or chemical nature; and includes the use of animal(s) in the production of reagents and products such as antigens and antibodies, routine diagnostics, testing activity and establishment of transgenic stocks, for the purpose of saving or prolonging life or alleviating suffering or significant gains in wellbeing for people of the country or for combating any disease whether of human beings or animals.

62 Rule 4 of BEA Rules, 1998

63 Rule 6 (a) of BEA (Amendment) Rules, 2001

64 Rule 8 of BEA Rules, 1998

Ethics Committee[65] ("**IAEC**") in the prescribed format to the Member Secretary of the Committee or the Institutional Animals Ethics Committee, as the case may be.

4. **How and in what manner can a breeder or an establishment stock animal?[66]**

   Animals can be stocked by the breeder and the establishment in the following manner:-

   a. in an animal house located in a quiet atmosphere undisturbed by traffic,
   b. the premises must be kept tidy, hygienic and the animals must be protected from drought and extremes of weather,
   c. animal cages for small animals and stables for large animals have to be such that animals are able to live in comfort and there is no overcrowding,
   d. cages/stables must be in conformation with the standards stipulated by Indian Standards Institution,
   e. animals attendants must be suitably trained and experienced in the duties allotted to them,
   f. animals must be looked after, before and after the experiments by a trained and experienced attendant;
   g. there must be satisfactory arrangement for looking after the animals during off hours and on holidays,
   h. detailed specifications for housing, feeding and maintenance of various species to be used in animal experimentation as notified by the Committee, must be adhered to by the registered establishment,
   i. The breeders and establishments must comply with the Indian National Science Academy Guidelines.

5. **What are the requirements to be fulfilled for performance of experiments on animals?[67]**

---

65 Section 2(f) of BEA Rules, 1998; "Institutional Animals Ethics Committee" means a body comprising of a group of persons recognised and registered by the Committee for the purpose of control and supervision of experiments on animal performed in an establishment which is constituted and operated in accordance with procedures specified for the purpose by the Committee.

66 Rule 7 of BEA Rules, 1998 and Amendment Rules, 2001

67 Rule 9 of BEA Rules 1998, and Amendment Rules 2006

In conducting experiments on animals, regard shall be had to the following conditions, namely:

a. Experiments in every case has to be done only by or under the supervision of a person duly qualified in that behalf;
b. experiments have to be performed with due care and humanity;
c. animals lowest on the phylogenetic scale which may give scientifically valid results should be first considered for any experimental procedure;
d. the experiment should be designed using minimum number of animals to give statistically valid results;
e. animals intended to be used for the experiments must be properly looked after both before and after experiments;
f. Personnel using experimental animal(s) should ensure welfare of animal(s) during their use in experiments and the investigators should provide for the aftercare and rehabilitation of animal(s) after experimentation.
g. Costs of aftercare and rehabilitation of animal(s) after experimentation has to be made part of research costs. Any rehabilitation treatment of an animal after experimentation should extend till the point animal is able to resume a normal existence;
h. experiments involving operative procedure more severe than simple inoculation or superficial venesection have to be performed under the influence of anaesthetic.
i. Anaesthesia should be administered by a Veterinary Surgeon or a Scientist/technician so trained for this purpose and who must remain present near the animal till the completion of the experiment;
j. animals if in the course of experiments under the influence of anaesthetic are injured such that their recovery would involve pain or suffering, such animal must be destroyed humanely while still under the influence of anaesthesia;
k. when there is reason to believe that an animal is suffering abnormal or severe pain at any stage of a continuing experiment, it should be painlessly destroyed at that stage without proceeding with the experiment;

l. the experiments not to be performed for the sole purpose of attaining or retaining manual skill except in schools, colleges and programmes duly scrutinized and permitted in registered establishments by the Committee;
m. experiments should not be performed by way of an illustration or as a public demonstration;
n. no paralyzing agent, including but not limited to curare, must be used or administered for the purpose of any experiment except in conjunction with anaesthetic of sufficient depth to produce loss of consciousness;
o. no experiment the result of which is already conclusively known, can be repeated without previous justification;
p. No chemical substance for the purpose of absorption through the conjunctival membrane or through the cornea can be applied on the eye of the animal which can cause pain;
q. dogs held for experimental purposes cannot to be debarked;
r. where experiments are performed in any institution, the responsibility is of the person in charge of the institution and in cases
s. where experiments are performed outside an institution by an individual qualified in that behalf, the-experiments, are performed on his responsibility.

6. **What are parameters to be adopted for application of euthanasia on animals?**
    a. When the animal is paralyzed and is not able to perform its natural functions; or
    b. it becomes incapable of independent locomotion; or
    c. it can no longer perceive the environment in an intelligible manner; or
    d. if during the experiment the animal has been left with a recurring pain wherein the animal exhibits obvious signs of pain and suffering; or
    e. where the non-termination of the life of the experimental animal will be life threatening to human beings or other animals;

7. **How can animals of experiment be transfer or acquired; who can transfer/from whom can such animals be acquired and who can acquire such animals?[68]:**
   a. A breeder cannot transfer any animal by sale or otherwise to an establishment which is not registered under the rules to conduct experiments on animals.
   b. (i) an establishment can acquire animal(s) for experiments from registered breeders only;
      (ii) in case of non-availability of animal(s) from registered breeders, the animal(s) can be procured from alternate legal sources after taking written permission from the authority competent to give such permission; and
      (iii) the establishment procuring such animal must maintain a record in this regard and produce the same before the Committee, whenever required;"
   c. For the acquisition of laboratory bred experimental rats and mice species of genetically defined strains not available within the country, the registered breeders or establishments have to apply for permission to the IAEC for the purpose of control and supervision of experiments on animals.
   d. After acquisition of animal(s) the establishment cannot transfer such animal(s) by sale or otherwise to any other establishment or person except to a registered breeder/ establishment.
   e. The animals used for experimentation in a production/ breed improvement programme may be given out by the breeder' institution for domestic use.
   f. In case an animal is not available from a registered breeder or from alternate legal sources within the country, genetically defined animals may be imported with permission of Directorate General of Foreign Trade.
   g. The aforesaid condition of non-availability within the country does not apply for laboratory bred rats and mice of genetically defined strains.

68 Rule 10 of BEA Rules, 1998 and Amendment Rules 2001 and 2006

h. A breeder/ an establishment must comply, with the directions given by the Committee for the purpose of controlling and supervising experiments on animals.

8. **Keeping of Records**[69]
   a. Every, establishment/IAEC has to maintain a record of the animals under its control and custody in the prescribed format.
   b. Every establishment/IAEC has to furnish such information, as the Committee may from time to time require in the prescribed format.
   c. All laboratories have to inform the exact number/ species of animals to the Member Secretary or any officer authorised in this regard by the Committee as per the prescribed format.

9. **Can a party carry on such experiments on animals on behalf of other party?**[70]
   Registered establishments are allowed to undertake contract research on behalf of any other agency in accordance with the PCA and the rules made thereunder.

69 Rule 11 of BEA Rules, 1998

70 Rule 12 of BEA Amendment Rules, 2006

GUIDELINES ISSUED BY THE UNIVERSITY GRANTS COMMISSION (UGC)

Guidelines for discontinuation of dissection and animal experimentation in Zoology/Life Sciences in a phased manner.

a. All educational institutions under the purview of UGC as per the guidelines have to prescribe laboratory curriculum involving animals in such a way to be compassionate with the animals, avoid experiments on animals, wherever possible, and use alternative in their place, experiments on animals are not performed merely for the purpose of acquiring manual skill, and not to use animals protected under Wildlife Protection Act, 1972. Animal's ethics should be included as a chapter in an appropriate course of study. Highlights of the PCA and Wild Life Protection Act must be displayed in the laboratories and elsewhere. Curriculum to be revised to accommodate the guidelines.
b. Dissection Monitoring Committee must be set up by the educational institutions coming under the purview of UGC which are engaged in dissection of animals and experiment using animals. DMC must ensure that animals that are permitted to be used for dissection/experiments in the guidelines are procured from ethical sources and not removed from the wild for these purposes, and transported to the laboratory without stress or strain to the animals if alive and anesthetized appropriately if they are used for dissection.
c. Institution are required to maintain appropriate records of procurement of animas, their transport if alive, number of animals used, use of anaesthesia/euthanasia if applicable.
d. Animals used in experiments should be, to the best extent possible, procured from laboratory bred sources, especially breeders approved by CPCSEA in which case their use will be under purview of IAEC.

e. For undergraduate programs, both major and allied levels the students per the guidelines shall not be required to dissect any animal. The teachers shall only demonstrate the dissection of one or more aspects of anatomy, which the students will observe and record. If found necessary the students may be required to flag specific parts in the specimens already dissected by the teachers and kept ready.
f. If animal anatomy is emphasized, the laboratory learning may make use of plastinated dissected specimens and/or digital alternatives, which are now available from commercial sources in plenty, such as ProDissector Frog, BioLab Frog, DigiFrog, Dissection works etc. Separate budgetary provisions should be made by the concerned institutions for the procurement of digital material and technology.
g. For post graduate students also the aforesaid guidelines are applicable however, the curriculum must provide for a choice to be expressed by the students whether to take to dissection of animals to go for a project related to biodiversity and/or biosystematics.
h. For those PG students who opt for dissection the curriculum may prescribe dissection of very few designated specimens.
i. PG students may be required to learn physiology and such other subjects in the laboratory using computer simulation learning devices and avoid use of animals in experiment and, this their removal from the wild for this purpose.

BAN ON EXPERIMENT ON ANIMALS

1. By notification in the Official Gazette, dated 13th January, 2014 Ministry of Health and Family Welfare brought into effect the Drugs and Cosmetic s (First Amendment) Rules, 2014 whereby after rule 148-B a new rules 148-C was inserted in the Drugs and Cosmetics Rules, 1945 which prohibits testing of cosmetics on animals and provides that; "No person shall use any animals for testing of cosmetics."
2. The Ministry of Health and Family Welfare notified the Drugs and Cosmetics (Fifth Amendment) Rules, 2014 in the Official Gazette vide notification dated 13th October, 2014. By the said amendment Rule 135-B was inserted after Rule 135-A of the Drugs and Cosmetics Rules, 1945 to prohibit the import of cosmetics tested on animals. Rule 135-B provides that; "No cosmetic that has been tested on animals after the commencement of the Drugs and Cosmetics (Fifth Amendment) Rules, 2014 shall be imported into the country."
3. Vide circular dated 12.04.2001 informed all the heads of the institutions affiliated to CBSE that all the experiments relating to dissection of animals in biology practical's shall be deleted from the Senior School Curriculum with immediate effect. No questions related to the dissection of animals will be asked in the practical examinations in Biology from March, 2002 examinations onwards.
4. Indian Medical Council (Professional Conduct, Etiquette and Ethics) Regulations, 2002 provide that no undue animal experimentations must be done. Any such experiments on animals should be done when these are necessary. Experiments must be done in a scientific and a humane way.

DO YOU KNOW THE LVING CREATURES THAT HAVE BEEN TO SPACE[71]?

Name of the animal	Year	Brief
1. Fruit Flies	1947[72]	This was done to help NASA address the effects of long-duration space missions on an astronaut's body and the way the body responds to new and stressful environments
	2015	Flies were chosen because of their genetic similarity to humans.
	2017	The FFL-01 mission studied the effects of spaceflight on the immune response to infection and also served as a test of the new hardware's performance[73].
		The Fruit Fly Lab-02 mission (FFL-02) was the second experiment to use NASA's Fruit Fly Lab hardware system aboard the International Space Station. This study explored the effects of spaceflight on cardiac disease and function[74].

71 https://history.nasa.gov/animals.html; last visited on 17.07.2020

72 https://www.nationalgeographic.com/news/2013/9/130918-animals-cats-dogs-monkeys-space-iran/; last visited on 16.07.202

73 https://www.nasa.gov/ames/fruit-fly-lab; last visited on 16.07.2020

74 *Ibid*

2. Monkey	1948 1949 1949	Albert I- a rhesus monkey. Lack of fanfare and documentation made Albert an unsung hero of animal astronauts. A live Air Force Aeromedical Laboratory monkey, Albert II, attained an altitude of 83 miles. The monkey died on impact. Albert IV a-It was a successful flight, with no ill effects on the monkey until impact, when it died.
3. Un-anaesthetized Mouse	1950	Did not survive the impact
4. Monkey named Yorik and 11 mice	1951	Yorick became the first monkey to survive space. Mice also were recovered.
5. Two Philippine monkeys- Patricia and Mike	1952	Patricia was placed in a seated position and Mike in a prone position to determine differences in the effects of rapid acceleration. Fired 36 miles up at a speed of 2000 mph, these two monkeys were the first primates to reach such a high altitude.
6. Dogs sent to space by Russia Dezik and Tsygan Dezik and Lisa	 1951 1952	 Successfully retrieved Dogs died A series of other successful and unsuccessful launches took place with dogs being recovered and dog fatalities respectively.
7. Laika stray dog (Soviet)	1957	She is one of the most popular amongst the animals launched in space. She launched in the space craft called Sputnik 2. In the U.S. she was eventually dubbed “Muttnik.” Laika was hastily trained and put aboard. There was no time to work out any re-entry strategy and Laika expired after a few hours of being in space. Sputnik 2 finally burned up in the outer atmosphere in April 1958.

8. Mouse	1958	Lost after rocket was destroyed. In a series of tests between1958-1959 several mice were lost.
9. Gordo a squirrel monkey	1958	Died on splashdown when a flotation mechanism failed.
10. Able, an American-born rhesus monkey, and Baker, a South American squirrel monkey	1959	Able died on the operating table from effects of anaesthesia, as doctors were about to remove an electrode from under her skin. Baker died of kidney failure.
11. Four Black mice	1959	Died
12. Sam, a rhesus monkey	1959	Recovered without any ill effects from the journey.
13. Miss Sam, a rhesus monkey	1960	Retrieved in good condition
14. Dogs (by Russia)	1960	2 dogs launched were killed due to booster explosion.
15. Ham a chimpanzee	1961	A post-flight medical examination found Ham to be slightly fatigued and dehydrated, but in good shape otherwise.
16. Goliath, a squirrel monkey	1961	Killed when rocket was destroyed
17. Enos a chimpanzee	1961	First chimpanzee to orbit the earth and was found overall in a good condition.
18. Félicette, a cat (France)	1963	Successfully retrieved from the first flight but died in the second.
19. Dogs Veterok and Ugoyok (Soviet Union)	1966	Hold a canine record of 21 days in space. It was to evaluate the prolonged effects during space travel of radiation from the Van Allen Belts on animals.
20. A payload of turtles, wine flies, mealworms, plants, seeds, bacteria, and other living matter (Soviet Union)	1968	First passengers of the new, manned moon ship of U.S.S.R.

21. Bonnie, pig-tailed monkey	1969	Bonnie died eight hours after he was recovered due to a heart attack brought about by dehydration.
22. Anita and Arabella, two common Cross spiders	1973	Successfully established the ability of spiders to spin webs in space.
23. Monkeys Lapik and Multik	1996	Mutik died which again raised questions as to the use of animals for research
Some other animals and living creatures which have been sent in space include: Rabbits, turtles, insects, spiders, fish, jellyfish, amoebae, and algae, tadpoles, guinea pig, insects, frog eggs, microorganisms, and plants.		

SLAUGHTER HOUSE RULES

Prevention of cruelty to animals (slaughter house) rules, 2000 ("**Slaughter House Rules, 2000**") were notified and became effective on 26th March, 2001 to regulate the area which can be used as slaughter house and specifications pertaining thereto, to regulate the manner in which animals can be slaughtered and to regulate the types of animals which can be slaughtered. It provides as is specified below.

1. **Where can animals be slaughtered[75]?**
   Any person can slaughter[76] an animal only in a recognised or a licensed slaughter house and in no other place in the municipal area.

2. **Which animal cannot be slaughtered[77]?**
   a. Animal which is pregnant; or
   b. Has an offspring less than three months old; or
   c. Is under the age of three months; or
   d. Has not been certified by a veterinary doctor to be in a fit condition to be slaughtered.

3. **Reception area or resting grounds for slaughter house[78] and Veterinary Inspection[79]**
   a. Slaughter house must have a reception area of adequate size which is sufficient for livestock subject to veterinary inspection.

---

75 Rule 3 of the Slaughter House Rules, 2000

76 Rule 2(b) "Slaughter" means the killing or destruction of any animal for the purpose of food and includes all the processes and operations performed on all such animals in order to prepare it for being slaughtered.

77 *ibid*

78 Rule 2(c) "Slaughter house" means slaughter house where 10 or more animals are slaughtered per day and is duly licensed or recognized under a Central, State or Provincial Act or any rules or regulations made thereunder.

79 Rule 4 of the Slaughter House Rules, 2000

b. Reception area must have proper ramps for direct unloading of animals.
c. It should have sufficient facility for feeding and watering of animals.
d. Separate isolation pens must be there in the slaughter house with water and food arrangements for the animals which are suspected to be suffering from contagious and infectious disease and for fractious animals.
e. As per the class of animals to be slaughtered adequate holding must be there in the slaughter house with adequate water and food arrangements.
f. Resting grounds must have overhead protective shelters.
g. Ante-mortem and pen area in slaughter house must be paved with impervious material, suitable to stand the wear and tear, having suitable drainage facilities, curbs of such material which is 150-300 mm high must be provided around the borders of livestock pen area, except at the entrance and pen must preferably be covered.
h. Veterinary doctor[80] must examine thoroughly 12 or less animals in an hour and 96 or less in a day.
i. After examining the animals' veterinary doctor must issue a certificate of fitness in prescribed format (**Annexure IX**).

4. **Lairages**[81]
   a. Every animal 24 hours before slaughter after being examined by veterinary doctor ought to be passed on to lairage for resting.
   b. Lairage must be of adequate size which is sufficient for the number of animals to be laired. It must have adequate water and food facilities.
   c. Pens of such lairage ought not to be less than 2.8 sq.mt. per large animal and 1.6 sq. mt. per small animal.
   d. Lairage must be constructed in a manner so as to protect animals from heat, cold and rain.

80 Rule 2 (d) "Veterinary doctor" means a person registered with the Veterinary Council of India established under the Indian Veterinary Council Act, 1984.

81 Rule 5 of the Slaughter House Rules, 2000

e. Animals must be kept in such lairage separately depending upon their type and class.

5. **Conditions for slaughtering animals and operating a slaughter house[82]**
   a. No animal can be slaughtered in sight of the other animals in the slaughter house
   b. There should be a slaughter hall in the slaughter house which is a separate section of adequate dimension sufficient for slaughter.
   c. Animal should not be administered any chemical, drug or hormone except the drug for treatment of any specific disease or ailment before the slaughter.
   d. Knocking section in slaughter house must be as it suits the animal and particularly the ritual slaughter.
   e. Knocking section and dry landing area associated with it must be so built that operator can easily escape from this section without allowing the animal to pass the escape barrier.
   f. A curbed-in bleeding area of the adequate size specified by the Central government must be provided in the slaughter house and must be so located that the blood does not splash on the other animals to be slaughtered or on the carcass being skinned.
   g. Blood drain and collection must be immediate and proper in slaughter house.
   h. A floor wash point must be provided in the slaughter house for intermittent cleaning.
   i. A hand-wash basin and knife steriliser must be provided for the sticker to sterilise knife and wash his hands periodically.
   j. Dressing of carcasses ought not to be done on the floor.
   k. Adequate means and tools for dehiding or belting of the animals should be provided with means for immediate disposal of hides or skins.

82 Rule 6 of the Slaughter House Rules, 2000

l. No hides and skin should be spread on the floor of the slaughter house for inspection and should be immediately transported in a closed wheelbarrow or a chute with self-closing doors.
m. In the dressing area of the slaughter house floor wash point and hand wash basins with steriliser must be provided along with means for immediate disposal of legs, horns, hooves, and other parts of animals.
n. Adequate space and facilities ought to be provided in the slaughter house for inspection of viscera of various animals slaughtered.
o. Slaughter house must have contrivances for immediate separation and disposal of condemned material.
p. Adequate arrangement must be there in the slaughter house for identification, inspection and correlation of carcass, viscera and head.
q. In the slaughter house a curbed and separately drained area or an area of sufficient size, sloped 33 mm per metre to a floor drain must be provided where carcasses can be washed with jet of water.

6. **Who can be engaged for slaughtering animals?**
   a. A person who possesses valid license or authorisation issued by municipal or other local authority.
   b. A person who is 18 years of age or above.
   c. A person suffering from communicable or infectious disease cannot be appointed and permitted to slaughter animals.

7. **How should the slaughter house building be constructed and structured?**

   Slaughter House building must be as per the specifications set out under Rule 7 of the Slaughter House Rules (**Annexure X**).

CIRCULAR TO PROHIBIT ILLEGAL KILLING AND SLAUGHTERING OF ANIMALS

1. Vide circular dated 4th July, 2016 and again vide circular dated 18th June, 2020 AWBI requested all the states to direct the concerned state authorities to take all precautionary measures to strictly implement the animal welfare laws to stop illegal killing of animals and to take stringent actions against the offenders violating the animal laws viz., PCA Act, 1960, Transport of Animals Rules, 1978, Transport of Animals (Amendment) Rules, 2001 and Slaughter House Rules 2001, municipal laws and directions of Food Safety and Standards Authority of India (**FSSAI**) for slaughtering of animals during Bark Id festival.

   AWBI noted that the FSSAI under the Ministry of Family Welfare has issued a direction in their LrNo.1-988/FSSAI/Import/2014 dated 06.08.2014 wherein it has defined animal as an animal belonging to any of the species specified below:

   - Ovines
   - Caprines
   - Suiliness
   - Bovines and includes poultry and fish

   It has directed that slaughtering of any animal other than of the species listed above is not permissible under the FSS Act and Regulation.

   This effectively means that camels cannot be at all slaughtered for food. Also wherever there is legislation prohibiting cow slaughter, slaughtering of cow is not allowed at all.

   Salient points of a few High Courts and Supreme Court Judgments regarding slaughter of animals were reproduced in the Circulars which are as follows:

a. In State of West Bengal etc. v. Ashutosh Lahiri and Ors.[83] the Hon'ble Supreme Court held that: "Slaughtering of healthy cows on Bakri Id day is not essential or required for religious purposes of Muslim, and accordingly, an order exempting slaughter of such cows from the operation of West Bengal Animal Slaughterhouse Control Act, 1950 was illegal.

   The slaughtering of healthy cows on Bakri Id is not essential or required for religious purposes of Muslims or in other words is not a part of religious requirement for a Muslim that a cow must necessarily be sacrificed for earning religious merit on Bakri Id.

   If there is no fundamental right of a Muslim to insist on slaughter of a health cow on Bakri Id day, it cannot be a valid ground for exemption by the State under Section of the West Bengal Animal Slaughter Control Act, 1950, which would in turn enable slaughtering of such cows on Bakri Id. Even Article 25 of the Constitution of India is not relevant in this context and cannot be resorted to."

b. In case of Siraj v. District Collector, the Kerala High Court held that: "for slaughtering any animal for the purpose of using its meat and food within the corporation limits, slaughter in a licensed slaughter house by a person licensed to slaughter is what would have to be resorted to.

   The Court further held that provision was available in their slaughter houses only for slaughtering cattle, goat, sheep and pig (at Kerala within the relevant municipal limits). There was none for slaughtering camel. Furthermore that there was no veterinary surgeon who could certify the fitness of camel or suitability of its meat for human consumption; or even any person licensed to slaughter and sell camel meat."

c. In the case of Animal Rights Funs v. State of Karnataka the Karnataka High Court noted that; "the petitioner had

83 Civil Appeals No. 6790 of 1983 with 6791 to 6794 of 1983, was as under

sought that the illegal transportation, and entry of camels into the State of Karnataka, particularly during festivals such as Bakri Id, for slaughter, be prohibited. Further, that the camels be transported to the habitat suited for them, within the State of Rajasthan.

The Hon'ble Lokayukta of Government of Karnataka has passed order dated 27.07.2015 on illegal slaughter of camels with direction to prevent cruelty to animals as well as illegal slaughtering of cattle and other animals with directions to prevent cruelty to animal as well as illegal slaughtering of cattle and other animals for effective implementation of the direction of the Hon'ble Supreme Court of India." The Court further noted that "the director of Animal Husbandry and Veterinary Services had issued a circular on 17th April, 1997, directing the Assistant Directors of the Taluk, Veterinary Hospitals, to prevent such illegal entry and slaughtering of camels under their official jurisdiction; and that a similar circular had been issued by Deputy Director, ANIMAL Husbandry on 31st May, 2006."

The Court required the State Counsel to ascertain as to whether the circulars were still in force, and upon learning that they were, took the view that no further circulars/ directions were required, while upholding those that had already been issued. The petition was then disposed of.

2. Again vide circular dated 20th July, 2016 AWBI took note of the fact that large number of animals are sacrificed and slaughtered on various occasion like Bali Pratha, Bakri Id festival etc, all over the country and during the transportation of animals rules for the transport of animals are not followed resulting in cruelty to animals. Illegal slaughtering is being carried out by unscrupulous persons in violation of laws and rules regulations thereunder.

   Vide the said circular AWBI requested all the states to direct the concerned state authorities to take all precautionary measures to strictly implement the animal welfare laws to stop illegal slaughtering/sacrificing of animals and to take stringent actions against the offenders violating the animal laws viz., PCA Act, 1960, Transport of Animals Rules, 1978, Transport of Animals (Amendment) Rules, 2001 and Slaughter House Rules 2001, Motor Vehicle Act, municipal laws and directions of Food Safety and Standards Authority of India (**FSSAI**) for slaughtering of animals during Bali Pratha, Bakri Id festival etc..

3. Vide circular dated 9th September, 2016 AWBI took note of the interim order passed by Madras High Court dated 18.08.2016 and 09.09.2016 in Writ Petition No. 13748, 13749, 11519, 13748 and 28899 of 2015 and W.P. No. 31476 of 2016 in the matter of E. Seshan and Ors. v. Union of India and Ors. and requested all the concerned authorities to take all the necessary action to stop illegal slaughter of camels as per the directions of the court. The court had in its order dated 18.08.2016 directed that; "in view of the stand of the Central Government and the provisions of the Central Act including Prevention of Cruelty of Animals Act, 1960 we cannot have a situation where such camel slaughtering is permitted especially in absence of facility for it."

BOMBAY SUBURBAN KHATIK ASSOCIATION V. MUNICIPAL CORPORATION OF GREATER BOMBAY; 2020 1 AIR BOM R 718

Facts: In the present case as per the petition, before 1973 slaughter house for sheep and goats was in Bandra Mumbai. The municipal authorities however, in order to ensure that slaughter houses were properly provisioned recommended construction of full-fledged abattoir and thus the slaughter house at Bandra was demolished and new abattoir near Deonar was constructed. However, the petitioners could not operate effectively at the abattoir and the municipal corporation after several representations of the petitioners and upon hearing them issued a communication dated 6th April, 1991 whereby each of the petitioners were informed that they are being granted individual licenses to slaughter at slaughter house in Bandra. On 20th July, 1991 municipal authorities issued another notification which was the impugned notification in the present case stating therein that the permission granted earlier was only for a period of three and that it was an experiment. The cancellation of the license was challenged to unfair, arbitrary, violative of the principle of natural justice.

Observed: The Court observed that; "... similar Writ Petition appears to have been filed by the All Maharashtra Khatik Association...in which following the Supreme Court decision... the municipal authorities were ordered not to issue licenses for slaughter of animals at any place other than recognised slaughter or licensed slaughter house."

Upon the analysis of the state laws and policies of the central government the Court observed that; "The law of the land, as enunciated and pronounced by the Supreme Court, left MCGM with no discretion to permit on any permanent or continued basis any such private slaughter-chambers. That would not only be contrary to the mandate of the statutes as noted above, but explicitly and directly in violation of the orders of the Supreme Court (which mandated immediate statutory conformity and compliance). To say, therefore, as the Petitioners before us do, that the withdrawal of the temporary permission is bad in law, unlawful or otherwise vitiated is a submission that does not commend itself in the least... We must therefore; hold which we do that it would have been wholly impermissible for MCGM to permit the continuance of the Petitioners' licenses. As a direct result the challenge to that continuance must fail..."

STATE OF GUJARAT V. MIRZAPUR MOTI KURESHI KASSAB JAMAT AND ORS.; (2005) 8 SCC 534

Issue/Facts: The Bombay Animal Preservation Act, 1994 was extended and made applicable to the state of Gujarat. The validity of the amendment to the said legislation i.e. the Bombay Animal Preservation (Gujarat Amendment) Act, 1994 imposing a complete ban on the slaughter of bulls or bullocks above the age of 16 years was challenged before the High Court of Gujarat. High Court allowed the writ petitions challenging the aforesaid legislation and struck down the impugned legislation as ultra vires the Constitution thereby lifting the total ban i.e. allowing the animals to be slaughtered consistent with the provisions of the Parent Act. Feeling aggrieved by the said decision State of Gujarat and Akhil Bharat Goseva Sangh filed the appeal against the said order.

The Court observed that:

> "137.... We have found that bills and bullocks do not become useless merely by crossing a particular age...cow and her progeny constitute the backbone of the Indian agriculture and economy. The increasing adoption of non-conventional energy sources like biogas plants justify the need for adoption of non-conventional energy sources like biogas plants justify the need for adoption of non-conventional energy sources justify the need for bulls and bullocks to live their full life in spite of their having ceased to be useful for the purpose of breeding and draught. This State of Objects and Reasons tilts the balance in favour of the constitutional validity of the impugned enactment. In Qureshi-I the Constitution Bench chose to bear it in mind, while upholding the constitutionality of the legislations impugned therein, insofar as the challenge

by reference to Article 15 was concerned that "the legislature correctly appreciates the needs of its own people." Times have changed; so, have changed the social and economic needs. The legislature has correctly appreciated the needs of its own people and recorded the dame in the preamble of the impugned enactment and the State of Objects and Reasons appended to it. In light of the material available in abundance before us there is no escape from the conclusion that protection conferred by the impugned enactment on cow progeny is needed in the interest of the nation's economy. Merely because it may cause "inconvenience" or some "dislocation" to butchers, restriction imposed by the impugned enactment does not cease to be in the interest of the general public…

140… we are unhesitatingly of the opinion that there is no apparent inconsistency between the directive principles which persuaded the State to pass the law and the fundamental rights canvassed before the High Court by the writ petitioners…

142. For the foregoing reasons, we cannot accept the view taken by the High Court. All the appeals are allowed. The impugned judgment of the High Court is set aside. The Bombay Animal Preservation (Gujarat Amendment) Act, 1994… is held to be intra vires the Constitution. All the writ petitions files in the High Court are directed to be dismissed."

STATE OF WEST BENGAL AND OTHERS V. ASHUTOSH LAHIRI AND OTHERS; (1995) 1 SCC 189

Facts: Respondents in the present appeal had filed a petition before the Calcutta High Court, challenging the validity of the exemption of slaughter of scheduled animal, namely, cows, from the operation of the West Bengal Animal Slaughter Control Act, 1950 on Bakri Id day. The Division Bench of the Calcutta High Court took the view that such slaughter of cows by members of Muslim community on Bakri Id day was not a requirement of Muslim religion and, therefore such exemption was outside the scope of Section 12 of the Act. The Division Bench allowed the petition and issued a mandamus to the State of West Bengal Respondent No.1 in the petition calling upon it and its delegate officers Respondents 2 to 16 in the writ, to forbear from giving exemption under Section12 of the Act in respect of slaughter of cows on the occasion of Bakri Id.

Issue: The present Appeal was filled by the Appellants challenging the aforesaid order of the Calcutta High Court.

Observed: The court in the present case observed that; "...when there is total ban under the Act, so far as slaughtering of healthy cows which are not fit to be slaughtered as per Section 4 (1) is concerned, if that ban is to be lifted, even for a day, it has to be shown that such lifting of ban is necessary for subserving any religious, medicinal or research purpose... Once the religious purpose of Muslims consists of making sacrifice of any animal which should be a healthy animal, on Bakri Id, then slaughtering of cow is not the only way of carrying out that sacrifice. It is therefore, obviously not an essential religious purpose but an optional one....For lifting the ban it should be shown that is essential or necessary for Muslims to sacrifice a healthy cow on Bakri Id day...But that is not the position.

We must therefore hold that before the State can exercise the exemption power under Section 12 in connection with slaughter of any healthy animal covered by the Act, it must be shown that such exemption is necessary to be granted for sub-serving an essential religious, medicinal or research purpose. If granting of such exemption is not essential or necessary for effectuating such a purpose no such exemption can be granted so as to bypass the thrust of the main provisions of the Act. We, therefore, reject ...that even for an optional religious purpose exemption can be validly granted under Section 12...

The contention of the learned counsel for the appellants that Article 25(1) of the Constitution deals with essential religious practices while Section 12 of the Act may cover even optional religious practices is not acceptable... We therefore entirely concur with the view of the High Court that slaughtering of healthy cows on Bakri Id is not essential or required for religious purpose of Muslims or in other words it is not a part of religious requirement for a Muslim that a cow must be necessarily sacrificed for earning religious merit on Bakri Id."

The former President of India Dr. Radhakrishnan in his speech on "**The Role of Cow in Indian Economy**"[84] has addressed as follows:

> "There is a great deal of sentiment for the cow; but in our daily life the welfare of the cow has been sadly neglected. There is a tendency among our people to maintain large numbers of cattle and to take pride in them, but adequate attention is not paid to their being properly fed and cared for. The result has been that the average productivity of the cow has remained low. In the changing economy of the country, there is increasing need for more productive cattle for both milk and draught.
>
> There is a large scope for non-official organizations supplementing the efforts made by the governmental agencies for cattle and dairy development in the country. Special

84 Bhartiya Govansh Raksham Sanverdhan Parishad v. Union of India; 2016 SCC OnLine HP 1290

mention may be made of the traditional institutions of *gaushalas and pinjrapoles* spread all over the country which, I think, have to play an increasingly important role in the field of protection and development of cattle. The *gaushalas and pinjrapoles,* as voluntary public bodies, have the advantage of being in direct contact with the people. With the advancement of science and the spread of education in the country, our people are becoming increasingly conscious of the need to apply improved methods in all fields of development. The gaushalas, which are reorienting their outlook on scientific lines, can carry the message of scientific development of cattle to the general public. Schemes for the development and reorganization of *gaushalas and pinjrapoles* as cattle-breeding-cum-milk production centres have been included in the Third Five Year Plan, and it is noteworthy that these institutions are availing themselves increasingly of the assistance provided under various schemes."

REGISTRATION OF CATTLE PREMISES

The Prevention of Cruelty to Animals (Registration of Cattle Premises) Rules, 1978 ("**RCP Rules, 1978**") have been made by the Central Government to regulate the registration of the premises on which cattle[85] i.e. oxen, buffaloes, cows, bullocks, and horses and their young ones are kept. Registering authority under the rules are the officers of veterinary department of the state government or a local authority as the state government may by special or general order specify[86]. It provides as is specified below.

1. **What premises needs registration under the said RCP Rules, 1978?**
   A premise in which not less than five heads of cattle are kept for the purpose of profit[87] must be registered.

2. **How to make application for registration?**
   Application has to be made to the Registering Authority with the following particulars for registration of cattle premises[88]:
   a. Full information regarding the number and types of animals kept or to be kept,
   b. The purpose for which they are kept or to be kept
   c. The provisions made with regard to floor space, flooring, ventilation, supply of food and water, disinfection, drainage, disposal of dung or unwanted matter, boundary walls.

3. **Validity of Certificate of Registration**[89]
   The certificate is valid for a period of three years from the date of the issue. It is however, renewable and may be renewed

85 Rule 2(a) of RCP Rules, 1978
86 Rule 2 (c) of RCP Rules, 1978
87 Rule 3 of RCP Rules, 1978
88 Rule 4 of RCP Rules, 1978
89 Rule 5 (ii) of RCP Rules, 1978

from time to time for a period of three years at a time, on application being made by the owner or in-charge of such premises within three months before the expiry date of the certificate.

4. **Need to display Section 12 of PCA**[90]
   If in any premises milch cattle is kept then the owner should display in or near the premises a copy of Section of 12 of PCA in language commonly understood in locality.

90 Rule 9 of RCP Rules, 1978

PERFORMING ANIMAL REGISTRATION RULES

The Performing Animal (Registration) Rules, 2001 ("**PAR Rules, 2001**") were made by the Central Government to regulate the laws pertaining to the performing animals' i.e. the animals which are used at or for the purpose of any entertainment to which the public are admitted through sale of tickets and provides as is specified below.

1. **Chapter V (Section 21-27) of PCA deals with the restrictions on exhibition and training of performing animals**
   a. "Exhibit" means exhibit at any entertainment to which the public are admitted through sale of tickets and "train" means train for the purpose of such exhibition, and the expression "exhibitor" and "trainer" have respectively the corresponding meanings[91].
   b. No person can exhibit or train any animal unless registered. Further no animal can be trained and exhibited as performing animal which the Central Government by notification in Official Gazette specify as animal which cannot be exhibited or trained as performing animals[92].

2. **Exemptions[93]:**
   a. Training of animals for *bona fide* military or police purposes or exhibition of trained animals.
   b. Any animal kept in zoological garden or by any society or association which has for its principal object the exhibition of animals for educational or scientific purposes.

91 Section 21 of PCA Act, 1960

92 Section 22 of PCA Act, 1960

93 Section 27 of PCA Act, 1960

3. **Offences**[94]

If any person:

a. Trains or exhibits any performing animal without registration;
b. Being registered exhibits or trains any performing animal with respect to which or in a manner with respect to which he is not registered;
c. Exhibits or trains any animal which cannot be so trained or exhibited because of the restrictions imposed by the central government;
d. Obstructs or wilfully delays any entry and inspection;
e. Conceals any animal to avoid inspection;
f. Being registered under the Act, fails to produce his certificates under the Act without any reasonable excuse;
g. Applies for registration when not entitled to be registered;
   Shall be punishable on conviction with fine which may extend to Rs. 500/- or with imprisonment which may extend to three months, or with both.

4. **Who is required to make an application for registration[95]?**

a. Any person who is desirous of exhibiting or training any performing animals[96].
b. The application must contain such particulars as set out in First Schedule (**Annexure XI**) to PAR Rules, 2001 and has to be made to the prescribed authority[97].
c. The application must be accompanied by a fee of Rs. 500/- which is payable in cash or in any other manner specified by the Board[98].

---

94 Section 26 of PCA Act, 1960

95 Rule 3 and Rule 4 of PAR Rules, 2001

96 Rule 2 (h) "performing animal" means an animal which is used at or for the purpose of any entertainment including a film or an equine event to which the public are admitted

97 2(g) PAR Amendment Rules, 2001; "prescribed authority " means the central government or such other authority including the Board or the State Government, as may be authorized by the central government.

98 Rule 2(b) Board means the Animal Welfare Board of India, established under section 4 and as reconstituted from time to time under section 5A of the Act;

5. **Use of animals in a film**[99]
   a. Every owner[100] who is desirous of hiring out or lending a performing animal in the making of a film[101] must give prior information to the prescribed authority in the prescribed format setting out there in the kind of animal, age of animal, physical health of the animal, the nature of performance to be done by the animal, the duration for which the animal shall be used for such performance, the duration and method of training of the animal for such performance and justification for the use of such animals in the film and such other information as may be required by that authority.
   b. Every such application has to be accompanied by a fitness certificate[102] issued by a veterinary doctor certifying that the health and fitness of the animal.
   c. A certificate of ownership is also to be attached in case the animal is covered under the Wildlife (Protection) Act, 1972.

6. **How can one inspect the register kept under the rules[103]?**
   a. During the office hours on any working day upon payment of fee of Rs. 20/-.
   b. A person can take extract from such register or request the prescribed authority to issue a certified copy of any entry in the said register on payment of fee of Rs.50/-.

7. **Variation of entries in the register**
   Application for the variation of any particular entered in the register maintained for the purpose of the rules has to be in the prescribed form set out in the Fourth Schedule (**Annexure**

---

99 Rule 7 of PPAR Rules, 2001

100 Rule 2(e) of PAR Rules, 2001 "owner" means the owner of an animal and includes any other person in possession or custody of such animal whether with or without the consent of the owner

101 Rule 2(c) of PAR Rules, 2001; film means a cinematograph film as defined in the Cinematograph Act of 1952

102 Rule 2 (d) of PAR Rules, 2001; fitness certificate means a certificate granted by a veterinary doctor to be nominated by the prescribed authority certifying the health and fitness of the animal;

103 Rule 10 of PAR

XII) of the rules and when any particular is varied the existing certificate of registration is cancelled and a new certificate is issued.

8. **Submission of report by veterinary doctor**[104]
   Every person who has been granted registration under the rules has to ensure that a monthly report of all the performing animals in the prescribed form in respect of their health, deaths and births duly certified by a veterinary doctor is submitted to the prescribed authority on or before the 7th of every succeeding month.

9. **Prohibition on exhibition and training of specified performing animals**[105]
   Performing animals whose performance has been prohibited under sub section (2) of section 22 of the Act cannot be trained or exhibited as a performing animal.
   In the exercise of the power under the aforesaid section by notification dated 14th October, 1998 the Government of India specified a list of the following animals which cannot be exhibited or trained as performing animals, with effect from the date of publication of the notification, namely:
   a. Bears
   b. Monkeys
   c. Tigers
   d. Panthers
   e. Lions

10. **Cancellation of Registration**[106]
   In case any owner registered as per the rules breaches any of the conditions of registration or any provision of PCA or the rules made the prescribed authority may suspend the registration pending enquiry and after granting an opportunity of hearing revoke the registration so granted or issue such orders or directions as it may consider proper or the welfare of the animals.

---

104 Rule 12 PAR Rules, 2001
105 Rule 13 of PAR Rules, 2001
106 Rule 16(3) of PAR Rules, 2001

11. Issue of duplicate copies of certificate[107]

Any person who has been granted registration under these rules may, on proof by him that the original certificate of registration has been lost or destroyed and on payment of a fee of Rs.100/-, be given a duplicate copy of the certificate of registration which shall have the same effect as the original certificate of registration.

CIRCULAR ISSUING ADVISORY TO THE MINISTRY OF ENVIRONMENT, FOREST AND CLIMATE CHANGE

Vide its circular dated 6th September, 2016 AWBI issued an advisory to the Ministry of Environment, Forest and Climate Change to ban the training, exhibition and use of elephants for performances in India. AWBI therein took note of the extreme cruelty to which captive elephants in India are subjected to when they are used for performances which involve training and exhibiting them and forcing them to perform tricks which are unnatural to them. It observed that in order to protect our national heritage animal, elephants need to be added to the list of wild animals banned from being used in performances in India. However, nothing has been done till date to prohibit the use of elephants as performing animals.

107 Rule 17 of PAR Rules, 2001

PEOPLE FOR ETHICAL TREATMENT OF ANIMALS (PETA) & ANR. V. UNION OF INDIA & ORS. 2005 SCC ONLINE BOM 997

Facts/Issue: People for Ethical Treatment of Animals (PETA) is a non-governmental organisation dedicated, to the welfare of animals. The Petitioners were aggrieved that the mandatory provisions contained in the Rules are observed in breach in the depiction of animals in cinematograph films, including those in the genre of commercial advertising. In order to consider the issues at hand in the aforesaid matter the Court analysed relevant provisions contained in the Performing Animals (Registration) Rules, 2001.

Observed: The court observed that; "… Board of Film Certification shall ensure that scenes "showing cruelty to or abuse of, animals are not presented needlessly."

> The court further held that: "The provisions which have been made in the Performing Animals (Registration) Rules, 2001, must be observed punctilious…in the entire process of training or exhibiting such animals including in the making of a film.
>
> …
>
> The Certification Rules framed under the Cinematograph Act, 1952 were amended on 12th November 1997, so as to require a declaration by the producer of a film that no cruelty was caused to the animal or to animals used during the shooting of a film. This provision was inserted prior to the notification of the Performing Animals (Registration) Rules, 2001. The Certification Rules framed under the Cinematograph Act, 1952, must be harmonized with the Performing Animals (Registration) Rules, 2001...

We are of the view that in order to ensure due observance of the Prevention of Cruelty to Animals Act, 1960, the Performing Animals (Registration) Rules, 2001 and the requirements laid down in the Cinematograph (Certification) Rules, 1983, certain directions are required to be issued in these proceedings. We accordingly issue the following directions:

(i) Consistent with the provisions that are enunciated…the Central Board of Film Certification shall hereafter in all cases where an applicant for certification of a film for public exhibition states that an animal has been used in the shooting of a film, require the production of a certificate from the Animal Welfare Board of India certifying that the provisions of the Performing Animals (Registration) Rules, 2001, have been complied with. Such a certificate shall be filed with the application for certification of a film for public exhibition and, in any event, before the film is certified for public exhibition;

(ii) …the Board shall process all applications for the grant of certificates for certifying compliance with the Performing Animals (Registration) Rules, 2001. This shall be done expeditiously within a period of two weeks of the submission of an application containing all the necessary particulars or, as the case may be, information as required by the Board;

(iii) We record the statement made by the Central Board of Film Certification on affidavit in these proceedings that the Board certifies films including all advertisements for public exhibition and that it observes the requirement of seeking a declaration to the effect that no cruelty was caused to animals during the shooting of a film produced in India and that the requirements stipulated in the Performing Animals (Registration) Rules, 2001 have been complied with from every producer while accepting applications for certification; and

(iv) The Central Board of film certification shall take steps to publish and/or circulate the aforesaid requirements in an appropriate manner to the concerned trade bodies."

MAHAVEER BISHNOI VS. STATE OF RAJASTHAN & ORS.; CIVIL WRIT PETITION (PIL) NO.6176/2014

Issue/Facts: Writ petition, was filed for banning Tonga Race on the ground that the race so organized was resulting in cruelty towards the animals under the Prevention of Cruelty to Animals Act, 1960 (hereinafter referred to as "the Act of 1960").

> **The Court held that**: "… horses that are forced to run on hard concrete road amidst speeding vehicles shouting spectators suffer mentally as well as physically. The desk research done during the study also indicates that no regulation can protect horses from cruelty and misery faced by them during the Tonga Races.
>
> Fear is worse than physical pain and the horses are terrorized by the entire atmosphere, which is created during the Tonga Races by the sheer presence of vehicles and large crowd yelling and screaming. In these circumstances, we cannot but agree with the report submitted by the Animal Welfare Board of India that "Tradition" is never a sufficient justification for cruelty, and a cruel tradition should never be allowed to define a culture. Traditions, like everything else, can – and must- evolve." Neither does this tradition have any religious significance. It simply arises out of economic gain to reap maximum money benefit, which results in the animal exploitation by using coercive methods and inflicting unnecessary pain, which is nothing but an evil practice.
>
> … the evaluation of the conditions shows that it is absolutely impracticable to control the suffering caused to the horses during the Tonga Races. We, therefore, hold that Animal Welfare Board of India (AWBI) was right in stand to ban the Tonga Race being organized in Nagaur district and such

events are in violation of Sections 3, 11(1)(a) and 11(1)(m)(ii) of the Prevention of Cruelty to Animals Act, 1960. Consequently, it is held that horses cannot be used for the Tonga Races in the State of Rajasthan.

We, therefore, make the following declarations and directions:

(1) The Collector, Nagaur and any other functionaries of the State of Rajasthan shall not permit any organisation, institution, body or person to hold 'Tonga Race' in the State of Rajasthan including the district Nagaur;
(2) The State of Rajasthan is directed to take appropriate steps to see that the persons-in-charge or care of animals, take reasonable measures to ensure the well-being of animals…
(3) The State must ensure the implementation of the Prevention of Cruelty to Animals Act, 1960 in its letter and spirit; and is scrupulously followed. The writ petition is disposed of with the aforesaid directions."

JUMBO CIRCUS V. UNION OF INDIA;
2000 SCC ONLINE KER 599

Issue: The writ petitions were in the present matter to over-reach the order dated 16-12-1998 by which the High Court of Delhi had upheld the validity of the notification dated 14-10-1998 prohibiting the exhibition and training of specified animals as performing animals with effect from the date of publication of the notification.

Observed: On consideration of all the contentions the court held that;

> "...Therefore, we have no hesitation in holding that the Government issued the impugned notification after forming an opinion upon consideration of the report which in turn is based on relevant materials. Hence, we have no hesitation in rejecting the contention of the learned Counsel for the petitioners based on absence of materials..."

Issue: Another contention was that was raised was that the impugned notification is discriminatory in so far as it is intended to ban exhibition and training of animals in circus only without bringing the zoos within its ken.

Observed: The Court held that; "In our considered opinion, the comparison sought to be made out is unrealistic and inexpedient... The inevitable conclusion, therefore, is that animals in zoos cannot be equated with animals in circuses and the contention to the contrary raised by the petitioners is devoid of merit and is accordingly rejected."

Issue: Another contention of the petitioners was that the impugned notification is arbitrary as it prohibits training and exhibition of animals only when the public are invited through sale of tickets, ...whereas, it does not prohibit training and exhibition of animals where the public can be admitted without sale of tickets.

Observed: The Court observed that; "...Section 21 defines the word 'exhibit' to mean 'exhibited' at any entertainment to which the public are invited through sale of tickets. Thus, persons who exhibit animals against sale of tickets are covered under this Chapter and those persons who may choose to exhibit animals without sale of tickets would fall under Section 11 of Chapter III of the Act... Thus, the impugned notification cannot be said to be arbitrary or discriminatory on the aforesaid ground."

Issue: It was then contended that the impugned notification invades the fundamental right of the petitioners to carry on their trade or business under Art. 19(1)(g) of the Constitution of India.

Observed: The Court held that; "This argument, in our opinion, proceeds on a fallacious premise which cannot be countenanced in the eye of law. The words 'trade' or 'business' as used in Article 19(1)(g) do not permit earring on of an activity whether commercial or otherwise, if it results in infliction of unnecessary pain and suffering on the specified animals... Neither the owners nor the employees of circus have a fundamental right to carry on trade or business in training and exhibiting endangered animals as the said trade is to such an obnoxious and pernicious activity geared towards mere entertainment which cannot be taken in the interest of general public to be a trade or business in the sense in which it is used in Article 19(1)(g) of the Constitution of India...

A Full Bench of the Delhi High Court in Ivory Traders and Manufacturers Association v. Union of India ruled as follows: "No citizen has a fundamental right to trade in ivory or ivory articles, whether indigenous or imported, assuming trade in ivory to be a fundamental right granted under Article 19(1)(g), the prohibition imposed thereon by the impugned Act is in public interest and in consonance with the moral claims embodied in Article 48-A of the Constitution; and the ban on trade in imported ivory and articles made therefrom is not violative of Article 14 of the Constitution and does not suffer from any of the mala fides namely, unreasonableness, unfairness and arbitrariness".

Issue: It was further contended that the impugned notification has violated the petitioners' fundamental right to life guaranteed under Article 21 of the Constitution of India.

Observed: The court held that; "Here again, we find no substance in the contention raised. In our considered opinion, right to life guaranteed under Article 21 does protect livelihood, but its application cannot be extended or stretched to the trade, business or avocation which is injurious to public interest or has insidious effect on public moral or public order. Accordingly, we reject the submission based on Article 21.

In conclusion, we hold that circus animals are being forced to perform unnatural tricks, are housed in cramped-cages, subjected to fear, hunger, pain, not to mention the undignified way of life they have to live, with no respite and the impugned notification has been issued in conformity with the changing scenario, values of human life, philosophy of the Constitution, prevailing conditions and the surrounding circumstances to prevent the infliction of unnecessary pain or suffering on animals. Though not homo-sapiens, they are also being entitled to dignified existence and humane treatment sans cruelty and torture. ...Many believe that the lives of humans and animals are equally valuable and that their interests should count equally. Their contribution to the health of humans is invaluable...In our considered opinion legal rights shall not be the exclusive preserve of the humans which has to be extended beyond people thereby dismantling the thick legal wall with humans all on one side and all non-human animals on the other side. While the law currently protects wild life and endangered species from extinction, animals are denied rights, an anachronism which must necessarily change.

Thus, on the whole, in the light of the foregoing discussion, we are satisfied that the impugned notification which is under challenge in this batch of writ petitions does not suffer from any of the infirmities as alleged and the same has only to be upheld. Accordingly, we uphold, the notification dated 14-10-1998 and dismiss these Writ Petitions."

N.R.NAIR AND OTHERS. V. UNION OF INDIA AND OTHERS; (2001) 6 SCC 84

Facts/Issue: In the present case appeals were filed from the judgment of Kerala High Court wherein it has upheld the validity of Section 22 of PCA and notification dated 14.10.1998 issued under Section 22 to the effect that no person shall train or exhibit any animals specified therein, namely bears, monkeys, tigers, panthers and lions. It inter alia, came to the conclusion that in the exercise of judicial review it was not possible for the court to examine the correctness of the decision of the government in issuing the said notification especially when it had not been shown that any relevant fact had been ignored or irrelevant fact taken into consideration.

Observed: In this case the court observed that; "In the very nature of things when the animals are used for performance in a circus, it required their training. It is for the Government to decide on the basis of the evidence on record and after taking into consideration other factors whether the training and exhibition of those animals would result in unnecessary pain or suffering being inflicted on them... it is the welfare of the animals which is of paramount consideration and it is only if the government is satisfied on the basis of the materials on record that unnecessary pain or suffering is inflicted on an animal during the course of training or at the time when it is exhibited that a notification under Section 22(ii) is issued. We are therefore unable to agree with the learned counsel for the appellants that the power contained in Section 22 is unguided...

It is true that the Act is silent with regard to the ownership of the animals with respect to whom a notification under Section 22 is issued, but inasmuch as the circus-owners keep the animals only for the purpose of training and exhibition it must follow that they cannot retain them for that purpose. We are informed by the learned Solicitor-General that rescue homes have been set up by the Central Government which are at zoological parks at Tirupathi, Visakhapatnam, Bangalore, Jaipur and Chennai."

The court held that the impugned notification was well within the parameters of PCA.

JADUGAR ANAND V. STATE OF M.P. AND OTHERS; 2002 SCC ONLINE MP 347

Facts: In the present case the challenge of the petitioner was respondents were not permitting him to stage magic shows which included a magic trick of converting bear into a lady pursuant to the notification dated 14.10.1998. Petitioner contended that the bear, is duly registered with Chief Wildlife Warden, Madhya Pradesh, Bhopal. For purposes of his profession of performing of magic shows, petitioner has to transport the bear from one place to another and certificate for this is issued under the provisions of Wild Life Protection Act from time to time.

The petitioner averred that the performing animal i.e. bear is not subjected to any kind of training nor any training for purposes of exhibition is given. Bear is simply brought at the stage of show and thereafter disappears from the stage. No act or action is done by the performing animal at any point of time, therefore, the notification in the present case is not at all applicable. The present notification though does not cover the case of petitioner is being made applicable to him and the authorities are not permitting the petitioner to include bear in his stage shows.

Petitioner further submitted that the restriction imposed by respondent authorities is violative of Articles 14, 19(1) (g) and 21 of the Constitution of India and infringe his fundamental rights to carry on his profession of magician.

Court Observed: On perusal of meaning of the term "Exhibit" and "Train" under section 21 of the PCA the court observed that "A bare reading of the...provision makes it clear that 'exhibit' means exhibit at any entertainment to which the public are admitted through sale of tickets and 'train' means train for the purpose of any such exhibition. Applying the said definition to the instant case, magic show is held by the petitioner and in that the bear is used as an exhibit, magic is a form of entertainment to which the public are admitted through sale of tickets for the purpose of exhibition.

Thus, the submission raised by learned counsel for the petitioner in magic show bear is not used as a performing animal, is not acceptable. When bear is used for conversion into a lady though not actually converted training has to be imparted to the bear for the part played by him and the bear is brought to the stage as an exhibit… the Government cannot be said to have acted unreasonably when the notification is read with section 21, the restriction is clearly just and reasonable and is within the parameter of the Act."

TRANSPORTING ANIMALS: RULES THAT MUST BE KEPT IN MIND

The Transport of Animal Rules, 1978 have been made by the Central Government to regulate various conditions subject to which different animals can be transported by rail, road, inland waterway, sea or air and provide as specified below.

A. TRANSPORT OF DOGS AND CATS OF ALL BREEDS WHETHER BY RAIL, ROAD, INLAND WATERWAY, SEA OR AIR.

1. **Certificate for transport**[108]
   a. A valid health certificate in the prescribed format (**Annexure XIII**) by a qualified veterinary surgeon to the effect that the dogs and cats are in a fit condition to travel by rail, road, inland, waterways, sea or air and are not showing any sign of infectious or contagious disease including rabies, must be accompanied with each consignment.
   b. The carrier cannot accept the consignment for transport without such certificate.

2. **Restrictions**[109]
   a. No dog or cat in an advanced stage of pregnancy can be transported.
   b. Dogs or cats to be transported in the same container must be of the same species and breed.
   c. Unweaned puppies or kittens cannot be transported with adult dogs or cats other than their dams.
   d. A female dog or cat in season (oestrus) cannot be transported with any male.

---

108 Rule 4 TAR, 1978

109 Rule 5, 6 and 7 TAR, 1978

 e. Any dog or cat reported to be vicious or exhibiting a vicious disposition has to be transported individually in a cage, muzzled and labelled to give warning to the handlers and in extreme cases, the dogs and cats must be administered with sedative drugs by a qualified veterinary surgeon.

3. **Conditions for transporting dogs and cats long distances[110]:** Dogs/Cats to be transported:
   a. Must be fed and given water at least two hours prior to their transport and should not be packed for transport if they are hungry or thirsty.
   b. They should be exercised as late as possible before dispatch.
   c. Should be given adequate water for drinking every four hours in summers and every six hours during winter.
   d. Should be fed once in twelve hours in the case of adult dogs or cats and once in four hours in the case of puppies and kittens in accordance with the instructions of the consignors if any.
   e. Adequate arrangements should be made for their care and management during the journey.
   f. When the dogs or cats are to be transported by rail involving a journey of more than six hours, an attendant must accompany the dogs or cats, to supply them with food and water on the way and the attendant should have access to the dogs or cats for this purpose at all stations and no dog or cat should be exposed to the direct blast of air during such journey.

4. **Conditions for transporting dogs or cats for short distance by road in a public vehicle[111]**
   a. They should be put in a cage and the cage should not be put on the roof of the vehicle but be inside the vehicle preferably near the end of the vehicle.

110 Rule 8 of TAR, 1978
111 Rule 9 of TAR, 1978

b. The transportation vehicle must as far as possible maintain constant speed, avoid sudden stops and reduce effects of shocks and jolts to the minimum.
c. At least one attendant must be present at all times during transit who ensures that proper transit conditions are observed and also replenishes food and water whenever necessary.

5. **Conditions for transporting dogs or cats by air**[112]
   a. Cages ought to be properly cleaned and disinfected before the dogs or cats are put in the cages.
   b. Sufficient paddy straw or saw dust or paper cuttings should be provided for cats in the cages as resting material.
   c. For international transport, the dogs or cats must be kept in pressurized compartment with regulated temperature.

6. **Other Conditions**
   a. The size and type of crates for transport of dogs and cats should confirm as clearly as may be to the size and type prescribed[113].
   b. All containers of dogs or cats should be clearly labelled showing the names address and telephone number (if any) of the consignor[114].
   c. The consignee must be informed about the train or transport arrival or flight number and its time of arrival in advance[115].

B. TRANSPORT OF MONKEYS FROM THE TRAPPING AREA TO THE NEAREST RAIL-HEAD.

1. **Certificate for transport**[116]
   a. A valid health certificate in the prescribed format (**Annexure XIV**) by a qualified veterinary surgeon to the effect that that the monkeys are in a fit condition to

112 Rule 10 of TAR, 1978
113 Rule 11 of TAR, 1978
114 Rule 12 of TAR, 1978
115 Rule 13 of TAR, 1978
116 Rule 16 of TAR, 1978

travel from the trapping area to the nearest unit-head and are not showing any sign of infectious or contagious disease including rabies, must be accompanied with each consignment.

b. The carrier cannot accept the consignment for transport without such certificate.

2. **Conditions of transport**[117]
   a. Monkeys from one trapping area should not be allowed to mix with monkeys from any other trapping area to prevent cross-infection.
   b. The time in transit from trapping area to the nearest rail-head should be as short as possible, by fastest means of transport available.
   c. Factors causing stress to monkeys during transit should be reduced to the minimum and the monkeys should not be left un-attended at any time during the journey.
   d. If the travel time is longer than six hours provision should be made to feed and to give water to the monkeys en route.
   e. During transit, precautions should be taken to protect the monkeys from extreme weather conditions and monkeys that die en route should be removed at the earliest available opportunity.
   f. Pregnant and nursing monkeys as well as monkeys weighing more than 5 kilograms should be transported in compartmented cages.
   g. All monkeys in the same cage should be of the same species and of approximately the same weight and size.

3. **Type of cage for transport**
   a. Monkeys captured within their natural habitat should be placed in new, sterilized or thoroughly cleaned cages and subsequent transfer, if any, should also be in new, disinfected or thoroughly cleaned cages.
   b. Monkeys should be transported in suitable wooden or bamboo cages, constructed in such a way that they do not

117 Rule 17, 19 ,20, 22, 23 of TAR, 1978

allow the monkeys to escape and at the same time permit sufficient passage of air for ventilation.

c. No nails, metallic projections or sharp edges should be exposed on the exterior or in the interior of the cages.
d. Each cage should be equipped with appropriate water and feed receptacles which are leak proof and capable of being cleaned and refilled during transit.
e. The floor of the cages should be made of bamboo reapers and the space between each reaper should range between 20 mm and 30 mm.
f. To facilitate carriage of these cages, provision may be made for rope loops at the four top ends.
g. The weight of any one loaded cage should not exceed 45 kilograms.
h. The cages of specified size should be used for specified number of monkeys of specific weight:
    - 910 x 760 x 510 mm = 12 or less monkeys, weighing between 1.8 - 3.00 kgs each or 10 monkeys weighing between 3.1-5.0 kgs each.
    - 710 x 710 x 510 mm = 10 or less monkeys weighing between 1.8 - 3.00 kgs each or 8 monkeys weighing between 3.1-5.0 kgs each.
i. The construction two types of cages has to be as per the dimensions and designs printed on page 5 of IS: 3699 (Part-I)-1966 published by Indian Standards Institutions **(ISI)**.
j. The wooden cages made as per the dimensions and design printed on page 6 of IS: 3059-1965 published by ISI can be used for carrying monkeys from the trapping area to the nearest rail head.

4. **Restrictions**[118]
    a. Monkeys that are not completely weaned, that is, less than 1.8 kilogram in weight, cannot be transported until specifically permitted by the Central Government.

118 Rule 18 and 19 of TAR, 1978

b. Pregnant and nursing monkeys cannot be transported except when specifically permitted by the Central Government.

AB. TRANSPORT OF MONKEYS FROM ONE RAIL-HEAD TO ANOTHER RAIL HEAD/ FROM RAIL-HEAD TO NEAREST AIRPORT

1. **Certificate for transport**[119]
   a. A valid health certificate in the prescribed format (**Annexure XV**) by a qualified veterinary surgeon to the effect that the monkeys are in a fit condition to travel from the one rail head to another or from a rail head to the nearest airport and are not showing any sign of infectious or contagious disease including rabies, must be accompanied with each consignment.
   b. The carrier cannot accept the consignment for transport without such certificate.

2. **Conditions for transport**[120]
   a. loading and unloading must be carried out quickly and efficiently.
   b. cages must be stored in such a manner that ventilation is adequate and the monkeys are not exposed to draught and direct heat or cold.
   c. Monkeys found dead must be removed as quickly as possible for suitable disposal.
   d. Due provision must be made by the sender for sufficient supply of food and water for the journey.
   e. In case the journey is over six hours an attendant must accompany the monkeys to supply them food, water and such other things, en route and he should have access to the monkeys for feeding, giving water and attention at all stations en route.
   f. The food and water containers must be checked at least every six hours and refilled, if necessary.

119 Rule 32 of TAR, 1978

120 Rule 25, 27, 28, 29, 30 of TAR, 1978

g. Monkeys must not be disturbed during the night hours.
h. Not more than one cage should be placed over the other.
i. Gunny packing must be placed between two cages, when one is placed over the other.
j. Monkeys should be brought to the airport sufficiently early.
k. Monkeys should be provided with food and water immediately before loading on the aircraft.
l. The cages must be clearly labelled showing the name, address and telephone number (if any) of the consignor and the consignee in bold red letters.
m. The consignee should be informed about the train in which the consignment of monkeys is being sent and its arrival time in advance.

BBB. TRANSPORT OF MONKEYS BY AIR

1. **Certificate for transport**[121]
   a. A valid health certificate in the prescribed format (**Annexure XVI**) by a qualified veterinary surgeon to the effect that the monkeys are in a fit to travel by air and are not showing any sign of infectious or contagious disease including rabies, must be accompanied with each consignment.
   b. The carrier cannot accept the consignment for transport without such certificate.

2. **Conditions for transport**[122]
   a. The time in transit must be as short as possible and factors causing stress to monkeys must be reduced to the minimum.
   b. Pregnant and nursing monkeys and monkeys weighing over 5 kilograms should be transported in specially designed individual cages.
   c. All monkeys in the same cage must be of the same species and of approximately the same weight and size.
   d. At no time during transit should the monkeys be left unattended when carried in a freighter aircraft.

---

121 Rule 42 of TAR, 1978

122 Rule 34, 37-39, 41, 43-45 of TAR, 1978

e. At least one attendant should be present at all times when the aircraft is on the ground.
f. To avoid danger of infection only monkeys of the same species should be transported in the same cabin or compartment of the aircraft.
g. The consignee should be informed in advance about the flight number of the freighter aircraft in which the consignment of monkeys is being sent and its arrival time.
h. The air must be changed not less than twelve times per hour and draughts must be avoided and there should be no dead pockets of air.
i. Monkeys except when being fed/given water must be made to travel in semi darkness to make them quieter giving them better opportunities of resting.
j. The food and water containers should be checked at every stop and refilled; if necessary.
k. A sufficient stock of suitable food should be available on the aircraft and at likely stopping places[123].
l. An empty cage of the usual dimensions with its sides covered except 50 mm at the top to allow for ventilation must be provided in the freighter aircraft for housing the monkeys which fall sick or are injured during the journey.

3. **Restrictions on Transport**[124]
   a. Monkeys that are not completely weaned, that is, are less than 1.8 kilograms in weight, cannot be transported except when specifically permitted by the Central Government.
   b. Pregnant and nursing monkeys cannot be transported except when specifically permitted by the Central Government.
   c. Apparently sick or disabled monkeys exhibiting external injuries or infested with parasites cannot be transported.

---

123 Rule 44 of TAR, 1978; Note: About 85 grams of food per monkey is required daily. Suitable foods are dry cereal grains or gram. Whole gram made into biscuits or wheat meal bread should be fed. A minimum of 140-ml. of water should be allowed for each monkey per day.

124 Rule 35, 36 and 38 of TAR, 1978

d. Other species of animals, birds, fish food stuff or poisonous materials, such as pesticides and insecticides, cannot be transported in the same cabin or compartment.

5. **Type of cage for transport**[125]
   a. Monkeys should be transported in suitable wooden cages, constructed in such a way that they do not allow the monkeys to escape and at the same time permit sufficient passage of air for ventilation.
   b. No nails, metallic projections or sharp edges should be exposed on the exterior or in the interior of the cages.
   c. Each cage should be equipped with appropriate water and feed receptacles which are leak proof and capable of being cleaned and refilled during transit.
   d. A suitable absorbent material such as saw dust should be kept in the dropping trays.
   e. The weight of any one loaded cage should not exceed 45 kilograms.
   f. The cages of specified size should be used for any such transport:
      - 460 x 460 x 460 mm = 10 or less monkeys weighing from 1.8- 3.0 kgs each or 4 monkeys weighing from 3.1-5.0 kgs each; and
      - 760 x 530 x 460 mm= 10 or less monkeys weighing from 1.8 -3.0 kgs each 8 monkeys weighing from 3.1-5.0 kgs each.
      - The construction of two types of cages should as per the dimensions and designs printed on page 6 of IS: 3059-1965 published by Indian Standards Institutions **(ISI)**.
      - The cages for transport of pregnant and nursing monkeys should be as per the dimensions and design printed on page 7 of IS: 3059-1965 published by ISI.
   g. The cages should be clearly labelled showing the name, address and telephone number (if any) of the consignor and the consignee in bold red letters.

125 Rule 40 and 41 of TAR, 1978

C. TRANSPORT OF CATTLE (COWS, BULLS, BULLOCKS, BUFFALOES, YAKS AND CALVES) BY RAIL

1. **Certificate for transport**[126]
    a. Each consignment for transport of cattle has to be accompanied by a valid certificate issued by a qualified veterinary surgeon in the prescribed format (**Annexure XVII**) to the effect that the cattle are in a fit condition to travel by rail or road and are not suffering from any infectious or contagious or parasitic diseases and that they have been vaccinated against rinderpest and any other infectious or contagious or parasitic diseases.
    b. If the consignment is not accompanies by such certificate then the carrier must refuse to accept the consignment for transport.

2. **Conditions for transport**[127]
    a. All batches of cattle must be accompanied by veterinary first-aid equipment.
    b. Each consignment must bear a label showing in bold red letters the name, address and telephone number (if any) of the consignor and consignee, the number and types of cattle being transported and quantity of rations and food provided.
    c. The consignee must be informed in advance about the train or vehicle in which the consignment of cattle is being sent and its arrival time.
    d. The average space for each cattle in a railway wagon or vehicle must be two square metres or more.
    e. Suitable rope and platforms must be used for loading cattle from vehicles.
    f. Cattle must be loaded after they are properly fed and given water.
    g. Cattle in advanced stage of pregnancy ought not to be mixed with young cattle in order to avoid stampede during transportation.

---

126 Rule 47 of TAR, 1978

127 Rule 48-55 of TAR, 1978

h. Water arrangements en route must be made and sufficient quantities of water must be carried with each consignment for emergency.
i. Sufficient feed and fodder with adequate reserve has to be carried to last during the journey.
j. Adequate ventilation must be ensured.
k. Wagon carrying cattle must have at least one attendant.
l. Cattle must be loaded parallel to the rails, facing each other.
m. Padding material such as straw which is at least 6 cm thick must be placed on the floor to avoid injury if a cattle lies down.
n. Rations for the journey must be carried in the middle of the wagon.
o. Cattle wagon should be attached in the middle of the train.
p. Cooking cannot be done in the wagons.
q. Hurricane lamps without chimneys cannot be used.
r. Two breast bars must be provided on each side of the wagon, one at height of 60 to 80 cm and the other at 100 to 110 cm.
s. Cattle-in-milk must be milked at least twice a day. The calves must be given sufficient quantity of milk to drink.
t. As far as possible, cattle may be moved during the nights only.
u. During day time, if possible, they should be unloaded, fed, given water and rested.

3. **Restrictions on transport of cattle by rail**[128]
    a. An ordinary goods wagon must not carry more than ten adult cattle or fifteen calves on broad gauge.
    b. It must not carry more than six adult cattle or ten calves on metre gauge.
    c. Further it must not carry more than four cattle or six calves on narrow gauge.

---

128 Rule 55 of TAR, 1978

AC. TRANSPORT OF CATTLE (COWS, BULLS, BULLOCKS, BUFFALOES, YAKS AND CALVES) BY GOODS VEHICLE[129]

a. Specially fitted goods vehicles with a special type of tail board and padding around the sides must be used.
b. On the floor of ordinary goods vehicles anti-slipping material, such as coir matting or wooden board must be laid and the superstructure, if low, should be raised.
c. Goods vehicle cannot carry more than six cattle.
d. Each goods vehicle must be provided with one attendant.
e. The goods, vehicles must not be loaded with any other merchandise while transporting the cattle; and
f. The cattle must preferably face the engine to prevent it from being frightened or injured.

D. TRANSPORT OF EQUINES (OF HORSES, MULES AND DONKEYS) BY RAIL, ROAD OR SEA

1. **Certificate for transport[130]**
   a. Each consignment must be accompanied with a valid health certificate in the prescribed format (**Annexure XVIII**) by a qualified veterinary surgeon to the effect that the equines are fit to travel by rail, road or sea and are not suffering from any infectious or contagious disease.
   b. The carrier cannot accept the consignment for transport without such certificate.

2. **Conditions for transport[131]**
   a. Each consignment must have a label showing in bold red letters the name address and telephone number (if any) of the consignor and consignee, the number and type of equines being transported and quantity of ratios and food provided.
   b. The consignee must be informed in advance about the train or vehicle or ship in which the consignment of equines is being sent and its arrival time.

129 Rule 56 of TAR, 1978
130 Rule 58 of TAR, 1978
131 Rule 59 and 60 of TAR, 1978

c. Pregnant and young equines must not be mixed with other animals.
d. Different species of equines must be kept separately.
e. Equines must be fed and given adequate water before being loaded.
f. Watering arrangements must be made en route and sufficient food must be carried to last during the journey.
g. All the batches of equines must be accompanied by veterinary first-aid equipment.
h. Adequate ventilation must be ensured.
i. Suitable ramps and platforms must be used for loading and unloading equines.

3. **Precautions to be taken while transporting equines by rail[132]:**
    a. Passenger or mixed trains only must be used for transport;
    b. When ordinary goods wagon is used for transportation it must not carry more than 8-10 horses or 10 mules or 10 donkeys on broad gauge.
    c. When ordinary goods wagon is used for transportation it must not carry more than 6 horses or 8 donkeys on meter-gauge.
    d. Water must be sprinkled by the railway authorities over the wagons containing equines to bring down temperature in extreme heat.
    e. Ice slabs in specially made containers may be placed inside the wagon, if recommended by a qualified veterinary surgeon.
    f. If the equines transported are more than two then it must have at least 2 attendants.
    g. Equines must be loaded parallel to the rails facing each other.
    h. Material such as paddy, straw with thickness of 6 cm or more must be placed on the floor to avoid injury to any animal in case it lies down.

132 Rule 61 of TAR, 1978

i. To provide adequate ventilation, upper door of the side of the wagon must be kept open and properly fixed.
j. The upper door of the wagon must have wire gauge closely welded mesh arrangements to prevent burning cinders from the engines entering the wagon and leading to fire break out.
k. Two breast bars must be provided on each side of the wagon, one at a height of 50 to 80 cm and the other at 110 cm.

4. **Precautions to be taken while transporting equines by goods vehicle[133]:**
   a. Specially fitted vehicles with a special type of tail board and padding around the sides must be used.
   b. It must be provided with anti-slipping material on the floor and the super structure, if low, should be raised.
   c. To prevent the animal from falling bamboo poles of at least 8 cm diameter between each animal and two stout batons at the back must be provided.
   d. To prevent horses from being frightened or injured their heads they should face left, away from the passing traffic.
   e. Each vehicle must not carry more than 4-6 equines.
   f. Each vehicle must be provided with one attendant.
   g. The vehicles must be driven at a speed of not more than 35km/per hour.

5. **Precautions to be taken while transporting equines by sea[134]:**
   a. Horses may be accommodated in single stalls and mules in pens. Each pen may hold 4-5 mules.
   b. For ventilation portholes must be kept and air trunks or electric blowers must be provided on all decks, and exhaust fans must be installed to blow out foul air.
   c. All animals to be transported must be athwart the ship with heads facing inwards.

133 Rule 62 of TAR, 1978
134 Rule 63 of TAR, 1978

d. To avoid distress especially during hot weather, the ship may go underway immediately after embarking. Disembarking must be done as early as possible after anchoring.
e. Colts and fillies should be kept on the exposed decks.
f. A pharmacy and spare stalls for five per cent of equines must be available.
g. Passage between two rows of pens must be 1.5 meters or more.

E. TRANSPORT OF SHEEP AND GOATS BY RAIL OR ROAD INVOLVING JOURNEYS OF MORE THAN SIX HOURS

1. **Certificate for transport**[135]
    a. Each consignment must be accompanied with a valid health certificate in the prescribed format (**Annexure XIX**) by a qualified veterinary surgeon to the effect that the sheep and goats are fit to travel by rail, or road and are not suffering from any infectious or contagious disease.
    b. The carrier cannot accept the consignment for transport without such certificate.
2. **Conditions for transport**[136]
    a. Each consignment must bear a label showing in bold red letters the name, address and telephone number (if any) of the consignor and consignee, the number and type of sheep or goats being transported and quantity of rations and food provided.
    b. The consignee must be informed in advance about the train or vehicle in which the consignments of sheep or goats are being sent and its arrival time.
    c. First-aid equipment must accompany the sheep or goats in transit.
    d. Suitable ramps must be provided for loading and unloading the sheep or goats.

135 Rule 65 of TAR, 1978

136 Rule 66-75 of TAR, 1978

e. In the case of a railway wagon, when the loading or unloading is done on the platform the dropped door of the wagon must be used as a ramp.
f. Sheep and goats must be transported separately. However if most of them are small special partition must be provided to separate them.
g. Rams and male young stock must not be mixed with female stock in the same compartment.
h. Sufficient food and fodder must be carried to last during the journey and watering facility must be provided at regular intervals.
i. Material for padding, such as straw, of not less than 5 cm thick must be placed on the floor to avoid injury if an animal lies down.
j. The animals must not be fettered unless there is a risk of their jumping out and their legs must not be tied down.
k. The space provided for goats and sheep must be as the same as that for a woolled sheep and the approximate space required for a sheep in goods vehicle or a railway wagon must be as below (space required in square meter/ weight in kg):

	Woolled	Shorn
• 1-20	0.18	0.16
• 21-25	0.20	0.18
• 26-30	0.23	0.22
• 30 or more	0.28	0.26

l. A railway wagon cannot accommodate more than the following sheep or goats:
   - Broad gauge
     - ➢ Area of wagon – less than 21.1 sq. mtr. – No. of sheep and goats: 70
     - ➢ Area of wagon – 21.1. sq mtr. or above- No. of sheep and goats: 100
   - Meter gauge
     - ➢ Area of wagon – less than 12.5 sq. mtr. – No. of sheep and goats: 50

- ➢ Area of wagon – 12.5 sq mtr. or above- No. of sheep and goats: 60
- Narrow gauge
  - ➢ Irrespective of the area of wagon – No. of sheep and goats: 25

m. Adequate ventilation must be provided in every wagon. Upper door of one side of wagon must be kept open and properly fixed.

n. Upper door of the wagon must have wire gauge closely welded mesh arrangements to prevent burning cinders from the engines entering the wagon and leading to fire breakout.

o. Goods vehicles of capacity of 5 or 4 ½ tons, which are generally used for transporting animals, must carry not more than forty sheep or goats.

p. In the case of large goods vehicles and wagons, partitions must be provided at every two or three metres across the width to prevent the crowding and trapping of sheep and goats.

q. In the case of ewes, goats or lambs or kids under six weeks of age, separate panels must be provided.

F. TRANSPORT OF POULTRY (DAY OLD CHICKS AND TURKEY POULTS, CHICKENS, QUAILS, GUINEA FOWLS, DUCKS, GEESE AND TURKEYS) BY RAIL, ROAD AND AIR

1. General conditions for transport[137]

a. The containers in which poultry is to be transferred must be properly cleaned and sterilised before the poultry is placed in them.

b. Poultry must not be exposed to the sunlight, rain and direct blast of air during transport.

c. Poultry must not be transported when the temperature exceeds 25 degree Celsius or when the temperature falls below 15 degree Celsius.

---

137 Rule 77 of Transport of Animals (Amendment) Rules, 2001

2. **Conditions for transport of day old chicks and poultry by rail, road and air**[138]
    a. Chicks and poults must be packed and dispatched immediately after hatching and must not be stored in boxes for any length of time before dispatch.
    b. They must not be fed or watered before and during transportation.
    c. Efforts must be made to ensure that chicks and poults arrive as quickly as possible at the dispatching site.
    d. It must be ensured that all consignments are kept out of direct sunlight, rain and heat.
    e. Care must be taken to carry the boxes in a level position so that chicks are not in danger of falling over on to their backs.
    f. No other merchandise must be put over and around chick boxes.

3. **Conditions for transport of poultry other than day old chicks and turkey poult by rail, road or air**[139]
    a. Poultry to be transported must be healthy and in good condition.
    b. It must be examined and certified by a veterinary doctor for freedom from infectious diseases and fitness to undertake the journey.
    c. Poultry transported in the same container must be of the same species and of the same age group.
    d. Poultry must be fed and watered properly before it is placed in containers for transportation and extra feed and water must be provided in suitable troughs fixed in the containers.
    e. Arrangements must be made for watering and feeding poultry during transportation and during hot weather. Watering must be ensured every six hours.
    f. Male stock must not be transported with female stock in the same container.

---

138 Rule 78 of Transport of Animals (Amendment) Rules, 2001

139 Rule 79 of Transport of Animals (Amendment) Rules, 2001

4. **Precaution while transporting poultry by road** [140]
   a. Container must not be placed one on the top of the other
   b. Container must be covered properly in order to provide light, ventilation and to protect from rain, heat and cold air.

5. **Precaution while transporting poultry by rail**[141]
   a. An attendant must accompany the consignment in case the journey is for more than twelve hours.
   b. Poultry must not be exposed to rain or direct blast of air.
   c. As far as possible poultry must be transported in wagons having adequate facilities for ventilation.
   d. No other merchandise which may result in mortality of birds be loaded in the same wagon.

6. **Precaution while transporting poultry by air or for international transport**[142]
   a. Containers carrying poultry must be kept in pressurised compartments with regulated temperature.
   b. Container must preferably be kept near the door.
   c. Containers must be unloaded immediately on arrival.

7. **Containers to be used for transportation**[143]
   a. Containers must be made of such material so that they do not collapse or crumble.
   b. They must be well ventilated.
   c. They must be designed to protect the health of poultry by giving it adequate space and safety.
   d. Containers must be so designed as to render it impossible for birds to crowd into the corners during transportation.
   e. They must be so designed to avoid the danger of boxes being stocked so close together as to interfere with ventilation.
   f. All the containers must be clearly labelled showing the name, address and telephone number of the consignor and the consignee.

140 Rule 80 of Transport of Animals (Amendment) Rules, 2001
141 Rule 81 of Transport of Animals (Amendment) Rules, 2001
142 Rule 82 of Transport of Animals (Amendment) Rules, 2001
143 Rule 83 of Transport of Animals (Amendment) Rules, 2001

g. The minimum floor space per bird and the dimensions of the containers for transporting poultry must be as specified below:

S.No.	Kind of Poultry	Minimum Floor Space cm^2	Dimensions (in cm)	No. in a container
1.	Month old chicken	75	Length:60 Width:30 Height:18	24
2.	Three month old chickens	230	Length:55 Width:50 Height:35	12
3.	Adult stock (excluding geese and turkeys)	480	Length:115 Width:50 Height:45	12
4.	Geese and Turkeys	900	Length:120 Width:75 Height:75	10 young
5.	Geese and Turkeys	1300	Length:75 Width:35 Height:75	2 growing
6.	Geese and Turkeys	1900	Length:55 Width:35 Height:75	1 grown up
7.	Chicks	---------	Length:60 Width:45 Height:12	80
8.	Poult	---------	Length:60 Width:45 Height:12	60

8. **Special requirement of containers for chicks and poults**[144]
   a. Wire mesh or a net of any material must not be used as a bottom for the containers.
   b. The container must be properly secured to avoid pilferage.
   c. The instruction namely "Care in Transit" must be printed on a label and fixed to the lid or printed directly on sides.
   d. The consignee must be informed about the train, transport or flight number and its time of arrival well in advance.
   e. Poultry must not be transported continuously for more than 6 hours and whole batch must be inspected at every 6 hours interval.
   f. The mode of transportation must not remain stationary for more than 30 minutes and during this period, it must be parked in shade and arrangements must be made for feeding and watering.
   g. All precautions against fire must be taken and fire extinguishers must be provided in transport.

G. TRANSPORT OF PIGS (PIGLETS, HOGS, HOGLETS AND ANIMALS OF PIGS FAMILY) BY RAIL OR ROAD INVOLVING JOURNEYS OF MORE THAN SIX HOURS

1. **Certificate for transport**[145]
   a. A valid health certificate by a veterinary doctor in the prescribed format (**Annexure XX**) to the effect that the pigs are in a fit condition to travel by rail or road and are not suffering from infectious or contagious or parasitic disease must accompany each consignment in the transport of pigs by rail or road.
   b. In the absence of such certificate the carrier shall refuse to accept the consignment for transport.

2. **Conditions for transport**[146]
   a. Each consignment must bear a label showing in bold red letters the name, address and telephone number (if any)

---

144 Rule 84 of Transport of Animals (Amendment) Rules, 2001

145 Rule 87 of Transport of Animals (Amendment) Rules, 2001

146 Rule 88-95 of Transport of Animals (Amendment) Rules, 2001

of the consignor and consignee, the number and type of pigs being transported and quantity of rations and food provided to them.

b. The consignee must be informed in advance about the train or vehicle in which the consignment of pigs is being sent and its arrival time.
c. First-aid equipment must accompany the pigs.
d. Suitable ramps must be provided for loading and unloading the pigs.
e. In case of a railway wagon, when the loading or unloading is done on the platform the dropped door of the wagon should be used as a ramp.
f. Male young stock must not be mixed with female stock in the same compartment.
g. Sufficient food and fodder must be carried to last during the journey and watering facility must be provided at regular intervals.
h. Material for padding, such as straw, of not less than 5 cm of thickness must be placed on the floor to avoid injury if an animal lies down.
i. Animals must not be fettered unless there is a risk of their jumping out and their legs must not be tied down.
j. No railway wagon must accommodate more number of pigs than specified below:
   - Broad gauge
     - Area of wagon – less than 21.1 sq. mtr. – No. of pigs: 35
     - Area of wagon – 21.1. sq mtr. or above- No. of pigs: 50
   - Meter gauge
     - Area of wagon – less than 12.5 sq. mtr. – No. of pigs: 25
     - Area of wagon – 12.5 sq mtr. or above- No. of pigs: 30
   - Narrow gauge
     - Irrespective of the area of wagon – not allowed
k. Adequate ventilation must be provided in every wagon.

l. The upper door of one side of wagon must be kept open and properly fixed.
m. Upper door of the wagon must have wire gauge closely welded mesh arrangements to prevent the burning cinders from the engines from entering the wagon and leading to breakout of fire.
n. Goods vehicles with capacity of 5 or 4.5 tons must not carry more than twenty pigs.
o. In large goods vehicles and containers, partition must be provided at every two or three metres across the width to prevent the crowding and trapping of pigs.
p. In the case of pigs under six weeks of age, separate panels must be provided.

TRANSPORT OF ANIMALS ON FOOT

Central Government has notified the Prevention of Cruelty to Animals (Transport of Animals on Foot) Rules, 2001 to regulate the transport of animals[147] by foot when distance from the boundary of village or town or city of the origin of such transport to the last destination is 5 km or more than 5 km (hereinafter "**TAFR, 2001**"). It provides as follows.

1. **Certificate for transport of animal on foot**[148]
   A certificate of a veterinary doctor in the prescribed format (**Annexure XXI**) in respect of each animal to be transported to the effect that such animal is in a fit condition for such transportation and is not suffering from any infectious, contagious or parasitic diseases and that it has been vaccinated against any infectious, contagious or parasitic diseases must accompany such animal.

---

147 Rule 2(a) of TAFR, 2001 animal means livestock and includes the following animals namely-

- (i) cattle including cow, bulls and bullocks, buffalo bulls and bullocks, cows, buffaloes, Mithuns, yaks and calves.
- (ii) equines includings horses, ponies, mules and donkeys.
- (iii) horse including entires (stallions), goldings, brood mares, colts and fillies
- (iv) goat including adult goat, male or female of two years age and above
- (v) ruck including male goat
- (vi) kid young goat below one year of age
- (vii) nanny female goat
- (viii) sheep including adult sheep, male or female of two years age and above
- (ix) ewe female sheep
- (x) lamb young sheep below one year of age
- (xi) ram male sheep
- (xii) wether includes male lamb that has been castrated before reaching sexual maturity
- (xiii) pig includes adult pig, male or female of one year of age or above
- (xiv) piglet includes young pig below one year of age

148 Rule 4 of TAFR, 2001

2. **List of animals which cannot be transported on foot**[149]
   a. New born animals of which the navel has not completely healed,
   b. any animal which is diseased,
   c. blind,
   d. emaciated,
   e. lame,
   f. fatigued, or
   g. has given birth during the preceding seventy two hours or
   h. is likely to give birth during transport

3. **Transport in on-farm social group**[150]
   Animal must be transported in their on farm social groups (established at least one week prior to journey)

4. **Conditions for transport of animals on foot**[151]
   a. Every animal to be transported on foot must be healthy and in good condition for such transport.
   b. First aid equipment must accompany animals transported on foot and the same has to be provided by the owner.
   c. In case the person transporting the animals on foot is not the owner of the animals then such person must carry a certificate as specified in the prescribed format (**Annexure XXII**) during such transportation.
   d. The owner must make watering arrangement en route.
   e. Sufficient feed and fodder with adequate reserve of such feed and fodder for the animals must be made available by the owner during the transport on foot.

5. **Prohibition of the use of whip, etc. during transportation of animals on foot**[152]
   a. A person cannot use a whip or a stick in order to force the animals to walk or to hasten the pace of their walk.
   b. A person cannot apply chillies or any other substance to any part of the body of the animal for the aforesaid purpose.

149 Rule 5 of TAFR, 2001
150 Rule 6 of TAFR, 2001
151 Rule 4, 7-10 of TAFR, 2001
152 Rule 11 of TAFR, 2001

c. If any animal needs to be tied it must be tied with a rope covered with suitable cushioning such as cloth around its leg.
d. Animals cannot be tied by their nose, all legs or any other part of the body except by their neck.
e. If more than one animal is to be tied adjacent to one another by a single rope the space between any two of such animals must be minimum two feet and animals so tied must be of similar physical condition and strength.
f. No more than two such animals can be tied adjacent to each other by a single rope.

6. **Certain Prohibition on transport of animals on foot**[153]
   a. No animal can be transported on foot:
      - before sunrise or after sunset
      - beyond the distance, time, rest interval and temperature specified for such animal
   b. After being provided with water every animal must be given a break of 20 minutes before the commencement of the transport of the animal on foot.
   c. After being fed every animal must be given one hour break before the commencement of the transport of the animal on foot.
   d. No animal can be made to walk under conditions of heavy rain, thunderstorms or extremely dry or sultry conditions.
   e. No animal can be transported on foot beyond the distance, time, rest interval and temperature specified for such animal in the table below:

153 Rule12 of TAFR, 2001

Species (Animal)	Maximum distance covered/ day/hour	Maximum no. of walking / day of hours (travelling) (in hours)	Period of rest (interval)	Temperature range (in degree Celsius) (max-min)
Cattle (Cows)	30km/day 4km/hour	8	At every 2 hours for drinking and at every 4 hours for feeding	12-30
Buffaloes	25km/day 3km/hr	8	At every 2 hours for drinking and at every 4 hours for feeding	12-30
Calves of cows and Buffaloes	16 km/day 2.5 km/hr	6	At every 1 and ½ hours for drinking and at every 3 hours for feeding	15-25
Horses, Ponies, Mules and Donkeys	45 km/day 6km/hr	8	At every 1 and ½ hours for drinking and at every 6 hours for feeding	12-30
Young ones (Foal)	25km/day 4km/hr	6	At every 2 hours for drinking and at every 4 hours for feeding	15-25
Goats and sheep	30 km/day 4 km/hr	8	At every 2 hours for drinking and at every 4 hours for feeding	12-30
Kids and lambs	16 km/day 2.5 km/hr	6	At every 1 and ½ hours for drinking and at every 3 hours for feeding	15-25
Pigs	15 km/day 2 km/hr	8	At every 1 and ½ hours for drinking and at every 3 hours for feeding	12-25
Piglets	10 km/day 1.5 km/hr	6	At every 1 and ½ hours for drinking and at every 3 hours for feeding	15-25

7. **Transportation of animals on foot only with shoes**[154]
   Animals whose hooves are not provided with shoes (as in the case of pack or draught animals) must not be transported on foot on hard cement, bitumen-coated or metalled roads, steep gradients or hilly and rocky terrain, irrespective of weather conditions (summer or winter).

154 Rule 13 of TAFR, 2001

RULES FOR RUNNING A PET SHOP

The rules called Prevention of Cruelty to Animals (Pet Shops) Rules, 2018 ("**Pet Shop Rules, 2018**") were made by the Central Government and have been notified by the Ministry of Environment, Forest and Climate Change in the Gazette of India setting out there in the rules and regulations which must be complied with for running a pet shop[155] for sale of pet animas[156] in India. They provide as follows.

1. **Registration for running a pet shop[157]**
   a. Any person can carry on or continue the business of sale or trade in pet animals, whether retail or whole sale and can establish or operate a pet shop or any other establishment in sale, purchase or exchange of pet animals by whatever name called after obtaining a certificate of registration in prescribed format (**Annexure XXIII**).
   b. The certificate of registration must be prominently displayed in the pet shop.
   c. The pet shop owner must keep the pet shop open for inspection by an inspector authorised in writing by the State Board or Society for prevention of Cruelty to Animals.

---

155 Rule 2(k) of Pet Shop Rules, 2018 "pet shop" means a shop, place or premise including a shop, place or premise in a weekly or other market, where pet animals are sold or housed, kept or exhibited for sale, or where any retail or whole-sale business involving the selling or trading of pet animals are carried out, and includes online platforms over which the sale and purchase of pet animals is carried out wherever the context permits.

156 Rule 2(j) of Pet Shop Rules, 2018 "pet animals" includes dogs, cats, rabbit guinea pig, hamster, rodents of the mice or rat category, pet birds and such other type of animals, the ownership of and the trade in which, is not prohibited by any other law, rules or regulations.

157 Rule 3 of Pet Shop Rules, 2018

2. **Application and eligibility criteria for registration**[158]
   a. In case of individual he must have attained the age of majority, must be of sound mind and must not be disqualified from contracting under any other law for the time being in force.
   b. In case of a corporation, company or any other association of person, it must be duly registered in accordance with any law for the time being in force.
   c. Application for registration in prescribed format (**Annexure XXIV**) has to be made to the State Board along with a fee of Rs.5000/- and affidavit stating there in that all the conditions for registration of pet shop have been fulfilled.
   d. A separate application has to be made with regard for each pet shop or premises used or intended to be used for sale or trade in pet animals whether retail or wholesale.

3. **The registration will not be granted by the State Board when**[159]**:**
   a. The information submitted by the applicant is found to be false; or
   b. Material and deliberate misstatements have been made in the application; or
   c. Falsified or fabricated records have been submitted to the State Board; or
   d. The applicant has, been before submission of application been convicted of any offence under the PCA, or the Wildlife (Protection) Act, 1972 (53 of 1972) or for any offence relating to animals under any other law for the time being in force; or
   e. The applicant refused to allow the inspector or the authorised representative of the State Board free and unimpeded access to his facilities; or
   f. The applicant was operating a pet shop without a valid certificate of registration, and failed to apply for the same resulting in sealing of his shop.

---

158 Rule 4 of Pet Shop Rules, 2018
159 *ibid*

4. **Validity, Transferability and Renewability of the Certificate**[160]
   a. A certificate of registration is valid for a period of five years.
   b. A certificate of registration issued is non-transferable.
   c. It is renewable upon application being made to the State Board together with a fee of five thousand rupees. An application for renewal of registration has to be made, at least thirty days prior to the expiry of the registration, to the State Board in the format attached hereto.
   d. The establishments registered and covered under the purview of the Breeding of and Experiments on Animals (Control and Supervision) Rules, 1998 for the purpose of experiments, breeding and trading of animals, are exempted from registration under these rules.

5. **Accommodation, infrastructure and housing**[161]
   a. A pet shop must be located within a permanent structure or building.
   b. It must have adequate arrangement for basic amenities such as water and electricity, and adequate power back up.
   c. A pet shop cannot be operated on a shanty, shack, pavement or any temporary or make shift arrangement.
   d. The enclosures or rooms or aviaries in a pet shop in which the pet animals for sale are displayed or housed must be of adequate size and space as prescribed (**Annexure XXV**), so as to permit—
      - the pet animal housed therein to stand, sit, lie down, turn around, stretch and make other normal postural adjustments without obstruction, interference or impediment occasioned by paucity of space;
      - the birds within to fly, hop, jump, climb and otherwise move about, and individually spread their wings, and perch in normal position without obstruction, interference or impediment occasioned by paucity

160 Rule 4 and 5 of Pet Shop Rules, 2018
161 Rule 6 of Pet Shop Rules, 2018

of space, and the water birds must be provided water troughs to wallow.

e. The floor of the enclosure or room for displaying or housing pet animals for sale must be constructed such that no injury to the animals' feet, or legs, or any other injury is caused to them.

f. Wherever mesh floors are used, a tray must be provided to avoid any organic matter falling into the cages below in case of stacking.

g. The temperature at the enclosures or rooms or aviaries in which pet animals are displayed or housed for sale must be comfortable, which may vary from animal to animal, and from breed to breed, and it is incumbent upon the pet shop owner to familiarise himself with the requirements of the breeds or species that he intends to deal in, and provide ambient and comfortable temperature for them.

h. Every pet shop owner must provide in the pet shop and particularly, in the enclosures or rooms or aviaries in which the pet animals are displayed or housed for sale, suitable drainage or a way to quickly eliminate waste and water when cleaning.

i. Every pet shop displaying or housing pet animals for sale must:
   - be adequately ventilated and a low noise exhaust fan or system should be installed;
   - be free from noise pollution, and must not be adjacent to areas where loud noises can be heard, or noxious fumes and odors emitted, including factories and other similar industrial establishments;
   - not be located within the vicinity of hundred meters from butcher shops, or butcheries, or abattoirs;
   - not allow the entry of other animals that may disturb or harm the pet animals housed or exhibited for sale in the pet shop;
   - install and make smoke-detection and fire-fighting equipment available and ready for use at the pet shop; and

- have an isolated or quarantine area where pet animals infected with a contagious disease or suspected of being infected can be segregated from the rest of the animals intended for sale.

6. Pet shop owner must comply with the conditions of general care of animals, veterinary care and other operational requirements as set out in **Annexure XXVI** hereto for running and operating a pet shop[162].

7. **Maintenance of records[163]**
   a. Every pet shop owner must maintain in a record book in prescribed format (**Annexure XXVII**), the particulars of breeders and suppliers of pet animals intended for sale, including name, address, contact details, and date of transaction, and the number of pet animals received, their breed or species, and bird band number if applicable.
   b. The pet shop owner must maintain a record in prescribed form (**Annexure XXVIII**) of customers buying pet animals from him in a record book, with names, addresses, contact details, and the details of pet animal purchased, and the price at which purchased, and the receipt issued.
   c. Every pet shop owner must maintain a record in prescribed form (**Annexure XXIX**) of the pet animals that die at the pet shop, with the day, date and time of death, and cause of death certified by a veterinary practitioner, and details of the medical attention and care provided to the deceased pet animal prior to its death certified in writing by a veterinary practitioner, and manner of disposal of carcasses.
   d. Every pet shop owner must maintain a separate record in prescribed form (**Annexure XXX**) of the pet animals that are euthanized, with the day, date and time of death, and cause of death certified by a veterinary practitioner, and details of the medical attention and care provided to

162 Rule 7 of Pet Shop Rules, 2018
163 Rule 8 of Pet Shop Rules, 2018

the deceased pet animal prior to its death, and manner of disposal of carcasses.

e. The records maintained must be available at the pet shop for inspection by the State Board or any intending purchaser.

8. **Reports by pet shop**[164]

   Every registered pet shop must:

   a. submit at the end of every year, a report to the State Board, consisting of the information as to the total number of animals sold, traded, bartered, brokered, given away, boarded, exhibited, died or euthanized, during the previous year;
   b. provide to the State Board, such information as may be required by the State Board, as the case may be from time to time.

9. **Effect of death of owner of a registered pet shop**[165]

   In the case the owner of a registered pet shop registered dies before the expiry of the period of registration, the registration in respect of the pet shop is deemed to have been granted to his legal heirs and remains valid till the end of a period of three months from the date of death of the owner. Thereafter a fresh application for registration of the pet shop must be made for continuing the pet shop.

10. **No license without registration**[166]

    No pet shop is granted a license by the local authority, unless the pet shop has obtained a certificate of registration from the State Board.

11. **Import of birds and animals**[167]

    a. Pet shop owner must ensure that the suppliers who supply imported, exotic breeds of birds and animals are importing these animals after obtaining all necessary approvals or license or both from the Director General of Foreign

164 Rule 12 of Pet Shop Rules, 2018

165 Rule 13 of Pet Shop Rules, 2018

166 Rule 14 of Pet Shop Rules, 2018

167 Rule 15 of Pet Shop Rules, 2018

Trade, Sanitary Import Permit and Permission from Regional or State Animal Quarantine and Certification Services, and

b. The pet shop owner must satisfy himself that the imports of live animals have been done through legal and appropriate channels.

Fun Fact! You love your pets/animals then get insurance for them. Yes pet/animal insurance is a thing and several insurance companies have now started to offer insurance for pets/animals ranging from pet dogs, to goat, pigs, camel, poultry, duck, rabbit, elephant, horse etc.

CAPTURE OF ANIMAL RULES, 1979

The rules called Prevention of Cruelty to Animals (Capture of Animal) Rules, 1979 were made by the Central Government and have been notified by the Ministry of Agriculture and Irrigation in the Gazette of India setting out there in the rules and regulations which must be complied with for capturing bird and other animals and provide as follows.

1. **Capture of Birds**[168]
   a. No bird is allowed to be captured for the purpose of sale, export or for any other purpose except by net method.
   b. A bird is said to be captured by the net method if in its capture the contrivance made of spun thread which is soft, pliable and sufficiently strong, like cotton, jute or any synthetic fibre, woven in such a way as to form a mesh of suitable size so that the bird is captured without any injury being caused to it used.

2. **Capture of Other Animals**[169]
   a. No animal is allowed to be captured for the purpose of sale, export of for any other purpose except by sack and loop method.
   b. An animal is said to be captured by the sack and loop method if in its capture the following contrivance is used, namely a strong canvas in the form of sack, not less than 92 cms in length and 138 cms in diameter, which has a smooth rope, not less than 5.5 meter in length passing through ten or more rings of not less than 4 cms. In diameter each attached at the open end, thus forming a loop, the sack having small holes at the convenient places to enable the animal to breathe during captivity, and the

168 Rule 2 of Prevention of Cruelty to Animals (Capture of Animal) Rules, 1979
169 Rule 3 of Prevention of Cruelty to Animals (Capture of Animal) Rules, 1979

animal is captured by the sack being thrown on it and secured by having the loop pulled.

c. An animal which cannot be captured by reason of its size, nature of other condition or circumstances by the sack and loop method, may be captured with the help of tranquiliser guns or by any other method which renders the animal insensible to pain before capture.

DRAUGHT AND PACK ANIMALS RULES, 1965 (DPA, RULES, 1965)

The Central Government made rules called the Prevention of Cruelty to Draught and Pack Animals Rules, 1965 (**DPA, Rules, 1965**) which shall come into force in any state on such date as the State Government may, by notification in the official Gazette, appoint.

1. **Meaning for the purpose of DPA Rules, 1965**[170]
   a. "Large bullock" or "Large Buffalo" respectively means a bullock or buffalo, the weight of which exceeds 350 kilograms;
   b. "Medium Bullock" or "Medium Buffalo" respectively means a bullock or buffalo, the weight of which exceeds 250 kilograms, but does not exceed 350 kilograms;
   c. "Small Bullock" or "Small Buffalo" respectively means a bullock or buffalo, the weight of which does not exceed 250 kilograms;
2. **Determination of weight of animals as specified above has to be by applying any of the following formulae, namely**[171]**:-**
   a. Length x Girth^2 in cms/10838 = Weight of animal in kgs. (Or)
   b. 9(Length in cms x Girth in cms^2) / 1,00,000
3. **Maximum loads for draught animals**[172]
   a. A person shall cause any animal specified in column 1 to draw a vehicle[173] of the kind described in column 2 only if it carries load of same or less weight specified in the corresponding entry in column 3 thereof.

170 Rule 2(a), (b) and (c) of DPA Rules 1965

171 Rule 2(2) of DPA Rules, 1965

172 Rule 3 of DPA Rules, 1965

173 Rule 2(e) of DPA Rules, 1965; "Vehicle" means a wheeled conveyance of any description, which is capable of being used as such on any street.

S.No.	1	2	3
1.	Small bullock or small buffalo	Two-wheeled vehicle: (a) if fitted with ball bearings (b) if fitted with pneumatic tyres (c) if not fitted with pneumatic tyres	 -1000 kgs. -750 kgs. -500 kgs.
2.	Medium bullock or medium buffalo	Two-wheeled vehicle: (a) if fitted with ball bearings (b) if fitted with pneumatic tyres (c) if not fitted with pneumatic tyres	 -1400 kgs. -1050 kgs. -700 kgs.
3.	Large bullock or large buffalo	Two-wheeled vehicle: (a) if fitted with ball bearings (b) if fitted with pneumatic tyres (c) if not fitted with pneumatic tyres	 -1800 kgs. -1350 kgs. -900 kgs.
4.	Horse or mule	Two-wheeled vehicle: (a) if fitted with pneumatic tyres (b) if not fitted with pneumatic tyres	 -750 kgs -500 kgs.
5.	Pony	Two-wheeled vehicle: (a) if fitted with pneumatic tyres (b) if not fitted with pneumatic tyres	 -600 kgs. -400 kgs.
6.	Camel	Two-wheeled vehicle	-1000 kgs

b. Where the vehicle to be drawn is a four-wheeled vehicle, weight specified in column 3 of the said table shall, in each case, be read as being one and a quarter times and, if the four-wheeled vehicle is one fitted with pneumatic tyres, as being one a half times, as much as the weight so specified.

c. Where the vehicle, whether two-wheeled or four-wheeled is to be drawn by two animals of either species referred to the entries in column 1, the weight specified in the corresponding entry in column 3 small be read as being twice, and if the vehicle is one fitted with pneumatic tyres, as being two and a half times as much as the weight so specified.

d. Where the route by which a vehicle is to be drawn involves an ascent for not less than one kilometre and the gradient is more than three meters in a distance of thirty meters, the weight specified in column 3 of the said table shall, in each case, be read as being one-half of what is so specified.
e. The weights specified herein shall be inclusive or the weight of the vehicle.
f. In calculating any weight for the purpose of this rule, fractions shall be disregarded

4. **Maximum load for certain pack animals**[174]
   No person can cause any animal to carry any load in excess of the weight specified herein:
   a. Small bullock or buffalo- 100 Kilograms
   b. Medium bullock or buffalo- 150 Kilograms
   c. Large bullock or buffalo -175 Kilograms
   d. Pony -70 Kilograms
   e. Mule -200 Kilograms
   f. Donkey- 50 Kilograms
   g. Camel- 250 Kilograms

5. **Maximum number of passengers for animal drawn vehicles**[175]
   A person in charge of any vehicle drawn by any animal referred to in column 1 of the table cannot allow more than four persons, excluding the driven and children below 6 years of age, to ride on the vehicle.

6. **General Conditions for use of draught and pack animals**[176]
   a. No person can use or cause to be used any animal for drawing any vehicle or carrying any load–
      - For more than nine hours in a day in the aggregate.
      - For more than five hours continuously without a break for rest for the animal

174 Rule 4 of DPA Rules, 1965
175 Rule 5 of DPA Rules, 1965
176 Rule 6 of DPA Rules, 1965

- In any area where the temperature exceeds 37 degree Celsius (99 degree Fahrenheit) during the period between 12.00 noon and 3.00 p.m.

7. **Animals to be disengaged after work**[177]
A person cannot continue to keep or cause to be kept any animal in harness, used for the purpose of drawing vehicles, after it is no longer needed for such purpose.

8. **Use of Spiked bits prohibited**[178]
A person cannot, use any spiked stick or bit, harness or yoke with spikes, knobs or projections or any other sharp tackle or equipment for the purpose of driving or riding an animal or causing it to draw any vehicle or for otherwise controlling it, which causes or is likely to cause bruises, swellings, abrasion or severe pain to the animal.

9. **Saddling of horses**[179]
A person cannot cause a horse to be saddles in such a way that the harness rests directly on the animal's withers without there being sufficient clearance between the arch of the saddle and the withers.

177 Rule 7 of DPA Rules, 1965
178 Rule 8 of DPA Rules, 1965
179 Rule 9 of DPA Rules, 1965

THE PREVENTION OF CRUELTY TO ANIMALS (LICENSING OF FARRIERS) RULES, 1965

The Central Government made the Prevention of Cruelty to Animals (Licensing of Farriers) Rules, 1965 (**Licensing of Farrier Rules, 1965**) which shall come into force in any State on such date as the State Government may, by notification in the official Gazette, appoint. Farrier[180] means a person who carries on the business of shoeing cattle[181]. The rules provide as follows.

1. **Farriers to be licensed[182]**
   A person after the commencement of the said rules can carry on the business of a farrier, only after obtaining a licence.

2. **Persons entitled to apply for license[183]**
   a. Who has completed the age of eighteen years, and
   b. has undergone any such training in the business of shoeing cattle as may be approved by the licensing authority; or has been carrying on the business of a farrier for not less than two years before the commencement of the said rules; shall be entitled to a license.

3. **Application for license[184]**
   a. Every person who intends to carry on such business of a Farrier has to apply in writing to the licensing authority[185]

---

180 Rule 2(b) of Licensing of Farrier Rules, 1965

181 Rule 2(a) of Licensing of Farrier Rules, 1965; Cattle means buffaloes, bullocks, horses, mules, or donkeys and includes other animals used for draught, pack or carriage purpose, which require shoeing;

182 Rule 3 of Licensing of Farrier Rules, 1965

183 Rule 4 of Licensing of Farrier Rules, 1965

184 Rule 5 of Licensing of Farrier Rules, 1965

185 Rule 2(d) of Licensing of Farrier Rules, 1965; "Licensing authority" means such officer of the veterinary department of the State or a local authority or any organization for the welfare of animals as the State Government may, by general or special order, specify in this behalf.

for a license giving his name, place of residence, place of business.

b. His qualifications for the license and such other particulars as the licensing authority may require.

4. **Tools and Implements required to carry on the business of Farrier**[186]

The tools and other implements which a person carrying on or intending to carry on the business of a farrier ordinarily has in his possession are the following:

a. Driving hammer with claws
b. Hand hammer
c. Drawing knife
d. Scorcher knife
e. Pincers
f. Buffer
g. Rasp
h. Chisel for cutting bar iron
i. Punch for making nail holes
j. Nails for shoeing
k. Twitch.
l. Wooden plank for finishing work
m. Iron anvil
n. Good quality wrought iron for shoes

5. **Term of license and renewal thereof**[187]

a. A license shall be valid for a period of two years from the date of its grant.
b. It may be renewed from time to time on application made by the licensee stating the period from which the license is to be renewed which shall not be more than 2 years.

6. **Issue of duplicate license**[188]

If a license is defected, lost or destroyed the licensing authority may after making such inquiry into the matter as it thinks fit, issue a duplicate.

---

186 Rule 6 of Licensing of Farrier Rules, 1965
187 Rule 7 of Licensing of Farrier Rules, 1965
188 Rule 8 of Licensing of Farrier Rules, 1965

7. **Farrier to exercise reasonable care and skill**[189]
   Every licensee under these rules must exercise reasonable degree of care and skill in the shoeing of cattle.

8. **Cancellation of license**[190]
   a. It is lawful for the licensing authority to enter the place of business of any licensee during normal working hours for the purpose of inspection; and if, in the opinion of the licensing authority the licensee is unable to exercise a reasonable degree of care and skill in the shoeing of cattle or is not properly equipped for the purpose of his business, after giving the licensee a reasonable opportunity of being heard, the licensing authority may cancel the licence.
   b. A licence may also be cancelled if the licensing authority is satisfied, after giving the licensee a reasonable opportunity of being heard that there has been a breach of any of the conditions of the licence.

9. **Issue of fresh licence after cancellation**[191]
   A person whose licence is cancelled may be granted a fresh license on application made in this behalf if the licensing authority is satisfied that having regard to the circumstances obtaining at the time of such application, there is no reason why the applicant should not be granted a fresh licence.[192]

189 Rule 9 of Licensing of Farrier Rules, 1965
190 Rule 10 of Licensing of Farrier Rules, 1965
191 Rule 11 of Licensing of Farrier Rules, 1965
192

PREVENTION AND CONTROL OF INFECTIOUS AND CONTAGIOUS DISEASES IN ANIMALS ACT, 2009

An Act to provide for the prevention, control and eradication of infectious and contagious diseases affecting animals[193], for prevention of outbreak or spreading of such diseases from one state to another, and to meet the international obligations of India for facilitating import and export of animals and animal products and for matters connected therewith or incidental thereto[194].

1. **Duties of the Owner/any other person in charge of the animal[195]:**
   a. If the owner, or any other person, NGO, public bodies or the village panchayat in charge of the animal if has a reason to believe that the animal is infected with any of the scheduled disease (**Annexure XXXI**) must report the same to the Village Officer or village panchayat inn-charge, who can then report the same to the nearest available Veterinarian.
   b. If the owner, or any other person, in charge of the animal if has a reason to believe that the animal is infected with any of the scheduled disease shall segregate and keep such animal in a place away from the other animals and prevent it from coming in contact with other animals.
   c. He shall confine such animal and prevent it from grazing in common place or drink water from a common source.

---

193 Section 2(a) of the Act, animals means:

(i) Cattle, buffalo, sheep, goat, yak, mithun;

(ii) Dog, cat, pig, horse, ass mule, poultry, bees; and

(iii) Any other animal or bird as the Central Government may by notification specify.

194 Preamble of the Act

195 Section 3, 4, 5, 6,7 and 21 of the Act

d. State government has the power to declare any areas as the controlled area for preventing, controlling and eradicating any scheduled disease and publish the same in a local newspaper in vernacular language and declare the same in loud voice and by beating of drums. In such case all animals in controlled area must be vaccinated by the owner/person in charge of the animal.
e. Any area may be declared by the state as free area where any scheduled diseases affecting any species is no longer prevalent. In such case no animal of the species or of any other susceptible species shall be allowed to enter free area unless duly immunised by vaccination.
f. Where any area is declared controlled area in relation to any disease affecting any species of animal, no animal belonging to particular species from controlled area can be moved from the place where it is kept.
g. The Director[196] may for controlling, preventing or for eradicating the scheduled disease in respect of any area prohibit the movement of all animals belonging to any specified species from place where it is kept to any other place and in such case no such animals shall be moved. However, animal may be moved to the nearest place where it can be immunised by vaccination.
h. Further such animal may be moved as along as the movement of the animal is accompanied with a certificate of vaccination to indicate that the animal is duly immunised against the particular disease and bears a proper mark of vaccination.

2. **Infected Areas**
   a. Veterinary Officer where is satisfied that any animal has been infected with any scheduled disease in any area or place within his jurisdiction can by notification publish in local newspaper in vernacular language and declare by loud voice and beating of drums such area to be an

196 Section 2(g) of the Act; "Director" in relation to a State means any officer in charge of the Department of Animal Husbandry or Veterinary Services, or both, notified by the State Government as such for the purpose of this Act.

infected area. Once area is declared as infected area then all the rules, regulations, and prohibitions as specified above for controlled area become applicable to infected area.

b. Owner/ person in charge must get any animal which is infected or reasonably believed to be infected in such area to be treated by veterinarian.
c. All the articles which are likely to have come in contact with the infected animal must be treated or disposed off.
d. Infected animal must be kept in isolation and owner/ person in charge must takes steps which may be necessary for the prevention, treatment and control of the disease directed by veterinarian.

3. **Vaccination**[197]
   a. To be administered by person competent under the law and issue a certificate of administration.
   b. The person vaccination shall cause to be put a mark by branding, tattooing or ear tagging, or in any such other manner as directed.
   c. Certificate of vaccination must specify the date of vaccination, date of manufacture and expiry of vaccine and date up to which vaccine shall be valid.

4. **Entry and exit into controlled, free and infected areas**[198]
   a. Where any area is declared as controlled area with regard to any disease affecting any species of animals, then no animal of that species can be taken out and no animal can be brought in that area.
   b. No carrier can carry animals from or out of a controlled area, free area or infected area by land, sea or air unless complies with specified requirements. However, it is not applicable to the carriage by railway of any anima through the controlled or infected area so long as the animal is not unloaded in such area.
   c. No person can take out of controlled area:

197 Section 8 of the Act
198 SECTION 10, 11, 12, 13 and 16 of the Act

    - Any animal alive or dead, which is infected with, or reasonably suspected to have been infected with, any scheduled disease.
    - Any kind of fodder, bedding, or other material which has come into contact with any animal infected with such disease or could, in any manner, carry the infection of the disease.
    - The carcass, skin or any other part or product of such animal.

   d. No person, organisation or institution can hold any animal market, fair or exhibition or carry on any other activity which involves grouping or gathering of any species of animals within a controlled area.
   e. No person can bring or attempt to bring into market fair, exhibition or congregation of animals or to any public place, any animal which is known to be infected with a scheduled disease.
   f. Where an animal belonging to species of animals with regard to which an area is declared controlled or free is vaccinated against that disease then such animal must be allowed to enter into or taken out of controlled or free area to any other place on production of a certificate to that effect and a period of at least 21 should have lapsed after the administration of vaccine.

5. **Quarantine Camps[199] (QC) and Check Posts[200] (CP)[201]**
   a. Director can establish as many QC and CP as may be required in the State.
   b. QC and CP are to be used for detention of animals suffering from scheduled disease or of animals which have come in contact with or have been kept in proximity of any infected animal and to prevent entry or exit from any controlled or infected area or free area.

---

199 Section 2(n) of the Act; "Quarantine Camp" means any place declared to carry out quarantine of animals and birds for the purpose of this Act.

200 Section 2(b) of the Act; "Check Post" means any place established as such by the Director to carry out checking of animals for the purpose of this Act.

201 Section 14 and 15 of the Act

c. Animal required to be detained, inspected, vaccinated or marked can be kept in QC for such period as directed by competent officer.
d. Any animal detained at QC has to be kept under the custody of the person in-charge of such QC and must be vaccinated and marked.
e. The officer in-charge of QC must at the time of release of an animal grant a permit to the person taking charge of animal and such person is bound to produce such permit wherever required.
f. Person in-charge of CP or QC must inspect any animal stopped at CP or detained in QC.
g. The manner of inspection and period of detention for administering vaccination, marking of animals, and the form and manner to permit entry of animal has to be as prescribed by the State Government.

6. **Infected animals: Powers and duties of veterinarian and veterinarian officer (VO)**
   a. Where on receipt of the report veterinarian has a reason to believe that any animal is infected with schedule disease he may by order in writing direct the owner/ person in charge to keep the animal segregated from other apparently healthy animals and to subject to the required treatment.
   b. Where in the receipt of the report of veterinarian the VO shall examine that and other animals which could have come in contact with the infected animal and submit such animals to test and medical examination.
   c. If after test and examination VO is of the view that animal is not infected he must issue a certificate to that effect.
   d. VO may draw such samples of the animal where it is of the opinion that the same is necessary to ascertain whether the suspected animal is actually infected or is susceptible to the infection or not.
   e. VO or any competent officer can draw samples to determine whether the animal was vaccinated or not and to check if the same was effective in conferring immunity.

f. In order to prevent the spread disease to other animals or to protect public health if the disease is of zoonotic importance the VO can direct euthanasia of the animal and immediate disposal of carcass.
g. Veterinarian or VO can order for post-mortem examination of a dead animal if in his opinion death was caused due to some infection and cause the carcass of the animal to be exhumed followed by proper disposal.
h. VO or any other competent officer can seize an infected animal where there is no owner or where owner/ person in-charge fails to comply promptly with the order issued with regard to such animal.

7. **Penalties**[202]
   a. Where any person, municipality or panchayat is required to take any measure with regard to any animal, carcass of any animal or any other thing and if he/it fails to such measures within specified time the authority which had issued such order can cause the measures to be taken at the cost of such person, municipality or panchayat as the case may be and costs of any measures is recoverable from such person, municipality or panchayat.
   b. Any person if issues a vaccination certificate without authority or competence in that behalf or administers a vaccine which he knows is defective in any manner is liable to be punished with fine of Rs.5000 or with imprisonment which may extend 1 month in case he fails to pay the fine. For any such subsequent offence he is liable to pay a fine of Rs.10,000/- and imprisonment which may extend to 3 months.
   c. Any person who contravenes the provisions of the Act or obstruct a competent officer in performing his duties is liable to be punished with fine which may extend to Rs. 1000/- or with imprisonment for a term which may extend to 1 month. For any such subsequent offence he is liable for a fine of Rs. 2000/- and with imprisonment for a term which may extend to 2 months in case of non-payment of fine.

202 Section 29, 31, 32 and 33 of the Act

d. Whoever places or causes or permits to be placed in any river, lake, canal or other water body, the carcass of any animal or any part of it which at the time of the death is known to be infected is liable to be punished for first offence with fine of Rs. 2000/- , or imprisonment of 1 month in case of non-payment of fine and for subsequent conviction with a fine of Rs. 5000/- or imprisonment for a term which may extend to 3 months or both.
e. Under the Act offender can be a company and the person in charge thereof.

8. **Precautionary measures on causative organism etc.**[203]
   a. Every institute, laboratory or clinic which is engaged in the manufacture, testing, research relating to vaccines, sera, diagnostic or chemotherapeutic drugs for prevention of scheduled diseases in animals must take adequate precautionary measures:
      - To ensure that the causative organism of any scheduled disease does not escape or otherwise gets released;
      - To guard against any such escape or release; and
      - To warn and protect everyone concerned in the event of any escape.
   b. Every animal used in manufacturing, testing or research or which is likely to carry or transmit any scheduled disease must be promptly administered euthanasia and disposed of by the person in charge of or having control of the institution, laboratory, or clinic as the case may be.
   c. In event of non-compliance of the aforesaid mandates every person who is in charge of or having control of an institution, laboratory or clinic becomes liable to be punished with fine which may extend to Rs. 20,000/- or imprisonment for a term which may extend to 6 months and in case the establishment is in commercial manufacturing of vaccines or medicines, a temporary suspension of license up to a period of one year can also be imposed.

203 Section 35 of the Act

KARNAIL SINGH V. STATE OF HARAYANA 2019 SCC ONLINE P&H 704

First specified herein are the directions that were issued by the Court to the State for the welfare of the animals and thereafter specified is the material that was relied upon by the court to arrive at the judgment.

1. **Following are the clarifications and directions that were issued by the Court:**
   a. The entire animal kingdom including avian and aquatic are declared as legal entities having a distinct persona with corresponding rights, duties and liabilities of a living person. All the citizens throughout the State of Haryana are hereby declared persons in loco parentis as the human face for the welfare/protection of animals.
   "Live and let live."
   b. Further the Court directed the State to ensure that the draught animals are not made to carry more load while driving vehicles than as prescribed, and clarified that the weight specified in the directions was to be inclusive of the weight of the vehicle.
   c. It directed the state to ensure that no person in charge of any vehicle drawn by any animal allows more than four persons, excluding the driver and children below 6 years of age to ride the vehicle.
   d. State was directed to ensure that animals are kept in proper conditions as prescribed.
   e. Use of spike stick or bit, harness or yoke with spikes, knobs or projections or any other sharp tackle or equipment which would cause pain and suffering to animals was banned throughout the State.
   f. Municipal Bodies were also directed to issue certificates of unladen weight of vehicles to avoid cruelty to animals

and to provide shelter of suitable size to horses, bullocks and camels driving vehicles.

g. The owners of bullock carts, camel carts, horse carts, tonga were ordered to put fluorescent reflectors in the front and back of the carts and also on the animals for their identification at night.
h. State was directed to ensure compliance with the TAR, 1978 read with Rule 93 of the Haryana Motor Vehicles rules, 1993, under the Prevention of Cruelty to Animals (Transport of Animals on Foot) Rules, 2001 and to enforce the provisions of the Prevention and Control of Infectious and Contagious Diseases in Animals Act, 2009.
i. All the Veterinary doctors throughout the State of Haryana were directed to treat the stray animals brought to them by the citizens, and in cases, where it is not possible to bring the sick animal/cattle to the Veterinary doctor, he/she was directed to personally visit and attend the stray cattle/animal without delay.
j. All the police officers throughout the State of Haryana were directed to ensure the due implementation of directions by taking the owner/incharge of the animal to the nearest weighing bridge to determine the weight of the load.
k. State was directed to constitute societies for prevention of cruelty to animals in each district, if not already constituted.
l. The cost of transporting the animal to an infirmary or pinjrapole, to be paid by the owner of the animal.
m. The Director Animal Husbandry to the State of Haryana was directed to ensure proper treatment of stray cattle and animals, throughout the State of Haryana by the duly qualified doctors.
n. All the Municipal bodies/Panchayati Raj Institutions, throughout the State of Haryana were directed to make sufficient provisions for housing the stray cattle and to provide them food/fodder and water.
o. All the Police Officers throughout the State of Haryana were directed to ensure that "Right of Way" is given to all the animal drawn carts.

p. The State of Haryana was directed to enforce the provisions of Prevention of Cruelty to Animals (Aquarium and Fish Tank Animals Shop) Rules, 2017; Prevention of Cruelty to Animals (Dog Breeding and Marketing) Rules 2017; and the Prevention of Cruelty to Animals (Pet Shop) Rules, 2018, in letter and spirit.

NARAYAN DUTT BHATT V. UNION OF INDIA; 2018 SCC ONLINE UTT 645

Facts: The present petition was filed pro bono publico for the protection and welfare of animals. Direction was sought to restrict the movement of horse carts/tongas from Nepal to India and from India to Nepal through Banbasa, District Champawat, India. Petitioner's case was that the provisions of Prevention of Cruelty to Animals Act, 1960 and the rules framed thereunder and the provisions of Prevention and Control of Infectious and Contagious Diseases in Animals Act, 2009 were not enforced and argued that the animals were transported in violation of Transport of Animals Rules, 1978.

Judgment: The Court held that:

a. "The entire animal kingdom including avian and aquatic are declared as legal entities having a distinct persona with corresponding rights, duties and liabilities of a living person. All the citizens throughout the State of Uttarakhand are hereby declared persons in loco parentis as the human face for the welfare/protection of animals."
b. The Nagar Panchayat, Banbasa was directed to regulate the plying of horse carts/tongas from Banbasa to Nepal. Government was directed to ensure the medical examination of all the animals including horses entering from Nepal to India as well as horses moving from Indian border to Nepal to check infectious and contagious diseases by setting the veterinary check-posts on the border.
c. The court directed constitution of a Committee to determine whether the maximum weight prescribed under Rules 3 and 4 of the Prevention of Cruelty to Draught and Pack Animals Rules, 1965 is reasonable or not, and the State was directed to make suitable amendment in Rules 3 and 4 of the Rules, 1965 as per the recommendations of the Committee

d. Further the court stated the weight/load limit for animals clarifying that the animals shall not be made to carry more or extra weight while driving vehicles.
e. State was directed ensure that no person in charge of any vehicle drawn by any animal allows more than four persons, excluding the driver and children below 6 years of age to ride the vehicle.
f. Use of spike stick or bit, harness or yoke with spikes, knobs or projections or any other sharp tackle or equipment which would cause pain and suffering to animals was banned throughout the State.
g. All the Municipal Bodies were directed to issue certificates of unladen weight of vehicles to avoid cruelty to animals and to provide shelter of suitable size to horses, bullocks and camels driving vehicles.
h. The owners of bullock carts, camel carts, horse carts, tonga were ordered to put fluorescent reflectors in the front and back of the carts and on the animals for their identification at night.
i. State was directed to ensure compliance with the TAR, 1978, Prevention and Control of Infectious and Contagious Diseases in Animals Act, 2009 and TAFR, 2001.
j. All the police officers throughout the State of Haryana were directed to ensure the due implementation of directions by taking the owner/incharge of the animal to the nearest weighing bridge to determine the weight of the load.
k. All the police officers were directed to enforce the provisions of Rule 14 of the Prevention of Cruelty to Animals (Transport of Animals on Foot) Rules, 2001.
l. State was directed to constitute societies for prevention of cruelty to animals in each district, if not already constituted.
m. State was directed to appoint infirmaries for the treatment and care of animals in respect of which offences have been committed. The cost of transporting the animal to an infirmary or pinjrapole, has to be paid by the owner of the animal.
n. The Director Animal Husbandry to the State of Uttarakhand was directed to ensure proper treatment of stray cattle and animals, throughout the State of Uttarakhand by the duly qualified doctors.

o. All the Veterinary doctors were directed to treat the stray animals brought to them by the citizens, in case, it was not possible to bring the sick animal/cattle to the Veterinary doctor, he/she was directed to personally visit and attend the stray cattle/animal without delay.

p. All the Municipal bodies, were directed to make sufficient provisions for housing the stray cattle and to provide them food/fodder and water.

q. All the Police Officers were directed to ensure "Right of Way" to animal driven carts to avoid inconvenience to the animals."

ARE BIRDS PROTECTED BY ANY LAW? CAN BIRDS BE CAGED?

ABDULKADAR MOHAMAD AZAM SHEIKH v. STATE OF GUJARAT AND ORS.[204]

Issue: Issue that was raised in the petition was "Whether do the birds have a right to live freely and/or Whether birds can be kept in illegal custody / cages and/or whether by keeping the birds in cages do their right to live freely is violated?"

The Court observed that:

> "8.01. ... It is an admitted position that the respective claimants, from whom 494 different birds have been seized, do not possess any licence as required under the provisions of Wildlife Protection Act. It is to be noted that most of the birds are Scheduled birds as per the provisions of Wildlife Protection Act, therefore, even for dealing with the same they are required to have licence. It is required to be noted that though the original claimants from whom the custody of the birds is taken are claiming ownership, have failed to even prima facie prove their ownership.
>
> 8.02. It is to be noted that even for the purpose of licence under the Wildlife Protection Act, 1972 and Wildlife (Protection) Licensing (Additional Matters for Consideration) Rules, 1983, if the licensing authority arrives at a finding of fact that applicant would not be able to carry on business of breeding of captive birds without hunting which includes trapping of birds, then the authority would be justified in refusing to grant licence.

---

204 SPECIAL CRIMINAL APPLICATION No. 1635, 1636, 1670, 2600, 2601, and 2602 of 2010

8.03. As observed by the Hon'ble Supreme Court in the case of Nasir Khan (supra), hunting includes trapping as per Section 2 (16) of the Wildlife Protection Act, 1972...

8.08. ... Prevention of Cruelty to Animal, 1960 is enacted with a view to prevent unnecessary pain or suffering to animals generally...

8.11. ... every bird / animal has a right to move freely and it cannot be disputed that so far as the birds are concerned, they have right to move freely in the open sky / air and they cannot be kept in cages at all and that too with such a brutality. To keep the birds in the cages would be illegal confinement of such birds against their wish which would be against the fundamental right of the birds to move freely. Even practically and physically it is not possible to keep the custody of the birds even to the institutions / NOGs for long time, as it will be too expensive as well as nobody knows when the trial will take place. Even environmentally also it is not safe and/ or in the interest of birds. Under the circumstances the only order which can be passed in such circumstances would be to enlarge the birds free in the sky / air and if such an order is passed it would be respecting the rights of the birds.

8.12...section 451 of the Code of Criminal Procedure confers powers upon the Court for custody and disposal of the property pending trial and the Court may make such order as it think fit for the proper custody of such property, pending conclusion of the inquiry or trial and if such property is subject to speedy and natural decay, or if it otherwise expedient to do so, Court may, after recording such evidence as it thinks necessary order it to be sold or otherwise dispose of. Considering the aforesaid provision and considering the fact that if birds in question are not ordered to be disposed of by way of enlarging them free in the air / sky, in that case looking to the hot weather, there are all chances that the birds may die. Under the circumstances also, it will be expedient and, in their interest, to enlarge the birds free..."

PEOPLE FOR ANIMALS V. MD MOHAZZIN & ANR; CRL. M.C. NO.2051/2015

Facts: Intimation was given to SHO PS Lajpat Nagar, New Delhi for violation of various provisions of Prevention of Cruelty (Capture of Animals) Rules, 1979 by the respondent. The birds were kept in small cages by the respondent though it was not sure whether their wings and tails were cut or not. More than thousands of birds were subjected to pain as the so-called owner-respondent had put them in small cages and sold them in the commercial market for his vested rights, despite of statutory and constitutional right to live with dignity.

Court held: After considering the facts and hearing both sides, the Court observed that; "…running the trade of birds is in violation of the rights of the birds. They deserve sympathy. Nobody is caring as to whether they have been inflicting cruelty or not despite of settled law that birds have a fundamental right to fly and cannot be caged and will have to be set free in the sky. Actually, they are meant for the same. But on the other hand, they are exported illegally in foreign countries without availability of proper food, water, medical aid and other basic amenities required as per law. Birds have fundamental rights including the right to live with dignity and they cannot be subjected to cruelty by anyone including claim made by the respondent. Therefore, I am clear in mind that all the birds have fundamental rights to fly in the sky and all human beings have no right to keep them in small cages for the purposes of their business or otherwise…"

OVERVIEW OF IMPORT AND EXPORT PROCEDURE FOR DOGS, CATS AND LIVESTOCK[205]

IMPORT PROCEDURE

1. Documents required to be submitted with the Application Form for import of livestock (pet under baggage rule for owners -dog/cat up to 2 number) dog and cat (as per custom circular no.15/2013 dated 08.04.2013)
    a. Accompanied Baggage: Ticket of the owner.
    b. Unaccompanied Baggage: Within1 month after arrival of owner- copy of Pass Port along with immigration stamp.
    c. Requirement of advance custom permission: For owners sending the pet more than 1 month after their arrival or before arrival.
    d. **For all above**: Visa copy/other document to establish continuous stay abroad for at least two years with proof of transferring the residence to India. In case of doubt/ procedural requirement advance custom permission may be asked to consider the pet under Baggage rule.
    e. Dog: Official health certificate from the country of origin certifying that the dog is free from clinical sign and symptoms of all infectious and contagious diseases including rabies, canine distemper, parvo virus infection, leptospirosis etc.
    f. Cat: Official health certificate from the country of origin certifying that the cat is free from clinical sign and symptoms of all infectious and contagious diseases including rabies, distemper, feline enteritis, feline panleukopenia, leptospirosis etc.

205 aqcsindia.gov.in/import-export-of-livestock-and-livestock-products.html; last visited on 25.07.2020

g. The dog (three months of age and older) and cat must be vaccinated against rabies more than one month, but within 12 months prior to actual embarkation and all details must be officially certified or mentioned in the official health certificate. Also, all other vaccination record/detail must be officially certified or mentioned in the official health certificate.
h. The name of owner in the official health certificate must match with the name as mentioned in the ticket of owner to establish ownership.
i. The name and address of the owner in the country of origin and in the country of arrival (import) must be mentioned on the health certificate.
j. The declaration from the owner that the dog/cat is bona fide pet with no commercial interest, gift and breeding purpose.
k. No additional feed, bedding etc. be allowed during the journey.
l. Copy of airway bill/journey details of pet/Bill of entry with custom (If coming under cargo).
m. Any other document if required during examination of application.
n. Authorization letter if owner is not approaching directly.

2. Documents required cum check list with application form for import of livestock (under DGFT licence/ sanitary import permit)- all livestock except pet (dog/cat up to two number with owner under baggage rule)
   a. Copy of valid DGFT Licence/Sanitary Import Permit (SIP)
   b. Bill of entry with custom reference.
   c. Official health certificate from the country of origin fulfilling all import health guidelines of India as per the notification/supplied protocol with license or SIP/AQCS requirement as the case may be. The description of livestock product must be mentioned in health certificate/ certified officially.
   d. Laboratory reports (not mandatory in each case).

e. The name and address of owner in the social health certificate must match with the Licence/SIP to establish ownership.
f. No additional feed, bedding etc. be allowed during the journey without permission.
g. Undertaking and declarations as per requirement.
h. Copy of airway bill/journey details of animal.
i. Any other document if required during examination of application.
j. Original health documents are mandatory on arrival for provisional clearance.
k. Authorization letter if owner is not approaching directly.
l. Advance NOC will be issued within 7 days of arrival based on the self-certified advance copies of all above documents. Original Health certificate will be retained by AQCS at the time of Provisional Clearance on arrival. Final Clearance will be issued as per the applicable post import Quarantine rule/regulation.

3. Documents Required cum check list with Application Form for import of livestock products
   a. Copy of valid DGFT Licence/Sanitary Import Permit (SIP)
   b. Bill of entry with Custom reference.
   c. Official health certificate from the country of origin fulfilling all import health guidelines of India as per the Notification/supplied protocol with license or SIP/AQCS requirement as the case may be. The description of Livestock product shall be mentioned in health certificate/ certified officially.
   d. Country of origin certificate.
   e. Laboratory Reports (if applicable).
   f. The name and address of consignor and consignee along with other details in the official health certificate must match with the Licence/SIP.
   g. Custom sealed samples/examination/sampling as the case may be.
   h. Undertaking and declarations as per requirement.

i. Copy of airway bill/cargo details/invoice/packing list of consignment.
j. Any other document if required during examination of application.
k. Original Health documents are mandatory on arrival for Provisional Clearance/Final clearance/Testing/ Examination as the case may be.
l. Authorization letter if owner is not approaching directly.
m. All attached documents with the application must be self-attested.
n. Sanitary Import Permit (SIP – issued for high risk products –list in notification no. SO 2666(E) dated 16.10.14) Issued by Ministry of Agriculture, Department of Animal Husbandry, Dairying Fisheries for Livestock Products like-
    - Meat & Meat products of all types
    - Aquatic Products and Meat
    - Egg products
    - Milk products
    - Embryos, Ova, Semen
    - Pet foods
    - Feathers, Pig Bristles
    - Serum
    - Bones and Horns Products.
k. DGFT License-Issued mainly for import of Livestock by Director General of Foreign Trade in consultation with Department of Animal Husbandry, Dairying & Fisheries.
l. All Livestock except pet under baggage (Dog and Cat) up to two numbers and livestock products (semen, embryos) are covered under DGFT License. Contains pre import and post import guidelines (checked by AQCS on arrival).
m. Entry points
    - Designated port: 6 (Airport and Sea port) and their connected ICDs (Inland Container Depots).
    - Vishakhapatnam and Cochin- Fish products only.
    - Patrapole land route (WB) - Fish only.

4. Import procedure
    a. Before arrival:

- Intimation (application) by the importer-DGFT/SIP
- Fulfilment of pre-import quarantine/sanitary requirements (As per the official health protocol)- Issue of advance NOC (for livestock)

b. Arrival: Examination of official health documents, inspection and sampling. Fulfilment of Post import protocol.
c. Clearances: Immediate, Provisional and on hold at port (as per risk analysis consignment wise)
d. Non-fulfilment of the import health guidelines: Deportation/destruction as the case may be.

EXPORT PROCEDURES

This section envisages provision of an internationally acceptable certification service for the export of livestock and livestock product to other countries from India confirming to the health requirements of the importing country and the health regulations prescribed in the International Zoo Sanitary code of OIE.

1. Export procedures
   a. International Animal Health Certification: All over the world including EU.
   b. Prevent ingress of exotic diseases from one territory to another.
   c. Ensures quality and satisfaction of importing country as per their requirement.
   d. Export Health Certificates: As per International Certification Procedure of OIE, Terrestrial Animal Health Code (chapter 5.2, article 5.2.1 to 5.2.4).
   e. AQCS Veterinarians: Official veterinarians as per OIE code.
2. Documents Required cum check list with Application Form for export of livestock
   f. Copy of valid Import/Export Licence or Permit as the case may be. If no permit/licence is required than undertaking from the exporter/owner in this regard.
   g. Official health requirement/format of the importing country. If no prescribed health requirement/format than undertaking from the exporter/owner in this regard.

h. Fulfilled health requirement of importing country including testing, treatment, vaccination etc. (if applicable).
i. Self-certified copies of present health documents including vaccination record of the animal.
j. Undertaking and declarations as per requirement.
k. Documents of origin, if applicable/asked.
l. Copy of airway bill/journey details of animal.
m. Any other document if required during examination of application.
n. Authorization letter if owner is not approaching directly.
o. All attached documents with the application must be self-attested.
p. Export Quarantine Certificate will be issued after physical examination/Quarantine observation of the animal as the case may be within 2-3 days before departure. If required the animal may be referred for detailed clinical examination including testing. If the animal is not healthy the Certificate will not be issued.
q. NOTE: All livestock meant for export must be micro chipped for better identification.

3. Documents Required cum check list with Application Form for export of livestock products
   a. Copy of valid Import/Export Licence or Permit as the case may be. If no permit/licence is required than undertaking from the exporter/owner in this regard.
   b. Official health requirement/format of the importing country. If no prescribed health requirement/format than undertaking from the exporter/owner in this regard.
   c. Fulfilled health requirement of importing country including testing, treatment, fumigation etc. (if applicable/asked).
   d. Registration certificate/Approvals of the exporting units.
   e. Undertaking and declarations as per requirement.
   f. Documents of origin of product, if applicable/asked.
   g. Copy of airway bill/Bill of lading/packing list/Invoice of the consignment.

h. Certificate/information from the local Government authorities and others wherever applicable.
i. Any other document if required during examination of application.
j. Authorization letter if owner is not approaching directly.
k. All attached documents with the application must be self-attested.
l. All application must be registered on/before the Bill of lading date.
m. Certificate will be issued on or before the lading date.

4. Exit points
   a. any port in India

5. Export
   Export certification is very important and must be as per International Certification Procedure of OIE, Terrestrial Animal Health Code (chapter 5.2, article 5.2.1 to 5.2.4). As per the procedure the Official Veterinarian (AQCS) of the Veterinary Authority (DAHDF, MOA&FW) of the Exporting Country sign the export Health certificate.

6. Points considered:
   Health requirements/guidelines of importing country request of the importer. Export rules of Government of India. Pre export quarantine and testing (as applicable) inspection and certification

7. Objective: To prevent the spread and introduction of diseases in new territories. To prevent the complaints from importing countries ensures quality certification and pre shipment inspection as per the requirement of importing country.

8. Auction
   Not recommended due to technical reasons (AQCS clearance is mandatory) reasons:
   Consignment may act as carrier/vehicle for dangerous exotic diseases. May harbour dangerous micro-organisms due to delay in reference by the Customs, clearance/deportation. Not t to use (adverse effect on animal/human health).

9. Re-import

   Points to consider:

   a. Reason of re-import. Other products in the carrier.
   b. Loading/unloading en-route.
   c. Shelf life of the product. Duration of stay in importing country.
   d. Place of holding in importing country.
   e. Health condition of the consignment.
   f. Fulfilment of pre-export requirements. Disease freedom status of importing country.

WILDLIFE PROTECTION ACT 1972

INTRODUCTION

A long time back an attempt was made to save wildlife by way of enacting Indian Forest Act, 1927 in India. It provided for hunting restrictions in protected and reserved forests. Art. 51-A (g) of Indian Constitution imposes a fundamental duty on every Indian citizen to protect and improve wildlife in the country.

The Wildlife (Protection) Act, 1972 (**WPA/Act**) is an Act passed by the Parliament of India on August 21, 1972, and later implemented on 9th September, 1972. This Act was enacted for the protection of plants, birds and animal species. The Act was necessitated as some wild animals and birds had already become extinct while some others were on the verge of extinction. The Act provides for the establishment of Wildlife Advisory boards and the appointment of wildlife wardens and other staff to implement the provisions of the Act. In several states, the office of the Chief Wildlife Warden and the Chief Conservator of Forests is united in a single post. The Act prohibits hunting of animals listed in Schedule I, II, III and IV of the Act. Under the Act, the state government may declare any area of adequate ecological, faunal, floral, natural, or zoological importance as a sanctuary or a national park. In both national parks and sanctuaries, public entry is restricted and the destruction of any wildlife or habitat is prohibited. This Act includes provisions for protection of plants and animals, hunting, harvesting and various other ancillary matters connected thereto. It has six schedules which extend to all over India. Under this Act, various kinds of penalties are also laid down for the violation of the laws contained therein. This Act contains 66 sections and six schedules.

SUMMARY OF PROVISIONS FOR THE PROTECTION OF ANIMALS UNDER THE ACT:

1. The act provides a comprehensive list of all endangered wildlife of the country and prohibits hunting of such endangered species.
2. This Act has six schedules which give varying degree of protection to the flora and fauna specified therein.
   e.g. Species of animals listed in Schedule I and Schedule II (Part II) of the WPA have absolute protection and offences against or with regard to such species attract maximum penalty and punishment. Whereas animal species listed in Schedule III and IV of the WPA are also protected, but the penalties and scale of punishment is lower. Schedule V includes the animals which may be hunted and these animals are referred to as vermin.
3. Scheduled animals are prohibited from being traded.
4. The Act provides for licenses for sale, transfer and possession of some wildlife species.
5. The Act provides for the establishment of Wildlife Sanctuary, National Parks, etc.
6. The Act provides for the formation of wildlife advisory board, wildlife wardens and specifies their duties, etc.
7. The National Board of Wildlife is constituted as a statutory organization.
8. The Act also provided for establishment of National Tiger Conservation Authority (giving a statutory authority to project Tiger launched in 1973).

OBJECTIVES OF WILDLIFE (PROTECTION) ACT, 1872

1. One of the main objectives is to prohibit the hunting of wild animals, various species of birds etc.
2. It lays down various punishments for the violation of rules and regulations to have proper control over the activities of human beings and to serve the various purposes of this Act.

3. Various Schedules contained under this Act give absolute protection to some endangered species so that they can be protected.
4. To provide shelter and protect the animals which are not in danger but need protection and security.
5. To specially protected animals that can be hunted like ducks, deer etc. For hunting such animals, the hunter has to obtain a license from the District Officer. If the license is granted, he would be given a certain restricted area to shoot the animals and in a particular season. Any of the acts which result in infringement of such a license will be cancelled.
6. One of the important objectives is to give powers in the hand of officers to punish the one who is guilty under this Act.
7. To help the state government and central government to declare any area as sanctuaries or national parks.
8. To plant trees and build protected animal parks so that such animals are protected in environment-friendly and natural areas.
9. To establish wildlife advisory boards, wildlife warden and to appoint the members with their duties and power.
10. To support the launching of the National component of UNESCO's Man and Biosphere Program, 1971.
11. To provide protection even for some endangered plants.
12. To impose a ban on trade and commerce of certain protected species.
13. To provide trade and commerce of some wild species by providing a license for possession, sale, and transfer.
14. To maintain the diversity of flora and fauna of the country and also to maintain a healthy ecological balance.

HUNTING OF WILD ANIMALS

Prohibitions, Restrictions and Permissions for hunting of wild animals are as follows:

1. **Prohibition:** No person can hunt any wild animal specified in Schedules I, II, III and IV of the WPA except as per the provisions of the Act[206].
2. **Permission[207]:**
   a. Any wild animal specified in Schedule I of WPA which becomes dangerous to human life or is so diseased or disabled as to be beyond recovery, then the animal can be hunted by the person permitted to do so or any other person appointed by such person upon the satisfaction and written order of the Chief Wild Life Warden (**CWLW**). Written order must be a reasoned order.
   b. However, no such order can be made if such animal can be captured, tranquilized or translocated. Any process of capture or translocation must be done in such a manner so as to cause minimum trauma to the animal.
   c. No captured animal can be kept in captivity if the animal can be rehabilitated. Any order if passed otherwise must be a reasoned order.
   d. Any wild animal or group of wild animals specified in Schedule II, III or IV of WPA which become dangerous to human life or is/are so diseased or disabled as to be beyond recovery, then the animal/group of animals can be hunted by the person permitted to do so or any other person appointed by such person upon the satisfaction and written order of the Chief Wild Life Warden (CWLW) or

206 Section 9 of the WPA

207 Section 11 of the WPA

any authorized officer. Written order must be a reasoned order.

e. Killing or wounding any wild animal in self-defence or in defence of some other person is an offence. However, the person should not be at the time of killing or wounding the animal acting in contravention of the Act or any rules made thereunder.
f. Any animal killed or wounded in defence of any person is government property.
g. The CWLW can subject to the conditions grant a written permit to any person on payment of prescribed fee to hunt any wild animal for the purpose of:
    - education
    - scientific research
    - scientific management[208]
    - collection of specimens:
        - for recognized zoos subject to the permissions
        - for museums and similar institutions
    - derivation or collection of such snake venom for manufacturing of life saving drugs.

No such permit can be granted by the CWLW without the previous permission of Central Government with regard to wild animals specified in Schedule I and of the State Government with regard to other wild animals.

208 WPA, Section 12, Explanation; "scientific management" means (i) translocation of any wild animals to an alternative suitable habitat; or (ii) population management of wildlife, without killing or poisoning or destroying any wild animals

TRILOK BAHADUR VS. STATE OF ARUNACHAL PRADESH 1979 CRLJ 1409 (GAUHATI)

Issue: The question that arose for consideration in the present case was whether the accused who had killed a tiger did so while acting in self-defence or not.

Facts: The brief facts of the case are that the petitioner was a guard in Changlai camp, when on sentry duty he observed the presence of a tiger. He reported the same to his Commander. Accordingly, he was ordered by his Commander to fire two or three rounds in the air. The tiger instead of fleeing came towards him and attempted to assault him. The accused had no option but to fire at the tiger. As a result, the tiger died. The Deputy Commissioner sentenced the accused for 6 months simple imprisonment under section 51 of the Wildlife Protection Act. A criminal revision petition was filed before the High Court.

Held: The basic question before the Court was to determine whether the accused killed the tiger in hunting or in self-defence. The Court observed that the ferocity of the animal would be relevant in that context and said that Tiger by nature is a dangerous animal. In the case of attack by '*ferae naturae*' the victim cannot be expected to weigh the chances in golden scale. The inference can be drawn that he was acting in good faith in defence of oneself and it cannot be said that the accused was committing any offence prior to shooting the tiger that charged at him. Therefore, he will be completely protected under sub-section (2) of Sec 11. Therefore, the court held that the impugned order of conviction and sentence is contrary to the provisions of Sec 11 of the Wildlife Protection Act and as such it is liable to be set aside.

PROTECTED AREAS

A. **Sanctuary**

1. **Declaration**[209]

State Government may by notification declare its intention to constitute any area as sanctuary if it considers such area is adequate ecological, faunal, floral, geomorphological, natural or zoological significance for the purpose of protecting, propagating or developing wildlife or is environment. Notification must specify as nearly as possible the situation and limits of such area such as by roads, rivers, ridges etc.

However, no area comprising of reserved forest or territorial waters can be declared as sanctuary.

2. **Restrictions on entry in sanctuary**[210]
   a. People who can enter a sanctuary:
      - Public servant on duty;
      - A person who has been permitted by CWLW/ authorized officer to live within the limits of sanctuary;
      - A person who has any right over immovable property within the limits of sanctuary;
      - Dependents of persons specified above; and
      - A person passing through sanctuary along a public highway.
   b. Duties of person residing in sanctuary
      - Prevent commission of offence against WPA in the sanctuary.
      - If there is a reason to believe that an offence against Act has been committed in sanctuary then to help in discovering and arresting the offender.

---

209 Section 18 of the WPA

210 Section 27 of the WPA

- To report death of any wild animal and to safeguard its remains until charge of the same is taken over by the CWLW/authorized officer.
- To prevent from spreading and extinguishing any fire in the sanctuary by lawful means
- To assist in preventing or investigation of any offence against the WPA.

c. All persons are restricted and prohibited from causing any damage to any boundary mark of a sanctuary or from causing wrongful gain by altering, destroying, moving or defacing the boundary mark of a sanctuary.

d. All the persons are prohibited and restricted from teasing or molesting any wild animal or littering the grounds of a sanctuary.

3. **Grant of Permit**[211]

CWLW may on application and upon payment of prescribed fee grant to any person a permit to enter or reside in a sanctuary for all or any of the following purposes:

a. Investigation or study of wildlife and purposes ancillary or incidental thereto;
b. Photography;
c. Scientific research;
d. Tourism;
e. Transaction of lawful business with any person residing in the sanctuary.

4. **Act prohibited in a sanctuary**

a. No person can except with the permit of CWLW[212]:
   - Destroy exploit or remove any wildlife including forest produce;
   - Destroy, damage or divert the habitat of any wild animal by any act whatsoever;
   - Divert, stop or enhance the flow of the water into or outside the sanctuary

211 Section 28 of the WPA

212 Section 29 of the WPA

No such permit can be granted until the State Government is satisfied that any such act is necessary for the improvement and better management of wild life therein, authorizes the issue of such permit.

b. No person can set fire to a sanctuary, kindle any fire or leave any fire burning in a sanctuary, in such manner as to endanger such sanctuary.[213]
c. No person can enter a sanctuary with any weapon except with the previous permission in writing of CWLW or the authorized officer[214].
d. No person can use in a sanctuary, chemicals, explosives or any other substances which may cause injury to, or endanger, any wildlife in such sanctuary[215].
e. No person can or cause to be taken any live stock in a sanctuary without getting it immunized. CWLW is responsible for taking all the measures as may be necessary for immunization against communicable diseases of the livestock kept in or within 5 kms of a sanctuary.[216]

5. **Registration of persons in possession of arms**
   a. Any person who holds a license under the Arms Act, 1959, for the possession of arms or is exempted from the provisions of the said Act and is in possession or arms and who resided in or within 10 km of any sanctuary has to within 3 months of declaration any area as sanctuary apply in the prescribed form and pay prescribed fee for registration of his name to the CWLW or the authorized officer. No new license can be granted within 10 kms of a sanctuary without prior concurrence of CWLW.

Mahesh Kumar Virjibhai Trivedi vs State of Gujarat[217]

In this case, the government allotted land in 1978 to the petitioners under a scheme for the rehabilitation of the

213 Section 30 of the WPA
214 Section 31 of the WPA
215 Section 32 of the WPA
216 Section 33-A of the WPA
217 Mahesh Kumar Virjibhai Trivedi vs State of Gujarat -AIR 2006 Guj. 35.

Pakistani Nationals who crossed over to India in 1971. Later, a Wild Ass Sanctuary was declared in 2001 under the Wildlife Protection Act, 1972 covering the land area allotted to the petitioners. They challenged this declaration and demanded that they may be permitted to live at the allotted land even if it may be inside the sanctuary. The court declared that the petitioners cannot claim any right to live there and continue to have possession of the land as the land was within the boundaries of the sanctuary.

B. **National Parks**

1. **Declaration of National Parks**
   a. Whenever it appears to the State Government that an area (within a sanctuary or not) is by reason of its ecological, faunal, floral, geomorphological or zoological association or importance, needed to be constituted as a National Park for the purpose of protecting, propagating, or developing wildlife therein or its environment, it may by notification, declare its intention to constitute such area as a National Park.
   b. The Notification must define the limits of the area which is intended to be declared as a National park.

2. **Prohibitions**
   a. No person can except with the permit of CWLW[218]:
   - Destroy exploit or remove any wildlife including forest produce from a National Park;
   - Destroy, damage or divert the habitat of any wild animal by any act whatsoever;
   - Divert, stop or enhance the flow of the water into or outside the National Park

   No such permit can be granted until the State Government is satisfied that any such act is necessary for the improvement and better management of wild life therein, authorizes the issue of such permit.

218 Section 29 of the WPA

b. No live stock can be grazed or be allowed to enter a National Park except where such livestock is used as a vehicle by a person authorized to enter such National Park.
c. The prohibitions as specified for a sanctuary are equally applicable to National Parks.

C. **Central zoo authority and recognition of zoos**

1. The Central Government is empowered under the WPA to constitute Central Zoo Authority (**CZA**).
2. The functions/duties of CZA are as follows[219]:
   a. Specify the minimum standards for housing, upkeep and veterinary care of the animals kept in a zoo;
   b. Evaluate and assess the functioning of zoos with respect to the standards or the norms as may be prescribed;
   c. Recognize or derecognize zoos;
   d. Identify endangered species of wild animals for purposes of captive breeding and assigning responsibility in this regard to a zoo;
   e. Co-ordinate the acquisition, exchange, and loaning of animals for breeding purposes;
   f. Ensure maintenance of study-books of endangered species of wild animals bred in captivity;
   g. Identify priorities and themes regarding display of captive animals in a zoo;
   h. Co-ordinate training of zoo personnel in India and outside India;
   i. Co-ordinate research in captive breeding and educational programmes for the purposes of zoos;
   j. Provide technical and other assistance to zoos for their proper management and development on scientific lines;
   k. Perform such other functions as may be necessary to carry out the purposes of this Act about zoos.
3. Recognition of Zoos[220]
   a. No zoo can operate without being recognized by CZA.

219 Section 38-C of the WPA
220 Section 38-H of the WPA

b. No zoo can be established without prior approval of CZA.
c. Application for recognition of any zoo must be made in prescribed form and fee to CZA.
d. Recognition if granted must specify the conditions subject to which applicant zoo can operate.
e. Recognition shall be granted by CZA only if after giving due regard to the interests of protection and conservation of wild life, and such standards, norms and other prescribed matters it is satisfied that recognition should be granted.
f. Reasonable opportunity of being heard has to be given to the applicant before application is rejected.
g. CZA may for recorded reasons suspend or cancel the recognition granted to a zoo after giving person operating zoo a reasonable opportunity of being heard.
h. Any appeal against such suspension or cancellation or refusal to recognize a zoo can be made before the Central Government within 30 days of the receipt of such communication.
4. Acquisition of animals by a zoo[221]
a. Zoo cannot acquire, sell, or transfer any wild or captive animal except from or to a recognized zoo.
b. Zoo cannot acquire, sell, or transfer any wild animal or captive animal specified in Schedules I and II except with the previous permission of the Authority.

5. Prohibitions

Teasing, molesting, injuring, or feeding of any animal or causing disturbance to the animals by noise or otherwise or littering the grounds in a zoo by any person is not permitted[222].

D. National Tiger Conservation Authority

1. Powers and functions of Tiger Conservation Authority[223]
    a. To approve the Tiger Conservation Plan prepared by the State Government under the provisions of the WPA.

221 Section 38-I of the WPA
222 Section 38-J of the WPA
223 Section 38-O of the WPA

b. Evaluate and assess various aspects of sustainable ecology and disallow any ecologically unsustainable land use such as, mining, industry and other projects within the tiger reserves.
c. Lay down normative standards for tourism activities and guidelines for project tiger from time to time for tiger conservation in the buffer and core area of tiger reserves and ensure their due compliance.
d. Provide for management focus and measures for addressing conflicts of men and wild animals and to emphasize on co-existence in forest areas outside the National Parks, sanctuaries or tiger reserve, in the working plan code.
e. Provide information on protection measures including future conservation plan, estimation of population of tiger and its natural prey species, status of habitats, disease surveillance, mortality survey, patrolling, reports on untoward happenings and such other management aspects as it may deem fit including future plan conservation
f. Approve, co-ordinate research and monitoring on tiger, co-predators, prey, habitat, related ecological and socio-economic parameters and their evaluation
g. Ensure that the tiger reserves and areas linking one protected area or tiger reserve with another protected area or tiger reserve are not diverted for ecologically unsustainable uses, except in public interest and with the approval of the National Board for Wild Life and on the advice of the Tiger Conservation Authority
h. Facilitate and support the tiger reserve management in the State for biodiversity conservation initiatives through eco-development and people's participation as per approved management plans and to support similar initiatives in adjoining areas consistent with the Central and State laws
i. Ensure critical support including scientific, information technology and legal support for better implementation of the tiger conservation plan
j. Facilitate ongoing capacity building program for skill development of officers and staff of tiger reserves

k. Perform such other functions as may be necessary to carry out the purposes of this Act regarding conservation of tigers and their habitat.
l. The Tiger Conservation Authority may, issue directions in writing to any person, officer or authority for the protection of tiger or tiger reserves and such person, officer or authority shall be bound to comply with the directions.
m. No such direction can however be issued to interfere with or affect the rights of local people, particularly the Scheduled Tribes.

2. Tiger Conservation Plan[224]
   a. The State Government, on the recommendation of the Tiger Conservation Authority, notifies an area as a tiger reserve.
   b. The notification must specify as nearly as possible, the situation and limits of such area.
   c. Duties of person residing in Tiger reserve
      - Prevent commission of offence against WPA in the tiger reserve.
      - If there is a reason to believe that an offence against Act has been committed in the tiger reserve then to help in discovering and arresting the offender.
      - To report death of any wild animal and to safeguard its remains until charge of the same is taken over by the CWLW/authorized officer.
      - To prevent from spreading and extinguishing any fire in the tiger reserve by lawful means.
      - To assist in preventing or investigation of any offence against the WPA.
   d. All persons are restricted and prohibited from causing any damage to any boundary mark of a sanctuary or from causing wrongful gain by altering, destroying, moving or defacing the boundary mark of a tiger reserve.
   e. All the persons are prohibited and restricted from teasing or molesting any wild animal or littering the grounds of a tiger reserve.

224 Section 38-V of the WPA

f. No person should set fire to a tiger reserve, kindle any fire or leave any fire burning, in a tiger reserve, in such a manner as to endanger such tiger reserve.
g. No person should use, in a tiger reserve, chemicals, explosives, or any other substance which may cause injury to, or endanger, any wildlife in such tiger reserve.
h. CWLW must take such steps as would ensure the security of wild animals in the tiger reserve and the preservation of the tiger reserve and wild animals therein.
i. CWLW can take such measures, in the interest of wild life, as it considers necessary for the improvement of any habitat.
j. The State Government must prepare a Tiger Conservation Plan including staff development and deployment plan for proper management of each such area to ensure:
    - Protection of tiger reserve and providing site specific habitat inputs for a viable population of tigers, co-predators and prey animals without distorting the natural prey-predator ecological cycle in the habitat.
    - Ecologically compatible land uses in the tiger reserves and areas linking one protected area or tiger reserve with another for addressing the livelihood concerns of local people, so as to provide dispersal habitats and corridor for spill over population of wild animals from the designated core areas of tiger reserves or from tiger breeding habitats within other protected areas.
    - The forestry operations of regular forest divisions and those adjoining tiger reserves are not incompatible with the needs of tiger conservation.
k. While preparing a Tiger Conservation Plan, State Government must ensure the agricultural, livelihood, developmental and other interests of the people living in tiger bearing forests or a tiger reserve is safeguarded. Tiger reserve for the purpose of this duty includes:
    - core or critical tiger habitat areas of National Parks and sanctuaries, where it has been established, on the basis of scientific and objective criteria, that such areas are required to be kept for purposes of tiger conservation,

without affecting the rights of the Scheduled Tribes or such other forest dwellers, and. notified as such by the State Government in consultation with an Expert Committee constituted for the purpose;

- buffer or peripheral area consisting of the area peripheral to critical tiger habitat or core area, identified, where a lesser degree of habitat protection is required to ensure the integrity of the critical tiger habitat with adequate dispersal for tiger species, and which aim at promoting co-existence between wildlife and human activity with due recognition of the livelihood, developmental, social and cultural rights of the local people, wherein the limits of such areas are determined on the basis of scientific and objective criteria in consultation with the concerned Gram Sabha and an Expert Committee constituted for the purpose.

l. No Scheduled Tribes or other forest dwellers should be resettled or have their rights adversely affected for the purpose of creating tiger conservation except as otherwise provided under the WPA.

3. Alteration and de-notification of tiger reserves[225]
   a. The boundaries of tiger reserve cannot be altered except on recommendation of the Tiger Conservation Authority and upon the approval of National Board for Wild Life.
   b. No state can de-notify a tiger reserve, except in public interest with the approval of the Tiger Conservation Authority and the National board of Wild Life.

4. Establishment of Tiger Conservation Foundation[226]
   a. The State Government must establish a Tiger Conservation Foundation for tiger reserves within the State in order to facilitate and support their management for conservation of tiger and biodiversity and, to take initiatives in eco-development by involvement of people in such development process.

225 Section 38-W of the WPA

226 Section 38-X of the WPA

b. The Tiger Conservation Foundation must, inter alia, have the following objectives:
    - to facilitate ecological, economic, social and cultural development in the tiger reserves;
    - to promote eco-tourism with the involvement of local stake-holder communities and provide support to safeguard the natural environment in the tiger reserves;
    - to facilitate the creation of, and or maintenance of, such assets as may be necessary for fulfilling the above said objectives;
    - to solicit technical, financial, social, legal and other support required for the activities of the Foundation for achieving the above said objectives;
    - to augment and mobilise financial resources including recycling of entry and such other fees received in a tiger reserve, to foster stake-holder development and eco-tourism;
    - to support research, environmental education and training in the above related fields.

Tarun Bharat Sangh, Alwar vs. Union of India[227]

The petitioner organization challenged the grant of 215 mining licenses in the area declared as Tiger Reserve in Alwar district of Rajasthan. The Supreme Court cancelled all the licenses as they were given in the tiger reserve area. In conclusion it was held that the legislature and judiciary in our country are both aware of significance of wildlife. With constantly shrinking forest cover, the survival of wildlife has been jeopardized. Still the citizens must do the best to protect the wildlife.

E. **Tiger and other endangered species Crime Control Bureau (CCB)**

The Central Government may constitute a Tiger and other Endangered Species Crime Control Bureau to be known as

227 Tarun Bharat Sangh, Alwar vs. Union of India (1993) Sup (3) SCC 115

the Wildlife Crime Control Bureau. The powers and functions of this crime bureau are as given below:[228]

1. collect and collate intelligence related to organized wildlife crime activities and to disseminate the same to State and other enforcement agencies for immediate action, so as to apprehend the criminals and to establish a centralized wildlife crime data bank
2. co-ordination of actions by various officers, State Governments and other authorities in connection with the enforcement of the provisions of this Act, either directly or through regional and border units set up by the Bureau
3. implementation of obligations under the various international Conventions and protocols that are in force at present or which may be ratified or acceded to by India in future
4. assistance to concerned authorities in foreign countries and concerned international organizations to facilitate co-ordination and universal action for wildlife crime control
5. develop infrastructure and capacity building for scientific and professional investigation into wildlife crimes and assist State Governments to ensure success in prosecutions related to wildlife crimes
6. advice the Government of India on issues relating to wildlife crimes having national and international ramifications, and suggest changes required in relevant policy and laws from time to time.

228 Section 38-Z of the WPA

M/S. MAA DASABHUJA FURNITURE UNIT *V.* STATE OF ORISSA & ORS. AIR 2006 ORI 63

Facts/Issue: In this case the office order passed by the Conservator of Forests, Berhampur Circle rejecting the petitioner's appeal for saw mill licence was challenged. The stand of the respondents was that the site proposed by the petitioner at Saradeipur (Uttara) is within 10 kms. radial distance from Kharija village forest and that in view of the Government notification no saw mill can be established within 10 kms. radial distance from any reserve or village forest.

Held: The court observed that; "The orders of the forest officials ... firmly indicate that the site proposed by petitioner is within 10 kms. radial distance from the above noted village forest.

> **7.** The Apex Court by order dated 30th October, 2002 in Writ Petition (Civil) No. 202 of 1995 directed closure of all licensed saw mills and prohibited opening of any new saw mill without prior approval of the Central Empowered Committee. Admittedly, permission of the Central Empowered Committee for the proposed saw mill of petitioner is not there. That apart, in the case of *T.N. Godavarman*, AIR 1998 SC 769 (supra) the Supreme Court prohibited opening of any saw mill within 10 Kms. radial from the boundary of any forest or forest area. In such a situation, there was absolutely no scope for opp. party No. 2 or 3 to grant a licence for establishment of a new saw mill at Sardeipur (Uttara) by petitioner. The rejection order Annexure-3 therefore, does not suffer from any illegality or perversity and thus does not call for any interference.
>
> **9.** In the result, therefore, the writ petition is bound to fail and is accordingly dismissed."

KAMLA KANT PANDEY V. STATE OF U.P. & ORS. AIR 2006 ALL 92

Facts: In the year1982 a notification under section 18(1) of the Wild Life Protection Act, 1972 was issued constituting Kaimur Wild Life Sanctuary. Boundaries of the Sanctuary were also described in the notification. Petitioner was carrying on mining activities and transport of minerals on the basis of lease. The lease was cancelled on the ground that the area leased by the Petitioner lies within the Kaimur Wild Life Sanctuary. It was contented on behalf of the State that the disputed land was a part of the Wild Life Sanctuary and so the lease in favour of the petitioner was rightly cancelled.

Issues: Court framed the following issues:

"(i) Whether the disputed leased area lies within the Kaimur Wild Life Sanctuary?

(ii) Whether permission should be granted to the petitioner to perform mining operation in the leased area under section 29 of the Wild Life (Protection) Act, 1972 if it is found that the disputed leased area is situate within the sanctuary?

(iii) Whether the petitioner is entitled to refund of the money deposited by him for obtaining the above lease if it is found that the leased area is situate within the sanctuary and that no permission should be accorded to him under section 29 of the above Act?"

Held:

"**22.** … that the leased is a part to Kaimur Wild Life Sanctuary. We agree with this finding and confirm the same.

…

24. … the permission is to be granted with prospective effect and not from retrospective effect, and so at the time of consideration of the matter, the amended section 29 shall have to be taken into consideration, and the question of grant of permission for mining sand… from the river bed shall be governed by its proviso which provides that it can be used only for meeting personal bona fide need of the people living in and around the Sanctuary and it cannot be used for any commercial purpose.

25. Since the matter of grant of permission under section 29 of the Act has not been properly considered and determined by the Government …, we remit this matter to the Government again for deciding this point taking into consideration the up to date amended law and the question of protection of wild life including Gharials, Muggars and fishes in the Son river...

26. … if it is found by the Government that the permission cannot be granted to the petitioner under section 29 of the Act, the Government shall return the money deposited by the petitioner for grant of lease after making rateable deduction in respect of the period for which the mining operations were done by the petitioner. We are further of the view that security money and the stamp duty realised by the Government from the petitioner for execution of the lease deed and for deposit of the security money should also be returned back in toto as the lease has been cancelled by the Government for no fault of the petitioner who offered his bid in response to an auction notice issued by the Government itself.

…

29. However, as the petitioner has been deprived of beneficial use of his money for no fault of his own he is certainly entitled to interest on the amount which is to be refunded to him by the Government. Section 34, C.P.C. provides for payment of interest on the principal sum adjudged, from the date of the suit to the date of the decree at such rate as the court deems reasonable, and for further payment of interest at 6% per annum from the date of decree to the date of actual payment.

32. The writ petition is, therefore, partly allowed. It is dismissed so far as it challenges the order passed by the Government holding that the disputed land lies within the area of Kaimur Wild Life Sanctuary. However, the writ petition is allowed to this extent that the matter of grant of permission to the petitioner under section 29 of the Wild Life (Protection) Act is remitted to the Government for reconsideration in the light of the observations made in the body of the judgment with a further direction that if the Government is of the view that no permission is to be granted to the petitioner under section 29 of the above Act, it shall pass suitable orders for return of money to the petitioner along with interest thereon as observed above in the body of the judgment…"

MOHD. HAZI RAFEEQ V. STATE OF UTTRANCHAL 2005 SCC ONLINE UTT 29

Facts: The petitioner received a letter from the Principal Chief Conservator of Forest, Uttaranchal stating that the petitioner's saw mill was located within 10 Kms. at an approximate aerial distance of 4 Kms. from the boundary of the forest and that such location of the saw mill was against the order passed by the Hon'ble Supreme Court and also against the terms and conditions regarding relocation of saw mill in the order of the Principal Chief Conservator of Forest. The petitioner was also directed to relocate his saw mill beyond an aerial distance of 10 Kms. from the boundary of the forest within 10 days. The petitioner did not comply with the above direction to relocate the saw mill beyond an aerial distance of 10 Kms. from the boundary of the forest. Therefore, the Principal Chief Conservator of Forest cancelled the permission granted to the petitioner for the saw mill.

Issue: The petitioner filed the said writ petition to challenge the order of cancellation passed by Principal Chief Conservator of Forest.

Held: The Court observed that;

> "...The Government of Uttaranchal framed the Uttaranchal Establishment and Regulation of Saw Mills Rules, 2004... from the Second Proviso to Rule 5 of the Uttaranchal Rules, it is clear that a saw mill cannot be located within 10 Kms. from an existing forest. It is also clear from the conditions of licence contained in the form of application. In addition to the above provisions in the Rules, there is a specific direction issued by the Hon'ble Supreme Court on 8-5-1997 that permission cannot be granted to relocate an existing licensed saw mill within 10 Kms. of any existing forest. It is in clear violation of the said direction of the Supreme Court that the

Principal Chief Conservator of Forest granted permission to relocate the petitioner's saw mill as per his order dated 22-2-2000. When the mistake came to his notice, he has rightly taken the action to cancel the said permission granted on 22-2-2000. The said action of the Principal Chief Conservator of Forest cannot be said to be illegal or arbitrary.

5. However, the contention of the learned counsel for the petitioner is that the distance of 10 Kms. should not be taken as aerial distance, but as road distance. We do not find any valid reason or justification for giving such an interpretation to the order of the Hon'ble Supreme Court. The object of prohibiting relocation of saw mills within 10 Kms. from any existing forest is to preserve and protect forests and to prevent illicit felling of trees and destruction of forests and also to avoid the adverse impact of pollution, if any, caused by saw mills, on the forests. Considering the above object, it is necessary and proper to understand the distance of 10 Kms. specified by the Hon'ble Supreme Court as aerial distance and not road distance... Therefore, we are of the view that the Principal Chief Conservator of Forest was right and justified in understanding the order of the Hon'ble Supreme Court as one which prohibits relocation of saw mills within ah aerial distance of 10 Kms. from an existing forest...

6. ... The Principal Chief Conservator of Forest has only acted in accordance with Article 48-A of the Constitution of India...

Hence, forests have to be preserved and protected even at the cost of the business interest of the petitioner.

7. ... the Central Empowered Committee constituted by the Hon'ble Supreme Court of India ... did not agree with the suggestion of the State Government of Uttaranchal to permit the Integrated Industrial Estate at Haridwar and the Growth Center at Kotdwar because they are not only very near the Rajaji National Park but also fall in the Rajaji Corbett Elephant Corridor. The Central Empowered Committee has reiterated the direction of the Hon'ble Supreme Court that permission to shift a saw mill from one location to another location can be granted only when the new site is more than 10 Kms. away from the boundary of the forest. According to the Central Empowered Committee, the identified Industrial Estate at Pant Nagar falls within the 10 Kms. range from the boundary of the forest...

...Hence, in the light of the decision of the Central Empowered Committee, the stand taken by the Principal Chief Conservator of Forest is fully justified..."

TRADE OR COMMERCE IN WILD ANIMALS, ANIMAL ARTICLES AND TROPHIES

1. Government Property
   Following shall be the property of the State Government property[229]:
   a. wild animal, other than vermin, which is hunted under Section 11 or Section 29 (1) or 35 (6) of the WPA (important ecological, fauna) or kept or bred in captivity or hunted in contravention of any provision of the WPA or any rule or order made there under or found dead, or killed by mistake.
   b. animal article, trophy or uncured trophy or meat derived from any wild animal in respect of which any offence against the WPA or any rule or order made there under has been committed.
   c. ivory imported into India and an article made from such ivory in respect of which any offence against the WPA or any rule or order made there under has been committed.
   d. vehicle, vessel, weapon, trap or tool that has been used for committing an offence and has been seized under the provisions of the WPA.

   Note: Where such animal is hunted in a sanctuary or National Park declared by the Central Government, such animals or any such animal article, trophy, uncured trophy or meat delivered from such animal or any vehicle, vessel, weapon, trap or tool used in such hunting is the property of the Central Government.

   e. No person shall, without the permission in writing of the Chief Wildlife Warden or the authorized officer
      a. acquire or keep in his possession, custody or control, or

229 Section 39 of the WPA

   b. transfer to any person, whether by way of gift, sale or otherwise, or
   c. Destroy or damage,

such Government property.

2. Declaration[230]
   a. Every person who at the commencement of WPA had custody, control or possession of:
      - any captive animal specified in Schedule I or Part II of Schedule II
      - animal article, trophy or uncured trophy derived from such animal
      - salted or dried skins of such animal
      - musk of musk dear
      - horn of a rhinoceros

      had to within 30 days of the commencement of WPA declare to CWLW/ authorized officer the number and description of the animal or article of the foregoing description under his control, custody or possession and place where such animal or article was kept. Not applicable to a recognized zoo subject to the provisions of section 38-I or to a public museum.
   b. No person must:
      - Acquire, receive, keep in his control, custody or possession,
      - sell, offer for sale or
      - otherwise transport any animal

      specified in Schedule I or Part II of Schedule II, or any uncured trophy or meat derived from such animal, or the salted or dried skins of such animal or the musk of a musk deer or the horn of rhinoceros except with the previous permission of CWLW/ authorized officer. Not applicable to a recognized zoo subject to the provisions of section 38-I or to a public museum.
   c. No person other than a person having a certificate of ownership, must, after the commencement of the WPA

230 Section 40 and 40A of the WPA

acquire, receive, keep in his control, custody or possession any captive animal, animal article, trophy or uncured trophy specified in Schedule I or Part II of Schedule II, except by way of inheritance. Not applicable to the live elephants

d. Every person inheriting any captive animal, animal article, trophy or uncured trophy must, within ninety days of such inheritance make a declaration to the CWLW or the authorized officer. Not applicable to the live elephant.
e. The State Government may, by notification, require any person to declare to the CWLW or the authorized officer any animal or animal article or trophy (other than a musk of a musk deer or horn of a rhinoceros) or salted or dried skins derived from an animal specified in Schedule I or Part II of Schedule II in his control, custody or possession in such form, in such manner, and within such time, as may be prescribed.
f. Central Government may, by notification, require any person to declare to the CWLW or the authorized officer, any captive animal, animal article, trophy or uncured trophy derived from animals specified in Schedule I or Part II of Schedule II in his control, custody or possession, in respect of which no declaration had been made by the State Government or by any person within 30 days of the commencement of the Act in such form, in such manner and within such time as may be prescribed.

3. Inquiry and preparation of inventory[231]
    a. CWLW or the authorized officer may, after such notice, in such manner and at such time, as may be prescribed
        - enter upon the premises of a person who at the commencement of WPA had custody, control or possession of:
            - any captive animal specified in Schedule I or Part II of Schedule II
            - animal article, trophy or uncured trophy derived from such animal

231 Section 41 of the WPA

  - ➢ salted or dried skins of such animal
  - ➢ musk of musk dear
  - ➢ horn of a rhinoceros
- make inquiries and prepare inventories of animal articles, trophies, uncured trophies, salted and dried skins and captive animals specified in Schedule I and Part II of Schedule II and found thereon; and
- affix upon the animals, animal articles, trophies or uncured trophies identification marks in such manner as may be prescribed.

b. No person must obliterate or counterfeit any identification mark referred to in this Chapter.

4. Certificate of ownership[232]
   a. The CWLW may, issue a certificate of ownership in such form, as may be prescribed to any person who, in his opinion, is in lawful possession of any wild animal or any animal article, trophy, uncured trophy and may, where possible, mark, in the prescribed manner, such animal article, trophy or uncured trophy for purposes of identification.
   b. Before issuing the certificate of ownership in respect of any captive animal, the CWLW must ensure that the applicant has adequate facilities for housing, maintenance and upkeep of the animal.

5. Regulation of transfer of animal, etc.[233]
   a. No person having in his possession captive animal, animal article, trophy or uncured trophy in respect of which he has a certificate of ownership should transfer by way of sale or offer for sale or by any other mode of consideration of commercial nature, such animal or article or trophy or uncured trophy.
   b. Where a person transfers or transports from the State in which he resides to another State or acquires by transfer from outside the State, any such animal, animal article,

232 Section 42 of the WPA

233 Section 43 of the WPA

trophy or uncured trophy in respect of which he has a certificate of ownership, he must, within thirty days of the transfer or transport, report the transfer or transport to the CWLW or the authorized officer within whose jurisdiction the transfer or transport is effected.

c. However, nothing specified in point and a and b above shall apply to:
   - to tail feather of peacock and the animal article or trophies made therefrom;
   - to transfer of captive animals between recognized zoos subject to the provisions of section 38-I, and
   - transfer amongst zoos and public museums.

6. Prohibition on dealing in trophy and animal articles without license[234]

   No person must except under and in accordance with a license granted

   a. commence or carry on the business as:
   - A manufacturer of or dealer in, any article;
   - A taxidermist;
   - A dealer in trophy or uncured trophy;
   - A dealer in captive animals; or
   - A dealer in meat

   b. Cook or serve meat in any eating-house

   c. Derive, collect or prepare or deal in snake venom.

   Note: Not applicable to the dealers in tail feathers of peacock and articles

7. Suspension or cancellation of licenses[235]

   The Chief Wildlife Warden or the authorized officer may, for reasons to be recorded by him in writing, suspend or cancel any license granted or renewed. Provided that no such suspension or cancellation can be made, except after giving the holder of the license a reasonable opportunity of being heard.

234 Section 44 of the WPA

235 Section 45 of the WPA

8. Restriction on transportation of wildlife[236]
   No person shall accept any wild animal (other than vermin), or any animal article, for transportation except after exercising due care to ascertain that permission from the CWLW or any other officer authorized by the State Government in this behalf has been obtained for such transportation.

9. Maintenance of Record
   A licensee must:
   a. Keep records and submit such returns of his dealings as may be prescribed to the director/any officer authorized by him in this behalf and to CWLW or the authorized officer.
   b. Make the records available on demand for inspection by such officer.

10. Purchase of animals
    a. No licensee can[237]:
       - Keep in his control, custody or possession:
         - Any animal, animal article, trophy or uncured trophy in respect of which a declaration under the provisions of WPA has to be made and not been made.
         - Any animal or animal article, trophy or uncured trophy, meat which has not been lawfully acquired under the provisions of WPA or any rule or order thereunder.
       - Capture any wild animal
       - Acquire, receive, keep in his control, custody or possession or sell or offer for sale or transport, any captive animal specified in Schedule I or Part II of Schedule II or any animal article trophy, uncured trophy or meat derived there form or serve such meat, or put under a process of taxidermy or make animal article containing part or whole of such animal.

236 Section 48-A of the WPA
237 Section 48 of the WPA

- A prior written permission of the Director/any officer authorized by him is required before acquisition, possession, control custody of animal or animal article or transport which entail transfer/transport from one State to another. No such permission must be granted unless the Director/authorized officer is satisfied that animal was lawfully acquired.

b. No person can purchase, receive or acquire any captive animal, wild animal, other than vermin, or any animal article, trophy, uncured trophy or meat derived there from otherwise than from a dealer or from a person authorized to sell or otherwise transfer the same under this Act.[238]

238 Section 49 of the WPA

PROHIBITION OF TRADE OR COMMERCE IN TROPHIES, ANIMAL ARTICLES, ETC., DERIVED FROM CERTAIN ANIMALS

This chapter elaborates on the prohibitions on dealings in trophies, animal articles, etc., derived from Scheduled Animals[239].

1. No person can:
   a. commence or carry on the business as:
      - A manufacturer of, or dealer in, scheduled animal articles.
      - A taxidermist with respect to any scheduled animals or any parts of such animals.
      - A dealer in trophy or uncured trophy derived from any scheduled animal.
      - A dealer in any captive animals being scheduled animals.
      - A dealer in meat derived from any scheduled animal.
   b. cook or serve meat derived from any scheduled animal in any eating-house.
2. A person holding a license to carry on the business as a taxidermist may put under a process of taxidermy any scheduled animal or any part thereof:
   a. For or on behalf of the Government or any corporation or society
   b. With the previous authorization in writing of the Chief Wildlife Warden, for and on behalf of any person for educational or scientific purposes[240].
3. Declaration by dealers
   a. Every person carrying on any business or occupation as specified herein in point 1 above must with 30 days from

239 Section 49A (a) "Schedules animal means an animal specified for the time being in Schedule I or Part II of Schedule II." (of the WPA)

240 Wildlife Protection Act- 1972|Section 49-B|pg. 39

the specified date declare to the CWLW or the authorized officer:

- His stocks, if any, as at the end of the specified date of:
  - Scheduled animal articles;
  - Scheduled animals and parts thereof;
  - Trophies and uncured trophies derived from scheduled animals;
  - Captive animals being scheduled animals;
  - Ivory imported into India or articles made therefrom.
- The place or places at which the stocks mentioned in the declaration are kept; and
- The description of such items, if any, the stocks mentioned in the declaration which he desires to retain with himself for his bona fide personal use.

b. Person making a declaration may express his desire to retain any items of stocks for bona fide personal use. In such case CWLW if is satisfied that person is in lawful possession of the items may with the prior written approval of the Director issue certificate of ownership in favour of such person with respect to all, or as the case may be, such of the items as in the opinion of the CWLW are required for the bona fide personal use of such person and affix upon such items identification marks in prescribed manner. The person making declaration can prefer an appeal in case CWLW refuses to grant certificate of ownership.

c. No such item can be kept in commercial premises.

d. A person must not counterfeit or obliterate any identification mark as specified in point (b) above.

e. Where any person who has been given such certificate in respect of any item:
   - Transfers such item to any person, whether by way of gift, sale or otherwise; or
   - Transfers or transports from the State in which he resides to another State any such items.

He must with thirty days of such transfer, transport, report the transfer or transport to the CWLW/authorized officer within whose jurisdiction the transfer or transport is effected.

f. No person other than the person to whom the certificate is issued can on or after the specified date keep under his control, sell or offer for sale or transfer to any person any scheduled animals, a scheduled animal article, or ivory into India or any article made therefrom.

BALRAM KUMAWAT VS. UNION OF INDIA AIR (2003) SC 3268

Issue

Whether 'mammoth ivory' imported in India will fall within the description of the words 'ivory imported in India' contained in Wild Life (Protection) Act, 1972 ('**Act**')?

Held

This Court held that;

> "10…the statutory authorities would be entitled to take possession of such ivory in terms thereof; the purpose and object of the Act are to impose a complete ban on trade in ivory. A complete prohibition has been imposed in the trade of ivory for the purpose of protecting the endangered species. Trade in ivory imported in India has been prohibited further with a view to give effect to the provisions contained in Article 48A as also Article 51A(g) of the Constitution of India."
>
> "14…The purport and object of the Act are that nobody can carry on business activity in imported ivory so that while doing so, trade in ivory procured by way of poaching of elephants may be facilitated. Parliament, therefore, advisedly used the word 'ivory' instead of elephant ivory. The intention of the Parliament in this behalf, in our opinion, is absolutely clear and unambiguous. We cannot assume that the Parliament was not aware of the existence of different types of ivory. If the intention of the Parliament was to confine the subject matter of ban under Act 44 of 1993 to elephant ivory, it would have said so explicitly.
>
> 15. As noticed hereinbefore, the objective of Parliament was not only to ban trade in imported elephant ivory but ivory of every description so that poaching of elephants can be

effectively restricted. An article made of plastic would by no means resemble ivory."

"There is a complete prohibition of trade in ivory. Such a complete prohibition is a reasonable restriction within the meaning of Clause (6) of Article 19 of the Constitution of India. The impugned Act is not unreasonable does not also attract the wrath of Article 14 of the Constitution of India."

PAYRELAL VS THE STATE DELHI ADMINISTRATION (AIR 1995 SC 1159)

Facts: The appellant was the owner of Haryana Novelty Emporium, Delhi. The Wildlife Inspector, on information, conducted a search of the premises and found lion-shaped trophies of chinkara skins meant for sale. The appellant was found guilty under Section 44 (prohibits any dealing in such trophies without a license) and Section 49 (lays down that no person shall purchase, receive or acquire any captive animal, wild animal other than vermin or any animal article, trophy, uncured trophy, or meat derived therefrom otherwise than from a dealer or from a person authorized to sell or otherwise transfer the same under this Act) which is punishable under Section 51 of the Wildlife (Protection) Act, 1972.

Plea of the, accused was that those trophies were made out of goatskin, after being painted and that the skins were not that of wild animals mentioned in the Schedule of the Act. The trial court convicted the appellant and sentenced him to undergo 6 months of rigorous imprisonment and to pay a fine of Rs. 500/- and in default of paying the fine to undergo 2 months of rigorous imprisonment.

Issue: Appeal was filed against the order of the trial court.

Held: The Court held that:

> "3…evidence thus establishes that was in possession of those trophies…
>
> 4…we are of the view that only the first part of Sub-section (1) of Section 51 was attracted and not the proviso. There is no evidence whatsoever when the accused came into possession…what is clear from the evidence is that there is only a contravention, namely that a declaration required under Section 40 was not made and that the act of dealing in the trophies by the appellant was without a licence… the

minimum sentence of 6 months as provided under the proviso is not attracted."

Moreover, the appellant had already been jailed for 2 months and his sentence was reduced to the period he had already undergone. Keeping the fine amount and default clause the same.

G.R. SIMON & ORS. V. UNION OF INDIA & ORS. 997 SCC ONLINE DEL 324

Facts/Issue: A batch of writ petitions were filed by the manufacturers, wholesalers and dealers engaged in retail trade of tanned, cured and finished skins of animals. Petitioners were also engaged in retail trade of articles made of skin. The petitioners had challenged the introduction of provisions of Chapter VA in the Wild Life (Protection) Act, 1972 by Wild Life (Protection) Amendment Act, 1986, together with notification issued thereunder as being violative of Article 19(1)(g) read with Articles 300 and 300A of the Constitution of India.

Held:

> "**9.** ...Each and every animal plays a role in maintaining the ecological balance and, therefore, the contention that certain animals have no role to play or are detrimental to human life is completely misconceived. Taking the case of even jackals, which are referred to by the petitioners as animals of no utility, these are natural scavengers who feed on offal and dead animals, thereby keeping the environment clean. Snakes which have been described by some petitioners as harmful and dangerous to human life feed on rats. The mortality rate in the country due to snake bites is less than 0.0005%, which is very low compared to the death and fatalities caused by other diseases and animal bites. Snakes are the natural killers of rats which cause loss of nearly 33 million tonnes of stored cereals, apart from dreaded diseases such as plague. Russel Wipers and Rat snakes are known to have fascination of rats for food. The above would show that even the most maligned animals which appear apparently to be of no utility, have a role to play in retaining ecological balance. Besides, it is only when human beings treat their natural habitat that animals react. The Wild Life (Protection) Act has provisions to deal

with and eliminate those animals which become harmful to human lives or properties. Thus, the argument that certain wild animals are harmful to life and serve no useful purpose is misconceived. It is to be recognized that Wild Life is an asset and heritage to be preserved for future generations…

12. … it was essential to bring in the amendment in the Schedule to save the endangered species from extinction as well as to protect others whose numbers were bring depleted by callous exploitation in trade...

13. The submission that Chapter V-A of the Act provides for acquisition and confiscation of property is not correct in as much as for the preservation of certain species in Schedules I & II after the prescribed period in the Act makes the possession and retention of the said animal articles an offence... It only provides for time period within which persons holding stock of such articles have to dispose of the said stocks and upon the expiry of the stipulated period it becomes an offence under Section. 49-C(7) of the Wild Life (Protection) Amendment Act to retain the Wild Life articles under Schedule I and II, except those for personal bona fide use…

22. …Wild animals and snakes involved in fur and snake skin trade are not killed only for their meat or any other purpose but only for their skins, used by Fur and Snake skin traders. It had led to extinction of many species wild life all over the world. The petitioners had been provided under the Act a period of two months to dispose of their stocks and as noticed above in fact as a result of petitions filed and orders passed, the petitioners have enjoyed the opportunity to sell for a period of nearly six years till February, 1993. Accordingly, the petitioners cannot have any legitimate grievance of denial of opportunity in this regard. We are of the considered view that neither the State nor the Bharat Leather Corporation and the State Trading Corporation are under any legal obligation to buy the stocks of the petitioners in acceptance of the one-time sale proposition advanced by the petitioners. The petitioners are also not entitled to any further time for disposal of stocks.

The stocks of the petitioners would, therefore, be liable to be dealt with in accordance with the provisions of the Wild Life (Protection) Act, 1972.

23. We hold that the provisions of Chapter V-A, introduced by the Amending Act of 1986 to the Wild Life Act of 1972 are valid and intra vires."

COTTAGE INDUSTRIES EXPOSITION LTD. & ANR. v. UNION OF INDIA & ORS. (2007) 143 DLT 477 (DB)

Issue: The main question raised in the petition was whether the phrase 'animal article' as defined under WPA excludes 'animal hair'.

Held:

> "…**31.** …the US Fish and Wildlife Service (USFWS) has listed the Tibetan Antelope or Chiru, as an endangered species under the authority of Endangered Species Act. The said Endangered Species Act prohibits the international commercial sale of any parts or products of these species. The Tibetan Antelope has also been provided the highest protection under the convention on international trade in endangered species, under Appendix I of the said convention. China has also provided the highest measure of protection under its laws to Tibetan Antelope or Chiru and has completely banned sale or purchase of any products or parts of this species. Thus, any intention to exclude the products derived from the said animal or any part of the said animal from the definition of 'animal article' would not only defeat the purpose and intent of the Legislature but would run contrary to the international concern expressed through the international legislation on the aforesaid subject.
>
> **32.** The product derived from 'Scheduled animal' has only been defined under 'Scheduled animal article' under Section 49A(b) as to be made from any captive or wild animal and includes an article or object in which the whole or any part of such animal has been used and specifically excludes tail feather of peacock and snake venom or its derivatives. Since no other exclusion has been specified by the Legislature

except the tail feather of peacock and its derivatives and the derivatives of snake venom, it is not open to this Court to add 'animal hair' to such excluded categories in Section 49A(b) merely on the basis of what is termed by the petitioner to be the inclusive definition of trophy.

33. 'Hair' has thus not been excluded from the definition of 'animal articles' and 'Scheduled animal articles' and was intended to be included by the Legislature in the definition of 'animal articles' as per Section 2(2) and of 'Scheduled animal articles' as per Section 49A(b) of the Act.

35. Secondly, the raw 'hair' under the wool of Chiru after treatment and processing would admittedly fall within the meaning of 'trophy'. The thread made from such processed wool including the shawl woven from such thread would be covered by the definition of 'animal article' as defined in Section 49A(b) in as much as both the thread and the shawl are articles which have been made by use of hair (wool) of a scheduled wild animal…

39. The Hon›ble Supreme Court in SLP (Civil) No. 12434/2003 in *Ashok Kumar* v. *State of J&K*, by its Order dated 22nd November, 2005, directed as under:

"There is a complete prohibition on dealing in trophies, animal articles derived from the Scheduled animals (Chiru) under Section 49B of the Act. It was directed that action be taken against those persons who are found to be carrying on trade in Shahtoosh. The Supreme Court is monitoring implementation of its directions. The sum and substance of the judgment of the Supreme Court is that no trade in Scheduled Animal Article of Chiru, commonly known as 'Shahtoosh' is permissible. Carrying on trade in Shahtoosh is an offence."

45. … The writ petition is dismissed accordingly."

M/S. IVORY TRADERS AND MANUFACTURERS ASSOCIATION & ORS. V. UNION OF INDIA & OTHERS

Issues: "Whether the ban imposed on trade of imported ivory and articles made therefrom under section 49B(1)(a)(ia) read with Section 49A(c)(iii) and Section 49C(7) of the impugned legislation violates Article 19(1)(g) of the Constitution and whether trade in ivory is pernicious and not covered by Article 19(1)(g) of the Constitution?"

"Whether section 39(1)(c) and 49C(7) read with section 51(2) of the impugned legislation are violative of Article 300A of the Constitution?"

While answering the said questions the court held that:

> **"21.** ...As already noticed, the Act is meant to protect and safeguard wild life...
>
> ...
>
> In this country ... the Amendment Act 44 of 1991 inserted sub-clause (ia) to Section 49-B (1)(a) of the Principal Act as a result whereof the trade in "imported ivory" and articles made therefrom were completely prohibited from the "specified date". It may be noted that legislature has used the words 'ivory imported into India and not African ivory, thus enlarging the area of operation of the Act. Now as to the meaning of the, words "specified date", ... means, ...dealers in imported ivory or articles made therefrom or manufacturers of such articles were required to liquidate their stocks and stop all activities relating thereto within six months of the commencement of the Wild Life (Protection) Act, 1991, i.e. April 2, 1992 (date of commencement of the Act being October 2, 1991 + six months therefrom).

... This was also in keeping with the global perception that the elephant must be saved from extinction…

28. Rights granted under Article 19(1) are not absolute rights but are qualified rights and restrictions including prohibition thereon can be imposed in public interest. There is high authority for the proposition that when it is reasonable in public interest, a trade could even be prohibited under Article 19(6) and such a prohibition would not fall foul of Article 19(1)(g)…

…

36…the ban imposed by the impugned legislation especially Section 49(B)(a)(ia) r/w, section 49(A)(iii) and section (49-C)(7) thereof is not violative of Article 19(1)(g) of the Constitution. It is also not in contravention of Article 14 of the Constitution as the ban does not suffer from unreasonableness, arbitrariness and unfairness…

58. The Amendment Act 44 of 1991 does not deal with the acquisition or requisitioning of the property for a public purpose. The right guaranteed by Article 300A of the Constitution relates to compulsory acquisition and requisitioning of property for a public purpose. None of the provisions of Chapter V-A deal with acquisition of property for a public purpose. As already noticed, the object and purpose of the provisions are meant for providing protection to the elephant which is a threatened species…

63. The above legislation which provides for extinction of the ownership of a person in imported ivory is not a law for the purpose of acquisition and requisitioning of property by the State. Its primary object is the preservation of the Elephant, and not for utilisation of the property for public purpose. This being so, Article 300A is not attracted. At this stage we may point out that the State had sufficient authority to enact the impugned law in exercise of its sovereign powers as distinguished from police powers of the State…

65. Having regard to the above decisions it is not necessary for the State to pay compensation to the petitioners for extinguishment of title of the petitioners in imported ivory or articles made there-from. Since the State is not under any obligation to buy the stocks of the petitioners in acceptance of the onetime sale proposition propounded by the petitioners, we cannot direct the State to either buy the same or pay compensation for it...

74. Thus the words 'ivory imported into India' occurring in Section 49B(1)(a)(ia) would include all descriptions of imported ivory, whether elephant ivory or mammoth ivory.

75. We are also of the view that the impugned legislation falls within the power and competence of the Parliament as the same is meant to protect the Indian elephant. In order to achieve that purpose, the Parliament has undoubted power to deal with matters which effectuate the same. It can legislate with regard to all ancillary and subsidiary subjects including the imposition of ban on trade in imported ivory of all descriptions, whether drawn from mammoth or elephant, for the salutary purpose of the preservation of the Indian elephant."

PREVENTION AND DETECTION OF OFFENCES

1. Power of entry, search, arrest and detention[241]
   a. The Director or any other officer authorised by him in this behalf or CWLW or the authorised officer or any forest officer or any police officer not below the rank of a sub-inspector, may, if he has reasonable grounds for believing that any person has committed an offence against WPA:
      - require any such person to produce for inspection any captive animal, wild animal, animal article, meat, trophy or trophy, uncured trophy, in his control, custody or possession, or any license, permit or other document granted to him or required to be kept by him under the provisions of the WPA;
      - stop any vehicle or vessel in order to conduct search or inquiry or enter upon and search any premises, land, vehicle or vessel, in the occupation of such person, and open and search any baggage or other things in his possession;
      - seize any captive animal, wild animal, animal article, meat, trophy or uncured trophy, or any specified plant or part or derivative thereof, in respect of which an offence against this Act appears to have been committed, in the possession of any person together with any trap, tool, vehicle, vessel or weapon used for committing any such offence and, unless he is satisfied that such person will appear and answer any charge which may be preferred against him, arrest him without warrant, and detain him:
      - Where a fisherman, residing within ten kilometers of a sanctuary or National Park, inadvertently enters on a boat, not used for commercial fishing, in the

241 Section 50 of the WPA

territorial waters in that sanctuary or National Park, a fishing tackle or net on such boat shall not be seized.

b. It is lawful for any of the officers specified above to stop and detain any person, whom he sees doing any act for which a license or permit is required under the provisions of WPA, for the purposes of requiring such person to produce the license or permit and if such person fails to produce the licence or permit, as the case may be, he may be arrested without warrant, unless he furnishes his name and address, and otherwise satisfies the officer arresting him that he will duly answer any summons or other proceedings which may be taken against him.
c. Any officer of a rank not inferior to that of an Assistant Director of Wild Life Preservation or an Assistant Conservator of Forests who, or whose subordinate, has seized any captive animal or wild animal may give the same for custody on the execution by any person of a bond for the production of such animal if and when so required, before the Magistrate having jurisdiction to try the offence on account of which the seizure has been made.
d. Any person detained, or things seized under the foregoing power, must forthwith be taken before a Magistrate to be dealt with according to law under intimation to the CWLW or the officer authorised by him in this regard.
e. Any person who, without reasonable cause, fails to produce anything, which he is required to produce under this section, is guilty of an offence against the WPA.
f. Where any meat, or uncured trophy, is seized, the Assistant Director of Wild Life Preservation or any other officer of a gazetted rank authorised by him in this behalf or the CWLW or the authorised officer may arrange for the disposal of the same in such manner as may be prescribed.
g. Whenever any person is approached by any of the officers [referred to in point (a)] for assistance in the prevention or detection of an offence against WPA, or in apprehending persons charged with the violation of WPA, or for seizure then it is the duty of such person or persons to render such assistance.

h. Any officer not below the rank of an Assistant Director of Wild Life Preservation or an officer not below the rank of Assistant Conservator of Forests authorised by the State Government in this behalf has the powers, for purposes of making investigation into any offence against any provision of the WPA:
- to issue a search warrant;
- to enforce the attendance of witnesses;
- to compel the discovery and production of documents and material objects; and
- to receive and record evidence.

i. Any evidence shall be admissible in any subsequent trial before a Magistrate provided that it has been taken in the presence of the accused person.

2. Penalties[242]
   a. Any person who contravenes any provision of the WPA except otherwise provided or any rule or order made thereunder or who commits a breach of any of the conditions of any licence or permit granted under WPA, shall be guilty of an offence against WPA, and is on conviction, punishable with imprisonment for a term which may extend to 3 three years, or with fine which may extend to twenty-five thousand rupees, or with both.
   b. Where the offence committed is in relation to any animal specified in Schedule I or Part II of Schedule II or meat of any such animal or animal article, trophy or uncured trophy derived from such animal or where the offence relates to hunting in a sanctuary or a National Park or altering the boundaries of a sanctuary or a National Park, such offence is punishable with imprisonment for a term which shall not be less than three years but may extend to seven years and also with fine which shall not be less than ten thousand rupees.
   c. In the case of a second or subsequent offence of the nature mentioned in this sub-section, the term of the

242 Section 51 of the WPA

imprisonment shall not be less than three years but may extend to seven years and also with fine which shall not be less than twenty-five thousand rupees.

d. Any person who contravenes any provisions of Chapter VA on prohibition of trade or commerce in trophies, animal articles, etc., derived from certain animals of the WPA, is punishable with imprisonment for a term which shall not be less than three years but which may extend to seven years and also with fine which shall not be less than ten thousand rupees.
e. Any person who contravenes the provisions of section 38J, is punishable with imprisonment for a term which may extend to six months, or with fine which may extend to two thousand rupees, or with both.
f. In the case of a second or subsequent offence the term of imprisonment may extend to one year or the fine may extend to five thousand rupees.
g. When any person is convicted of an offence against WPA, the Court trying the offence may order that any captive animal, wild animal, animal article, trophy, uncured trophy, meat, ivory imported into India or an article made from such ivory, in respect of which the offence has been committed, and any trap, tool, vehicle, vessel or weapon, used in the commission of the said offence be forfeited to the State Government and that any license or permit, held by such person under the provisions of this Act, be cancelled.
h. Such cancellation of license or permit or such forfeiture shall be in addition to any other punishment that may be awarded for such offence.
i. Where any person is convicted of an offence against WPA, the Court may direct that the license, if any, granted to such person under the Arms Act, 1959 (54 of 1959), for possession of any arm with which an offence against this Act has been committed, shall be cancelled and that such person shall not be eligible for a license under the Arms Act, 1959, for a period of five years from the date of conviction.

j. Nothing contained in section 360 of the Code of Criminal Procedure, 1973 (2 of 1974), or in the Probation of Offenders Act, 1958 (20 of 1958), is applicable to a person convicted of an offence with respect to hunting in a sanctuary or a National Park or of an offence against any provision of Chapter VA unless such person is under eighteen years of age.

3. Certain conditions to apply while granting bail[243]
   a. When any person accused of, the commission of any offence relating to Schedule I or Part II of Schedule II or offences relating to hunting inside the boundaries of National Park or wild life sanctuary or altering the boundaries of such parks and sanctuaries, is arrested under the provisions of the Act, then notwithstanding anything contained in the Code of Criminal Procedure, 1973 (2 of 1974) no such person who had been previously convicted of an offence under the WPA shall, be released on bail unless:
      - the Public Prosecutor has been given an opportunity of opposing the release on bail; and
      - where the Public Prosecutor opposes the application, the Court is satisfied that there are reasonable grounds for believing that he is not guilty of such offence and that he is not likely to commit any offence while on bail.

4. Attempts and abetment[244]
   Whoever attempts to contravene, or abets the contravention of, any of the provisions of the WPA or of any rule or order made thereunder is deemed to have contravened that provision or rule or order, as the case may be.

5. Punishment for wrongful seizure[245]
   If any person, exercising powers under the WPA, vexatiously and unnecessarily seizes the property of any other person on

243 Section 51A of the WPA
244 Section 52 of the WPA
245 Section 53 of the WPA

the pretence of seizing it for the reasons mentioned in Section 50 of the WPA he shall, on conviction, be punishable with imprisonment for a term which may extend to six months, or with fine which may extend to five hundred rupees, or with both.

6. Power to compound offence[246]
    a. The Director of Wild Life Preservation or any other officer not below the rank of Assistant Director of Wild Life Preservation empowered by the Central Government or CWLW or any officer of a rank not below the rank of a Deputy Conservator of Forests empowered by the State Government, accept from any person against whom a reasonable suspicion exists that he has committed an offence against the WPA, payment of a sum of money by way of composition of the offence which such person is suspected to have committed.
    b. On payment of such sum of money to such officer, the suspected person, if in custody, must be discharged and no further proceedings in respect of the offence can be taken against such person.
    c. The officer compounding any offence has the power to order the cancellation of any license or permit granted under the Act to the offender. However, if not empowered to do so, can approach an officer so empowered, for the cancellation of such license or permit.
    d. The sum of money accepted or agreed to be accepted as composition must, in no case, exceed the sum of twenty-five thousand rupees.
    e. No offence, for which a minimum period of imprisonment has been prescribed in Section 51 of the WPA shall be compounded.

7. Cognizance of offences[247]

    No court shall take cognizance of any offence against the WPA on the complaint of any person other than:

246 Section 54 of the WPA
247 Section 55 of the WPA

a. the Director of Wild Life Preservation or any other officer authorised in this behalf by the Central Government; or
b. the Member-Secretary, Central Zoo Authority in matters relating to violation of the provisions of Chapter IVA; or
c. Director of the concerned tiger reserve; or
d. the Chief Wild Life Warden, or
e. any other officer authorised in this behalf by the State Government subject to such conditions as may be specified by that Government; or
f. the officer-in-charge of the zoo in respect of violation of provisions of section 38J; or
g. any person who has given notice of not less than sixty days, in the manner prescribed, of the alleged offence and of his intention to make a complaint, to the Central Government or the State Government or the officer authorised as aforesaid.

8. Operation of other laws not barred[248]
Nothing in this Act shall be deemed to prevent any person from being prosecuted under any other law for the time being in force, for any act or omission which constitutes an offence against the WPA or from being liable under such other law to any higher punishment or penalty than that provided by the WPA. However, no person can be punished twice for the same offence.

9. Presumption to be made in certain cases[249]
Where, in any prosecution for an offence against the WPA, it is established that a person is in possession, custody or control of any captive animal, animal article, meat, trophy, uncured trophy, it shall be presumed, that such person is in unlawful possession, custody or control of such captive animal, animal article, meat, trophy, uncured trophy, specified plant, or part or derivative thereof until the contrary is proved. The burden of proving the contrary shall lie on the accused.

---

248 Section 56 of the WPA
249 Section 57 of the WPA

10. Offences by Companies[250]
    a. Where an offence against the Act WPA is committed by a company, every person who, at the time the offence was committed, was in charge of, and was responsible to, the company for the conduct of the business of the company as well as the company, shall be deemed to be guilty of the offence and shall be liable to be proceeded against and punished accordingly.
    b. Any such person if proves that the offence was committed without his knowledge or that he exercised all due diligence to prevent the commission of such offence then he shall not be liable to such punishment.
    c. However where an offence against the WPA is committed by a company and it is proved that the offence has been committed with the consent or connivance of, or is attributable to any neglect on the part of, any director, manager, secretary or other officer of the company, such director, manager, secretary or other officer shall also be deemed to be guilty of that offence and shall be liable to be proceeded against and punished accordingly[251].

250 Section 58 of the WPA

251 Section 58 of the WPA; Explanation.—For the purposes of this section,— (a) "company" means any body corporate and includes a firm or other association of individuals; and (b) "director", in relation to a firm, means a partner in the firm.

SANSAR CHAND v. STATE OF RAJASTHAN [2010 (11) JJ 518 (SC)]

Facts: Sansar Chand, the appellant in the present case had a long history of criminal activities, starting with a 1974 arrest for 680 skins including tigers, leopards and others. The appellant and his gang were allegedly accused in 57 wildlife cases between 1974 and 2005. The present was one such case. The police had arrested one Balwan in January 2005 who was travelling with a carton containing Leopard's skin. During investigation, he made a disclosure statement (Extra Judicial Confession) to the Station head officer that the two leopard skins were to be handed over to Sansar Chand in Delhi. Sansar Chand was charged sheeted and was convicted by Additional Chief Judicial Magistrate (Rajasthan). He made an appeal which was dismissed by Special Judge under SC/ST (Prevention of Atrocities Act). Furthermore, he filed for a revision petition which was dismissed by Rajasthan High Court.

Issue: Whether or not the appellant (Sansar Chand) could have been convicted based on an extra judicial confession?

Held: The court held that the letter of confession written by Arvind Kumar at the instruction of Balwan and with his thumb print was sent while he was on bail, hence the letter cannot be said a result of coercion.

> "27...In our opinion it cannot be held that the accused Balwan was under any pressure of the police..."

Physical evidences like nails of animals and weapons used for killing the animals were also found with the appellant. Properties in Delhi in his and his wife's name were found which were results of the earnings from his illegal activities were. The court mentioned several times that it becomes difficult to find the leaders of poaching cartels due to lack of evidence but in this case they found.

The court also stated that "there is no absolute rule that an extra judicial confession can never be the basis of a conviction, although it should be corroborated with other evidences." Hence, the court dismissed the appeal and found the appellant guilty and affirmed the High Court Verdict.

BHIMA VS SHRI PRAGDEESH (WILDLIFE INSPECTOR) NEW DELHI AND OTHERS[252]

Facts: Wildlife officer along with his team reached the place where informant told the exchange of wildlife contraband was going to take place. The suspect identified by the informant was found carrying 2 plastic bags which contained tiger skin, bones and two live turtles. The accused did not have any documents on him and was immediately detained. The accused revealed the weapons used for committing the crime and the same was recovered from the forest. The accused also revealed that he had killed a tiger before this with his associates, who were both arrested earlier for committing wildlife crime. It was further noted that he was previously involved in wildlife crimes and was a repeated offender. He was charged with crimes under section Sections 9,39, 51,44, 49A (the scheduled animal as an animal specified for the time being in schedule-l like Tiger) and 40 (no person other than a person having a certificate of ownership shall deal in wildlife activities like capturing or selling trophies etc.) of Wildlife Protection Act, 1972.

Issue: Whether or not the accused can be convicted merely based on an extra judicial confession?

Held: The court while relying on **Khusia Happy Vs. State of Punjab**[253] held that the main foundation for the conviction in the extra judicial confession is that it is made by the accused. The onus is upon the prosecution to establish that the confession made was true, and evidence of the same must be produced. It must be

252 Bhima vs Shri Pragadeesh (Wildlife inspector) New Delhi and Others-Case No:06 of 2012

253 Khusia Happy Vs. State of Punjab-2007 RCR (criminal) 557

shown that such confession is free from any kind of coercion and was given at the accused's will.

> The court held that; "31...the prosecution must establish (1) that a confession was made, (2) evidence of it can be given and (3) that it is true. Two rules of caution in the matter of acting upon extra judicial confession are (1) that the evidence of confession must be reliable and free of infirmity and (2) it must find corroboration...."
>
> It was found in the present case that enough evidence was put forth the court to establish that the accused committed the crime. The court observed that "32...In the present case the evidence of confession of accused was found to be reliable and does not suffer with any infirmity and was duly corroborated with the recovery, discovery, and the deposition of the prosecution witnesses."

The accused in the said case was hence convicted of all the crimes and the court took a special note and stated that crimes against wildlife animals are serious offences and must not be ignored.

WILDLIFE CRIME CONTROL BUREAU (WCCB) v. MOHD. HASIN [CRL. A NO. 57/13]

Facts: The accused was found in possession of tiger skin. Since, the accused failed to produce any legal source of procurement of the above skin and a license or authority to possess or keep the same, therefore, recovered skin was seized. The accused was charged with Section 40(2), 49, 49 B (1) read with Section 39 and 65 of the said Act which is punishable u/s 51 of the Act. FIR was registered, and the accused was arrested. The lower court however acquitted the accused due to the lack of public witnesses and for non-production of the property after seizure. The present appeal was filed by WCCB against the acquittal.

Issues: Whether lack of public witnesses and non-production of the case property immediately after seizure can be grounds for acquittal?

Held: The court held that; "9…it is always appreciated that public witnesses are joined in the investigation in order to prove the truthfulness of the investigation but it does not mean that in any case where there are no public witness joined, the case will always be a false case…

> 10…Mere fact that artificial skin of tiger might be available in the market does not prove that the skin recovered from the possession of the accused in the present case was also artificial skin…Hence I am of the opinion that the Ld. Trial Court had based his order of acquittal on incorrect appreciation of evidence."

The court also relied on the judgement held by Hon'ble Supreme Court in **Ajmer Singh Vs State of Haryana**[254], wherein it was held that the non-joining of independent witness is not fatal

254 Ajmer Singh Vs State of Haryana - 2010 (2) RCR, Crl. 132

to the prosecution case particularly when efforts were made by the investigating party to join public witness but none was willing. It was held that accused cannot be acquitted merely because no independent witness was produced.

The court also found that the case property was produced before the then lower court on the very next day of the seizure. And it was the lower court which ordered that property be kept in police station for safe custody. Therefore, requirement of Section 50 (4) Wildlife Act has been fulfilled by the police officials. "14… settled preposition of law that on mere technical grounds accused is not to be acquitted unless it has specific bearing or affect the root of the case as held in **Chittranjan Das vs State of West Bengal**[255]…".

Hence, the accused was convicted under section 40(2), 49, 49 B (1) read with section 39 and 65 of the Wildlife (P) Act, 1972 which is punishable u/s 51 Wildlife (P) Act, 1972.

255 1963 SCR 237

FORFEITURE OF PROPERTY DERIVED FROM ILLEGAL HUNTING AND TRADE

The provisions contained in this chapter are applicable only to the following persons:

a. Person who has been convicted of an offence punishable under the WPA with imprisonment for a term of three years or more;
b. Every associate of said person
c. Any holder of any property which was at any time previously held by a person referred to in point 'a' or point 'b' above unless the present holder or, as the case may be, anyone who held such property after such person and before the present holder , is or was a transferee in good faith for adequate consideration.

1. Prohibition of holding illegally acquired property
   a. It shall not be lawful for any person to whom this chapter applies to hold any illegally acquired property either by himself or through any other person on his behalf.
   b. Where any person holds such property, the property shall be liable to be forfeited to the State Government.
   c. No property shall be forfeited if such property was acquired by a person before a period of six years from the date on which he was charged for an offence relating to illegal hunting and trade of wild life and its products.

2. Identifying illegally acquired property
   a. An officer not below the rank of Deputy Inspector General of Police duly authorized by the Central Government or as the case may be, the State Government, on receipt of a complaint from the competent authority about any person having illegally acquired property, must proceed to take all steps necessary for tracing and identifying any property illegally acquired by such person.

b. The steps may include any inquiry, investigation or survey in respect of any person, place, property, assets, documents, books of account in any bank or financial institution or any other relevant step as may be necessary.
c. Any inquiry, investigation or survey referred to has to be carried out by an officer in accordance with such directions or guidelines as the competent authority may make or issue in this behalf.

3. Seizure or freezing of illegally acquired property[256]
   a. Where any officer conducting an inquiry or investigation has reason to believe that any property in relation to which such inquiry or investigation is being conducted is an illegally acquired property and such property is likely to be
      - concealed,
      - transferred or
      - dealt with in any manner which may result in frustrating any proceeding relating to forfeiture of such property

      he may make an order for
      - seizing such property and
      - where it is not practicable to seize such property, he may make an order that such property shall not be transferred or otherwise dealt with, except with the prior permission of the officer making such order, or of the competent authority

        and a copy of such order shall be served on the person concerned.

256 Section 58F of the WPA; Explanation.—For the purposes of this section, "transfer of property" means any disposition, conveyance, assignment, settlement, delivery, payment or other alienation of property and, without limiting the generality of the foregoing, includes— (a) the creation of a trust in property; (b) the grant or creation of any lease, mortgage, charge, easement, licence, power, partnership or interest in property; (c) the exercise of a power of appointment, of property vested in any person not the owner of the property, to determine its disposition in favour of any person other than the donee of the power; and (d) any transaction entered into by any person with intent thereby to diminish directly or indirectly the value of his own property and to increase the value of the property of any other person.

A copy of such an order must also be sent to the competent authority within forty-eight hours of its being made.

b. Any order made shall have no effect unless the said order is confirmed by an order of the competent authority within a period of thirty days of its being made.

4. Notice of forfeiture of property
   a. If having regard to the value of the properties held by any person, either by himself or through any other person on his behalf, the competent authority for reasons recorded in writing believes that all or any of such properties are illegally acquired properties, it may serve a notice upon such person calling upon him within a period of thirty days:
      - To show cause why all or any of such properties, should not be declared to be illegally acquired properties and forfeited to the State Government and
      - to indicate the sources of his income, earnings or assets, out of which or by means of which he has acquired such property, the evidence on which he relies and other relevant information and particulars.
   b. The competent authority must give a reasonable opportunity of hearing to such person/ any other person holding property on his behalf.
   c. If the person affected (and in a case where the person affected holds any property specified in the notice through any other person, such other person also), does not appear before the competent authority or represent his case before it within a period of thirty days specified in the show cause notice, the competent authority may proceed to record a finding ex parte on the basis of evidence available before it.
   d. Where the competent authority is satisfied that some of the properties referred to in the show cause notice are illegally acquired properties but is not able to identify specifically such properties, then, it shall be lawful for the competent authority to specify the properties which, to

the best of its judgment, are illegally acquired properties and record a finding accordingly within a period of ninety days.

e. Where the competent authority records a finding under this section to the effect that any property is illegally acquired property, it shall declare that such property shall, stand forfeited to the State Government free from all encumbrances.
f. In case the person affected establishes that the property specified in the notice issued is not an illegally acquired property and therefore not liable to be forfeited under the WPA, the said notice shall be withdrawn and the property shall be released forthwith.
g. Where any shares in a company stand forfeited to the State Government, the company shall, forthwith register the State Government as the transferee of such shares.
h. In any proceedings, the burden of proving that any property specified in the notice served is not illegally acquired property is on the person affected.

5. Fine in lieu of forfeiture
    a. Where the competent authority makes a declaration that any property stands forfeited to the State Government and it is a case where the source of only a part of the illegally acquired property has not been proved to the satisfaction of the competent authority, it shall make an order giving option to the person affected to pay, in lieu of forfeiture, a fine equal to the market value of such part.
    b. Before making an order imposing a fine the person affected must be given a reasonable opportunity of being heard.
    c. Where the person affected pays the fine due under within such time as may be allowed in that behalf, the competent authority may, by order revoke the declaration of forfeiture and thereupon such property would stand released.

6. Procedure in relation to certain trust properties
    If the competent authority, on the basis of the information and materials available to it, for reasons to be recorded in writing

believes that any property held in trust is illegally acquired property[257], it may serve a notice upon the author of the trust, or as the case may be, the contributor of the assets calling upon them within a period of thirty days specified in the notice, to explain the source of money or other assets and all the provisions of this Chapter shall apply accordingly.

7. Certain transfers to be null and void
   Where after the making of an order or the issue of a notice any property referred to in the said order or notice is transferred by any mode whatsoever, such transfer shall, for the purposes of the proceedings under this Chapter, be ignored and if such property is subsequently forfeited to the State Government, then, the transfer of such property shall be deemed to be null and void.

8. Appeals
   a. Any person aggrieved by an order of the competent authority can, within forty-five days from the date on which the order is served on him prefer an appeal to the Appellate Tribunal.
   b. The Appellate Tribunal has the discretion to entertain an appeal after the said period of forty-five days, but not after sixty days, from the date aforesaid if it is satisfied that the appellant was prevented by sufficient cause from filing the appeal in time.
   c. Appellate Tribunal may, after giving an opportunity of being heard to the appellant, if he so desires, and after making such further inquiry as it deems fit, confirm, modify or set aside the order appealed against.
   d. The Appellate Tribunal may regulate its own procedure.

257 Section 58L of the WPA; Explanation.—For the purposes of this section "illegally acquired property" in relation to any property held in trust, includes— (i) any property which if it had continued to be held by the author of the trust or the contributor of such property to the trust would have been illegally acquired property in relation to such author or contributor; (ii) any property acquired by the trust out of any contributions made by any person which would have been illegally acquired property in relation to such person had such person acquired such property out of such contributions.

e. On application to the Appellate Tribunal and on payment of the prescribed fee, the Appellate Tribunal may allow a party to any appeal or any person authorized in this behalf by such party to inspect at any time during office hours, any relevant records and registers of the Appellate Tribunal and obtain a certified copy or any part thereof.

9. Notice or order not to be invalid for error in description
No notice issued or served, no declaration made, and no order passed under this Chapter shall be deemed to be invalid by reason of any error in the description of the property or person mentioned therein if such property or person is identifiable from the description so mentioned.

10. Bar of jurisdiction
No order passed or declaration made shall be appealable except as provided therein and no civil court shall have jurisdiction in respect of any matter which the Appellate Tribunal or any competent authority is empowered by or under this Chapter to determine, and no injunction shall be granted by any court or other authority in respect of any action taken or to be taken in pursuance of any power conferred by or under this Chapter.

11. Power to take possession
    a. Where any property has been declared to be forfeited to the State Government, or where the person affected has failed to pay the fine within the time allowed the competent authority may order the person affected as well as any other person who may be in possession of the property to surrender or deliver possession thereof to the Administrator or to any person duly authorized by him in this behalf within thirty days of the service of the order.
    b. If any person refuses or fails to comply with such order the Administrator may take possession of the property and may for that purpose use such force as may be necessary.
    c. The Administrator may, for the purpose of taking possession of any property requisition the services of any police officer to assist him and it shall be the duty of such officer to comply with such requisition.

12. Punishment for acquiring property in relation to which proceedings have been taken under this Chapter
    Any person who knowingly acquires, by any mode whatsoever, any property in relation to which proceedings are pending under this Chapter shall be punishable with imprisonment for a term which may extend to five years and with fine which may extend to fifty thousand rupees.

ANIMAL LAWS IN INDIA: SERVING THE PURPOSE, ARE THEY?

The animals in our country have mythological significance and are worshipped in several parts of India. Further numerous laws, rules and regulations have been enacted in India to safeguard animals. Indian judiciary has also been playing an active role in passing progressive judgments to protect the animals. However, it is shocking that the ground realty continues to remain the same and the cruel behaviour that is meted out to the animals is unceasing.

There have been several reports of gruesome inhuman acts towards animals lately. A dog in Mumbai was sexually abused and raped with its mouth tied with a rope[258]. This obnoxious incident was followed by a similar rape case in just eight weeks in the same city. Multiple legislations for animal rights and security have been rendered ineffective due to the lack of proper execution and follow up actions. People commit such ghastly acts and roam freely without any guilt as there is no fear of any gruesome punishment which may correspond to their act of cruelty. There have been several reported incidences of abuses, each more shocking than the last. Dogs are poisoned, cows have been burned with acid and elephants have been fed crackers and many more.

Propagating for increased penalties and fines

Since 2014, the Supreme Court of India has been consistently taking steps forward to recognize the animal laws and prodding the government to formulate adequate penalties and punishment. However, punishment for the cruelty to animals has not seen enough change since the primitive laws were enacted. What the legislature over the years has failed to recognize is that the amount

258 *See* https://www.timesnownews.com/mumbai/article/mumbai-horror-labourer-rapes-female-dog-after-tying-up-her-mouth-with-rope/678577, *Last visited on 17/12/2020.*

of penalty according to section 11 of PCA, 1960 should have been increased with time according to the valuation today. Animal welfare organizations and activists have constantly been pushing for stringent laws for over several years by the way of campaigns and protests. "**No more than 50**"[259] was name of the campaign that was started by several MPs like Shashi Tharoor, Meenakshi Lekhi and Varun Gandhi for increasing the fine amounts. Organizations like PETA have continued campaigning for almost 20 years in India for welfare of the animals. They have written open letters to the Centre for addressing the issue of weak animal protection laws and demanding jail time, significant increase in fine amount and counselling for the culprits[260]. These protests have led to the environment ministry in process of preparing draft amendment to the PCA.

Ineffective implementation of laws and minimal penalties to be alone blamed for existing situation?

India has had a rich royal history. The kings and queens of different provinces considered it to be a matter of pride to kill animals and decorate their parts like ornaments as a display of their bravery. They continued doing so along with the colonial British government. This tradition has been passed on through generations with minor modifications and now has set a trend of dead animals being displayed by the uber rich and royals as bags and shoes. One cannot just blame the legislature for non-implementation of stringent laws but also needs to question the morals of individuals and the different money-making industries that exploit the animals. For example, the Fashion Industry has always portrayed wearing or accessorizing animal skin is a way of presenting chic couture. What the industry fails to realize is that they display cruelty. The number of animals killed for fur and leather in different parts of the world is innumerable. It is no doubt that one of the causes of rampant illegal poaching of animals in

259 *See* https://theprint.in/india/governance/modi-govt-hikes-penalty-for-cruelty-to-animals-by-120-times/164044/, *Last visited on 17/12/2020.*

260 *See* https://secure.petaindia.com/page/31656/action/1?locale=en-GB, *Last visited on 17/12/2020.*

our country is to make money by selling animal skin and parts to serve the fashion industry.

Despite the fact that the various rules and regulations enacted pursuant to PCA provide greater penalty than PCA which merely provides penalty ranging from Rs.10-Rs.50 for the first offence and Rs.25-Rs.100 for any subsequent offence the illegal acts against animals and the ill-treatment meted out to them continue. We till date find it difficult to protect the animals. The reason for such constant failure is also largely attributable to the lack of awareness. People are not aware about the laws; as a result they are not aware of the forums and organizations which can be approached in case there is any violation of the existing laws or in case they witness any ill-treatment to animals. People may be conscious about taking care of animals by providing them food and shelter however, they are not aware as to how they can protect them and ensure peaceful co-existence.

The continuous exploitation of other natural resources such as forests, rivers and oceans have left the animals vulnerable resulting in extinction of so many species and so many of them being on the verge of extinction. Non-strict application of laws and low penalties have further added to the already wane situation. The reporting of illegal acts which are being committed in violation of the prescribed laws, rules and regulations is very minimalistic. Further there is no reward or incentive attached to reporting such violation and hence lack of perks also play a vital role in non-reporting of illegal activities being done and committed by the people against the animals.

What is required is that the NGOs and other non-profit organizations are engaged by governments for organizing awareness programs which are interactive and help people understand as to how they can play an active role in protection of animals. Initiatives by the Governments in India both at the Centre and States is a must to ensure the effectiveness of the already elaborate laws. Plethora of laws shall be of no use unless put to work and applied effectively. The animals are one of the most beautiful creations of the nature and it is our duty to protect and safeguard them.

Animals are a part of our world. The least that can be expected is empathy towards them if not anything else. Let us not forget that they all are speechless creatures and individuals like us must take steps every day to help them out for the sake of saving the little humanity that is still within us. Hence, this compilation is our little initiative to sensitize the entire matter around the animal rights and to create as much awareness as possible. The present compilation intends to encourage people "to do it themselves" i.e., the idea is to compile all the laws in a simpler fashion so that everyone can read and understand the laws on their own and take steps to comply and ensure compliance of the said laws on everyday basis.

DO IT YOURSELF!

Compassion without Action is EVIL.[261] Animal cruelty is an offence under Section 11 of the PCA (as detailed on page 7-9 of this book) and under different provisions of Indian Penal Code, 1860 (**IPC**). A few steps which one can and should take in order to protect the animals from being subjected to cruelty or to ensure that they get requisite care if any cruelty has been committed on them are as follows:

a. **Spread Awareness**: It is rightly said that prevention is better than cure. Instead of sitting back and waiting that you will help if cruelty is committed on any animal the better way to approach the whole situation is that you create awareness. One should not feel hesitant in educating other people about the rights they hold as an animal lover, about the duties they owe towards the animals owned by them, about the penalties and imprisonments they can be subjected to if they commit cruelty on animals whether or not owned by them or on stray animals. One can organise seminars and activities in their schools, colleges, societies etc, to create consciousness among people about the rights of animals and obligation of care towards them. This is likely to ensure greater sensitivity towards the animals. Short notes can also be put on the notice boards of buildings, apartments and societies to make people aware of their duties towards animals whether as owners or otherwise and of their rights as animal lovers.
b. **Teach yourself before you teach others**: Before you venture out to create awareness it is important that you have requisite knowledge about all the laws, circulars, policies which are in place, and about the action that can be taken in case one

261 https://www.peopleforanimalsindia.org/pfa-units.php last visited on 04.01.2021

witnesses cruelty being committed on any animal. Thus, know it yourself first.

c. **Act and not only preach**: Preaching is not enough. What is required is that each person must take positive steps to prevent cruelty being committed on animals and safeguard the animals by acquiring proper veterinary care in case cruelty has already been committed on any animal. Acting on what a person is preaching is very important to ensure effective implementation of rights and obligations, of and towards, animals.

d. **Get help**: Sometimes any short delay can also result in death of animal on which cruelty has been committed. If you can't do it alone take help. If it is not possible for you to ensure the safety of any animal alone then don't hesitate in taking help of other people and organisations in order save or safeguard any animal. People for Ethical Treatment of Animals (**PETA**) is one of the organisations which has been working extensively to create awareness in this aspect. On its website it provides a helpline number which can be used in order to report any incidence of cruelty and in order to procure assistance to help any animal in distress. There are several other organisations which are working on national, state and local level to protect animals and can be contacted for help[262]. Another such organisation is People For Animals (**PFA**). It is a Non-Governmental Organization which works all over India[263]. One can also take recourse to the reliefs available under the law. Many lawyers are very compassionate about animals and may offer to provide legal assistance for free or at bare minimal cost.

e. **Document the crime**[264]: Law functions only on the basis of evidence. In case of uncorroborated crimes it is often difficult to establish the act and to get the conviction of the accused or bring the case to justice. Hence, other than extending help to the distressed animal it is important that evidence is secured by taking photos, videos etc. with the help of other people so

---

262 https://www.petaindia.com/blog/helpinganimalsindistress/ last visited on 04.01.2021

263 https://www.peopleforanimalsindia.org/pfa-units.php last visited on 04.01.2021

264 https://www.petaindia.com/blog/9-things-to-do-if-you-witness-cruelty-to-animals/ last visited on 04.01.2021

that the accused can at later stage be recognised and be held liable for its acts of cruelty.

f. **Report the Crime[265]:** In case one witnesses any offence being committed towards animals then he/she can report the same to the police. Some important aspects of filing the FIR are as follows:
   i. Every information relating to the commission of a cognizable offence (offence punishable with imprisonment of 3 years or more), if given orally to an officer in charge of a police station, has to be reduced to writing by such officer or under his direction.
   ii. Such information has to be read over to the informant.
   iii. Every such information, whether given in writing or reduced to writing as aforesaid, has to be signed by the person giving it.
   iv. A copy of such information has to be given forthwith to the informant, free of cost.
   v. If the officer in charge of a police station refuses to record such information then in such case informant can send the substance of such information, in writing and by post, to the Superintendent of Police concerned, approach the court [Section 482/156 of Criminal Procedure Code (**CrPC**)] or make a private complaint (Section 200 of CrPC).
   vi. When information is given to an officer in charge of a police station regarding the commission of a non-cognizable offence (punishable with imprisonment with of less than 3 years), then he has to enter or cause to be entered the substance of the information in a book to be kept by such officer in such form as the State Government may prescribe in this behalf, and refer the informant to the Magistrate.
   vii. No police officer can investigate a non-cognizable case without the order of a Magistrate having power to try such case or commit the case for trial.
   viii. Where a case relates to two or more offences of which at least one is cognizable, the case shall be deemed to be a cognizable case.

265 Section 154-156 of Criminal Procedure Code, 1973 (**CrPC**)

g. **IPC provisions under which complaint can be made:**
   i. Section 47 of the IPC defines word "animal" to include any living creature other than a human being.

   Section 289, 428, 429, 503 and 506 of IPC read as under:

   ii. Section 289-Negligent conduct with respect to animal: "Whoever knowingly or negligently omits to take such order with any animal in his possession as is sufficient to guard against any probable danger of grievous hurt from such animal, shall be punished with imprisonment of either description for a term which may extend to six months, or with fine which may extend to one thousand rupees, or with both."
   iii. Section 428-Mischief by killing or maiming animal of the value of ten rupees: "Whoever commits mischief by killing, poisoning, maiming, or rendering useless any animal or animals of the value of ten rupees or upwards, shall be punished with imprisonment of either description for a term which may extend to two years, or with fine, or with both."
   iv. Section 429- Mischief by killing or maiming cattle, etc., of any value or any animal of the value of fifty rupees: "Whoever commits mischief by killing, poisoning, maiming or rendering useless, any elephant, camel, horse, mule, buffalo, bull, cow or ox, whatever may be the value thereof, or any other animal of the value of fifty rupees or upwards, shall be punished with imprisonment of either description for a term which may be extended to five years, or with fine, or with both."
   v. Attempts to interfere with or harass persons who choose to look after and feed community dogs can tantamount to very grave offence of criminal intimidation. (Section 503 read with Section 506 IPC)
   vi. Section 503- "Whoever threatens another with any injury to his person, reputation or property, or to the person or reputation of any one in whom that person is interested, with intent to cause alarm to that person, or to cause that person to do any act which he is not legally bound to do, or to omit to do any act which that person is legally

entitled to do, as the means of avoiding the execution of such threat, commits criminal intimidation."

vii. Section 506 "Whoever commits the offence of criminal intimidation shall be punished with imprisonment of either description for a term which may extend to two years, or with fine, or with both. If threat the threat be to cause death or grievous hurt, or to cause the destruction of any property by fire, or to cause an offence punishable with death or imprisonment for life, or with imprisonment for a term which may extend to seven years, or to impute unchastity to a woman, shall be punished with imprisonment of either description for a term which may extend to seven years, or with fine, or with both."

h. **Some important provisions to be kept in mind regarding FIR are as follows[266]:**
   i. If information discloses commission of cognisable offence then registration of FIR is mandatory and no preliminary inquiry is permissible in such situation.
   ii. If information does not disclose commission of cognisable offence and indicates necessity to conduct inquiry. Then in such case preliminary inquiry can be committed only to ascertain whether cognisable offence is committed or not.
   iii. If such preliminary inquiry discloses commission of cognisable offence then FIR must be registered.
   iv. If preliminary inquiry ends in closing the complaint, then copy of entry of such closure has to be supplied to informant within 1 week of such closure disclosing therein reasons in brief for closing the complaint and not proceeding further.
   v. Police officer cannot avoid his duty to register offence if cognisable offence is disclosed.
   vi. Action can be taken against erring officers also.
   vii. Any preliminary inquiry has to be made in a time bound manner not exceeding 7 days.

266 Lalita Kumari v. State of Uttar Pradesh (2014) 2 SCC 1

www.ingramcontent.com/pod-product-compliance
Ingram Content Group UK Ltd.
Pitfield, Milton Keynes, MK11 3LW, UK
UKHW041842190726
13854UKWH00002B/672